DRAMACONTEMPORARY

FRANCE

THE DRAMACONTEMPORARY SERIES

DramaContemporary is a series specializing in the publication of new foreign plays in translation, organized by country or region. The series developed in response to the increasing internationalism of our age that now links world societies more closely, not only economically, but culturally as well. The last twenty years, in particular, is characterized by cross-cultural references in writing and performance, East and West and throughout the Americas. The new drama series is designed to partake of this movement in world patterns of culture, specifically in the area of our specialty, theatre.

Each volume of DramaContemporary features a selection of recent plays that reflects current social, cultural, and artistic values in individual countries. Plays are chosen for their significance in the larger perspective of a culture, as a measure of the concerns of its artists and public. At times, these plays may find their way into the American theatrical repertoire; in other instances, this may not be possible. Nevertheless, at all times the American public can have the opportunity to learn about other cultures—the speech, gestures, rhythms and attitudes that shape a society—in the dramatic life of their plays.

The Publishers

IN PRINT:

DramaContemporary: Czechoslovakia
DramaContemporary: Spain
DramaContemporary: France

IN PREPARATION:

DramaContemporary: Latin America
DramaContemporary: Hungary
DramaContemporary: Poland
DramaContemporary: Germany
DramaContemporary: Russia
DramaContemporary: India

DRAMACONTEMPORARY
FRANCE

plays by

Marguerite Duras
Nathalie Sarraute
Michel Vinaver
Gildas Bourdet
Enzo Cormann
Jean-Claude Grumberg

Edited, with an Introduction, by
Philippa Wehle

PAJ Publications
(A Division of Performing Arts Journal, Inc.)
New York

© 1986 Copyright by PAJ Publications

Vera Baxter: © 1980, copyright by Editions Abatros; translation © 1985 copyright by Philippa Wehle
Over Nothing At All: © 1982 copyright by Editions Gallimard; translation © 1985 copyright by Philippa Wehle
Chamber Theatre: © 1978 copyright by L'Arche; translation © 1979 copyright by Paul Antal
The Gas Station: © 1985 copyright by Les Editions Solin; translation © 1985 by Judith G. Miller
Exiles: © 1985 copyright by Thomas Sessler Verlag; translation © 1985 copyright by J.G. Strand
The Workroom: © 1975 copyright by Theatre Ouvert; translation © 1982, 1984 copyright by Daniel A. Stein and Sara O'Connor
All rights reserved

Second printing, paperback, 1992

Distributed by The Johns Hopkins University Press
701 West 40th Street, Baltimore, Maryland 21211-2190
The Johns Hopkins Press Ltd., London

Library of Congress Cataloging in Publication Data
DramaContemporary: France
CONTENTS: *Vera Baxter, Over Nothing At All, Chamber Theatre, The Gas Station, Exiles, The Workroom*
Library of Congress Catalog Card No.: 85-63861
ISBN: 0-933826-93-1 (cloth)
ISBN: 0-933826-94-X (paper)

Design: Gautam Dasgupta
Printed in the United States of America

Publication of this book has been made possible in part by a grant from the National Endowment for the Arts, Washington, D.C., a federal agency, and public funds received from the New York State Council on the Arts.

General Editors of the DramaContemporary Series:
Bonnie Marranca and Gautam Dasgupta

Contents

"text" of the production was written down only after months of preparation. Consequently in the Soleil productions of the 70s (*1789, 1793,* and *L'Age d'Or*) it is not the text that is of primary interest, but the gestural, the spectacular and the immediacy of the relationship between artists and audience.

Others such as Jacques Kraemer's Théâtre Populaire de la Lorraine created plays collectively for and with suggestions from a specific audience (the miners of the Lorraine, in their case). Here again, the playscript, collectively developed, was only of secondary importance. Still other groups eliminated the written text altogether, substituting vocal sounds–screams, yells and moans–and gestural language in their striving for politically effective theatre.

Even Armand Gatti, one of France's finest playwrights, author of a dozen major plays throughout the 60s, and still a believer in the value of the poetic text, turned away from the literary to the production of "spectacles" created by non-professionals. Traveling throughout Belgium, Germany and France, Gatti and his "Tribe" worked with locals, spending months in villages and rural areas to prepare their "spectacles without spectators." From the "Durutti Column Experiment" in an abandoned factory in the suburbs of Brussels (1972), which told the story of the Catalonian Republican Army's attempt to stop Franco's advance using large posters as scenery, to their "Brabant-Walloon Work," a 28-hour show created with the 3,000 residents of this Belgian rural region, Gatti's aim was to break the passivity of the public and help the "people"–underprivileged, marginal, inarticulate–express themselves creatively.

Elsewhere, centers of experimentation like the Théâtre National de Strasbourg absorbed the solitary author into a collective endeavor of another type. Under the leadership of Jean-Pierre Vincent (1975-1983), the TNS created a research team of directors, actors, designers and dramaturg/writers who worked together to create new forms of "scenic writing." Together they produced major historical pieces (*Vichy Fictions; La Peste [The Plague]*) of which original playscripts by resident dramaturgs Michel Deutsch and Bernard Chartreux are an integral part. But, although these plays can stand alone, they are fully effective only in the larger context of the production for which they were written.

Towards the close of the 70s, Mnouchkine, the Salamandre and others seemed to resume their interest in the literary text. They turned, however, not to the work of contemporary authors, but to the adaptation of non-dramatic texts. (In 1978, the Théâtre de la Salamandre staged Jack London's *Martin Eden*, based on collective improvisations, and in 1979, the Soleil adapted Klaus Mann's novel *Mephisto*.) Such stage adaptations, pioneered in the early 70s by Antoine Vitez and Simone BenMussa, provided new possibilities in theatre writing and were an important trend in the 70s. In fact, the challenge of transfering descriptive narrative to the stage and projecting the inner voices of memory and thought in scenic terms tempted most of the experimental directors of the time.

* * * * *

Eden Cinema to the comedic patter of *Les Eaux et Forêts* (*The Rivers and Forests*). *Des Journées entières dans les Arbres* (*Whole Days in the Trees*) [1965 and 1975], for example, is drama of family conflict, couched in the form of a series of realistic tableaux and three acts. Duras's most characteristic style, however, is the elegantly elliptical, concentrated dramatic form of *La Musica* (first and second versions), *Savannah Bay* and *Véra Baxter*. These are the modern tragedies of contemporary French theatre.

Véra Baxter is the tragedy of fidelity, of a wife forced by her husband to betray her marriage vows. Fidelity had been Véra Baxter's vocation, her definition. She had been the faithful wife through better and worse, throughout Jean Baxter's numerous adulteries and gambling passions. But now, as the play opens, she has taken a lover because her husband wanted her to; he in fact has paid the man to sleep with his wife. Jean Baxter hoped to bring back his desire for her in this way; for her, it has brought only despair and a radical break with the past. For Véra must now leave her husband, her lover and in effect her former self.

The play centers on this charged moment of leave-taking when one world is ending and another, possibly, beginning. Such moments are sheer purgatory in Duras's plays. Clearly, Vèra may not even survive the terror and pain of it. She has shut herself up in the summer villa she has come to rent and where she now wants to die. These closed rooms are where Vèra must live her passion. Duras excels in evoking their oppressive atmosphere; the stifling, enclosed spaces which mirror Véra's cloistered inner world. In contrast to these still, dead rooms, the "Outside Turbulence," made up of the noises and sounds of a lively party, calls to her. Like the wind, it gusts and lulls, invades her private world, then recedes and fades away. This turbulence is a fifth presence in the four character drama; "a potentional contradiction," as Duras calls it, which may or may not effect Véra's decision to die.

The final scene of the play hints at possible salvation through Véra's retelling of her story in her own words and in her own version. For this an interlocutor is needed, an "interrogator," who will draw her out and listen to what she says. Thus "The Stranger" prods her, gently and lovingly, to reveal herself. It is a labored and painful process. For Véra Baxter, like other of the author's women, doesn't know how to use words. She doesn't know how to talk about love or how to evoke the past. Hence the reticence, the pauses and the silences of Duras's dialogue. A connection with another can only come through language, however, and Véra seems to achieve this by the end of the play, striving to articulate her inner world.

Nathalie Sarraute

Over Nothing At All [1982], which premiered in New York in June 1985 and in Paris in February 1986, is Nathalie Sarraute's sixth play. A pioneer of the "new novel" group of post-war writers, Sarraute did not turn to the theatre until 1967, and only then at the urging of Jean-Louis Barrault who convinced her that her fictional world of sub-conversations was indeed a theatrical world of mini-dramas. The dramatic substance of such novels as Le Planétarium [1959] and Martereau [1953] is the delicate minute rhythms, the amorphous movements beneath the words of ordinary conversation. Set into motion by an antagonist, these tropisms (the title of Sarraute's 1939 masterpiece) advance, recoil and evolve without reference to psychology of character or physical appearance. Consequently, Sarraute admits finding it difficult to visualize her characters. This explains why her plays were first written as radio dramas and why her characters are usually anonymous men and women; He and She or M. 1 and W.

All of Sarraute's plays explore this hidden underworld of sensations, reactions and reflexes. They probe the undercurrents of meaning to question the bonds of human relations and unmask the conventional appearances of reality and truth. In Le Silence (Silence) [1967], for example, five anonymous characters try to find out why a sixth, Jean-Pierre, remains silent. In appearance, the subject is Jean-Pierre's mutism; in reality, it is the inner preoccupations of the others: their need to fill the silence with their words.

In Sarraute's theatre, actions are minimal; the dramatic tension lies between the apparent banality of the spoken and the enigmatic reverberations of the unspoken. For this reason, the pauses and rhythmic patterns are most important. Yet, although most characters have no name, there are recognizable differences between them. In Over Nothing at All, for example, two male friends, one confident, agressive, the other, passive, somewhat dreamy, have had a falling out "over nothing at all," and call in two neighbors as arbiters of the grievance. Their exchange reveals a life-long hostility between the two men, covered up for years by their proclamation of undying friendship. One small phrase and the way it was pronounced has served as catalyst to their quarrel. As they explore the implications of this chink in their relationship, it becomes clear that underneath the surface, a sub-conversation has long festered, composed of envy, condescension and contempt. In order to terminate their friendship, however, they must petition a jury of good citizens who they know will find no reality to their dispute and the play ends with the two still arguing over nothing and everything.

Michel Vinaver

Michel Vinaver had already published two novels when he wrote his first play Aujourd'hui ou les Coréens (The Koreans), in 1955. He had joined the Gillette International Razor Company the year before. For a while he managed to combine both artistic and business careers (and indeed his experience of a multinational corporation provided the writer with his basic materials). His plays were staged in the 50s by both Roger Planchon and Antoine Vitez and he wrote reviews and articles for important journals of artistic criticism: *Théâtre Populaire* and *Travail Théâtral* among them. He gave up playwriting in the 60s when the demands at Gillette became too arduous, but returned full strength to dramatic production with his epic farce *Par-dessus bord* (*Overboard*), written in 1967-1969 and staged by Roger Planchon at the TNP in 1973. Since then, Vinaver has written six more plays; all of them masterpieces of a new kind of theatre of daily life, frequently rich in insights into the operations of large and small business firms as these affect the texture of human relations.

For although Vinaver's theatre uses the ordinary language of salesmen, secretaries and office managers, it goes beyond the surface banality of shop talk and business deals to form a mosaic of phrases, fragments of speech and bits of conversation reorganized in such a way as to create a theatre of poetic possibilities arising from the shrewd and careful juxtaposition and succession of these fragments.

Les Travaux et les Jours (*A Smile at the End of the Line*) [1977], is a particularly happy blending of these techniques. It is "minimal theatre" (the term is Vinaver's) at its most coherent. Its five characters (three secretaries, an office manager and a blue-collar worker) work in the Customer Serice department of a small coffee grinder company. The women exchange typical office gossip and chatter between phone calls while the men are more involved with the fate of the company and of the Customer Service department as rumors circulate that the company is for sale and its workers are on strike. Their snatches of conversation alternately intersect, bypass each other, and comment on unrelated threads of discourse. Meaning evolves not so much from what is left out as from the overall composition, the montage of polyphonic discourse. The result is stroboscopic, illuminating in rapid flashes the underpinnings of corporate politics and private lives.

In his *Chamber Theatre*, composed of *Dissident, il va sans dire* (*Dissident, Goes Without Saying*) and *Nina, c'est autre chose* (*Nina, It's Different*) [1978], Vinaver creates miracles of another sort. These are families (a mother and a son in *Dissident*; two brothers and one brother's girlfriend in *Nina*) and the fragile but unbreakable bonds that connect them are the substance of these intimate plays. Life goes on for Helen and Philip, as it does for Charles and Sebastian without any truly dramatic interruptions, or so it appears. The upsets in these ordinary lives are so subtly stated that they seem almost taken for granted, as it were, or accepted out of habit or passivity. Events matter little. Unexpressed for the most part, except for a gesture here and there (Nina's offer to wash Sebastian's back; the Mother's suggestion that the police can wait while she puts on some music), the fabric of intimacy *is* the fabric of these deftly constructed chamber pieces.

Gildas Bourdet

Gildas Bourdet is artistic director of the Salamandre, one of France's five national theatres. It is located in the northern, Pas de Calais region. He writes exclusively for the Salamandre company and with specific actors in mind. *The Gas Station* [1985], his fourth play, continues in the comic style he has been developing since his widely successful *Le Saperleau*.

From a working class family, Bourdet had little experience of the theatre when he became set and stage designer for Le Salamandre, a company in his home town of Le Havre. From this he moved to acting, then directing and playwriting.

Like other May '68 companies, the Salamandre became a workers' cooperative, developing its material collectively in an attempt to reach a popular audience. In his writing as well as his stagings, Bourdet has remained committed to this goal. With the exception of his first play *Didascalia* (1981), a highly experimental piece composed entirely of stage directions, his work seeks to bridge the gap between high and low culture through the theatre. His treatment of Gorki's *The Lower Depths*, for example, was based on taped conversations with workers in the cafés of Tourcoing, which he transcribed, adapted and placed in a basement set in this northern area of France.

Le Saperleau features three grotesques caught in a classic love triangle and one narrator. Performed in and out of a plexiglass house, with the audience seated inside, the play is a vigorous, lusty comedy, charged with Bourdet's irreverent linguistic inventions (borrowings from old French, Latinisms, deformed words and foreign phrases reminiscent of the richness and texture of Rabelais's French). The play works on two levels: as a farce complete with broad strokes and broad humor and as an indirect warning about the impoverished state of official language.

Reminders of the made-up language of *Le Saperleau* are found in *The Gas Station*, in the lines given to young Tut-Tut, the retarded son of Thérèse, a schoolteacher and grandson of Madeleine, the owner of a run-down gas station in rural France. His distorted words and mispronounced syllables deflate the seriousness of other characters. A poetic little figure, ignoring all social conventions (peeing freely on the stage and going out naked in the middle of the night to talk to the moon), Tut-Tut gives the play its irreverent tone.

The Gas Station draws on the popular techniques of conventional boulevard comedy and nineteenth-century melodrama to portray the disintegration of a lower class family trying to make the best of their poverty and bad luck. The play switches from the corrosively comic to the pitiable, from the cruel to the tender, as it moves at a dizzying pace through the reversals, coincidences and recognition scenes of established comedy. Bourdet's intention, however, is not to copy but to subvert. His characters are not the mechanical, one-dimensional figures of bourgeois comedy. They are full and human. And there is an earthiness about them which gives the play its special coloration.

Enzo Cormann

The author of over twelve plays in the six short years since he began writing, Enzo Cormann is one of France's best new playwrights. Keenly in tune with his generations' fear for our planet's survival, his dramatic world is a world of impending cataclysm. His thought often centers on the rise of Nazism as a metaphor of global catastrophe. Like the ravaged figures of the painter Francis Bacon (Cormann's favorite), his characters project their gnarled, violent inner worlds before us. Their universe is a closed one (four bare walls in *Exils* (*Exiles*) [1984]; the sordid ruins of a burned house in *Le Rodeur* (*The Drifter*) [1982], or the basement hovel where Gretl hides from the horror of Berlin's destruction in *Berlin, ton danseur est la Mort* (Berlin, Your Dance is the Dance of Death) [1981]. Such are the places where these solitary figures hide from their nightmares. The outside world is only vaguely perceived, filtered through the fear and insecurity of the central characters.

Nothing is certain in Cormann's dramatic universe. Carl Sturm, of *Exiles*, is a pseudonym; Jo, of *The Drifter*, has no last name. The identity of characters shifts as well. Is the woman in *Exiles* the employee of a publishing house or a fictional recreation of Annah, Sturm's former mistress? Is the time now or in the past?

A number of Cormann's plays are small-scale pieces; one character playlets like *Credo, The Drifter, Exiles,* and *Temporalia*. Others, like *Noises* (1983), with a cast of nine characters, or *Kè Voî?*, a full-length play commissioned by Philippe Adrien in 1985, are more complex experiments. In *Noises* (which in French means quarrels), Cormann assembles men and women at a party and, framing their encounters like a series of polaroid camera shots, he lets their chatter reveal the vanity of their discourse.

In *Exiles*, one of Cormann's most successful attempts to break with the constraints of traditional dialogue, Carl Sturm, an unpublished poet, deprived of his German citizenship in 1933, lives his nightmare of banishment in an unfriendly Paris, triply exiled from home, country and himself. His story is born of the poem at the beginning of the play and from this comes the narrator's voice. Soon a different voice separates off from the narrator's, a "She" who begins to enact his imagined dialogue. As this dialogue between "She" and "You" becomes more intense, the "You" switches to "Me," creating a plurality of voices which weave in and out of the narrative, returning always to the poem and its evocation of the ritual murder of a woman.

Jean-Claude Grumberg

Jean-Claude Grumberg, actor and playwright, has been writing plays since 1965. His most recent work, *L'Indien sous Babylone* (*The Indian in Babylonian Captivity*) [1985], his twelfth play, is a witty, biting dissection of the motives behind government sponsored art and the parasitism of artists. Its hero, César

Bysminski, an aging and ailing playwright, finds himself mysteriously incarcerated in a sordid basement office of the Ministry of Culture of an unknown state. An unctuous official is forcibly urging him to accept a government commission to write "*the* great contemporary play." Reminiscent of Grumberg's early plays (black farces dealing with themes of violence, power and persecution), *L'Indien sous Babylone* illuminates the concrete dilemma of artistic creation and poetic sterility in the form of a Kafkaesque nightmare. Grumberg's other style, more realistic, more historically oriented, is best illustrated by his plays *Dreyfus* (1974), *En R'venant d'l'Expo* (*On the Way Back from the Expo*) [1975] and *L'Atelier* (*The Workroom*) [1976].

Set in Poland in 1930, *Dreyfus* centers on a Jewish theatre company's rehearsals of a play about the unfortunate Captain. As discussions among the actors of how to present a play about anti-semitism evolve, their ignorance about the anti-semitism surrounding them becomes blatantly clear. Skillfully constructed with eight swiftly paced scenes, Dreyfus demonstrates Grumberg's gift for authentic coloration and dialogue. *En r'venant d'l'Expo* similarly places its events in an historical setting, the Universal Exhibition of 1900, and artfully interweaves the contrasting modes of a frivololus "café concert" and syndicalists' discussions of impending war.

Like *Dreyfus*, *The Workroom* returns to the enclosed space of a single set, this time a tailor's workroom in post-war Paris. The owners are Jewish as is one of the workers, Simone, whose husband was executed by the Nazis. As she waits to get a government certificate testifying to her husband's death, the years go by, and life goes on in the workshop. There is little action; the characters remain basically unchanged except for Héléne, the tailor's wife who is outraged at the bureacratic injustices of post-war France and the insensitivity of those around her. By the end of the play, Simone is in the hospital, a victim of overwork and exhaustion. *The Workroom* is a fine and subtle evocation of "ordinary moments in ordinary lives" (Grumberg).

Véra Baxter

or

The Atlantic Beaches

Marguerite Duras

VERA BAXTER
Théâtre de Poche (France)
Directed by Jean-Claude Amyl

CHARACTERS:

Michel Cayre
M. Combès
Customer
Véra Baxter
The Stranger

I. THE BAR AT THE HÔTEL DE PARIS IN THIONVILLE-SUR-MER

(*Three o'clock in the afternoon. Wintertime. White light. The place is large, empty, dark, luxurious. Three people, three men. Behind the bar, a bartender. Seated at the table in the room, the hotel guest: "The Stranger." Seated at the bar, a third man: Michel Cayre. A rather long pause. Then a telephone rings [the ring sounds like a stage phone ring]. The bartender gets up and goes out to answer it.*)

BARTENDER: (*Off.*) No . . . she hasn't come back yet . . . no, nobody (*silence*) . . . that's all right . . . goodbye, sir . . . you're welcome. (*The bartender goes back behind the bar, he looks at Michel Cayre. Awkward silence.*) He's called four times since noon.
CAYRE: (*Pause.*) From Paris . . .
BARTENDER: From Chantilly.
CAYRE: (*Pause.*) Where's the house?
BARTENDER: On the Thionville estates. (*Pause.*) It's called "The Colonnades." (*Turbulence. Dance music, music of laughter and shouts combined. Sounds of a lively, violent party. We'll call these sounds the OUTSIDE TURBULENCE. Michel Cayre moves off in the direction of the telephone.*)
BARTENDER: (*To the customer.*) It belongs to some people from Rouen . . . they had it built and then, something happened . . . They don't come here anymore except for her sometimes she comes at Easter. They rent it out in the summer . . . (*OUTSIDE TURBULENCE.*)
BARTENDER: The real estate agent tried calling too. She doesn't answer the phone.
CUSTOMER: What's her name?
BARTENDER: Baxter. Véra Baxter. They've been coming here for ten years now. He's in promotional work. Jean Baxter . . . You've never heard of him?
CUSTOMER: No.
BARTENDER: (*Pointing in the direction of Cayre offstage.*) He's a reporter. Michel Cayre. (*Silence. Michel Cayre comes back. He is facing front.*)

CAYRE: (*In a low voice.*) You're right. She doesn't answer.

BARTENDER: (*Hesitant.*) You're going to go over there . . . (*Silence. A woman has come in. Monique Combès. She looks at the two men who don't move and walks over to Michel Cayre.*)

M. COMBES: We've met before.

CAYRE: (*Reticent.*) I think so. (*The customer is listening and watching. He listens somewhat abstractly, neutrally. Whispered conversation between M. Combès and Michel Cayre.*)

M. COMBES: You know why I've come . . .

CAYRE: (*Pause.*) I don't know any more than you do. (*Pause.*) She went out this morning around ten o'clock. I was asleep. (*Silence. They sit down. Slowness of their movements. Silence before they speak.*)

M. COMBES: (*Pause.*) She was supposed to meet you?

CAYRE: (*Pause.*) Yes. At noon, here.

M. COMBES: It's three-thirty.

CAYRE: (*A rather long silence.*) What did she tell the real estate agent? (*The whispered conversation is heard perfectly well by the customer.*)

M. COMBES: That she wanted to think it over before renting . . . that she felt the price was very high . . . (*pause*) that in any case she had to discuss it with Jean Baxter before she could decide.

CAYRE: (*Silence.*) The house has already been rented . . . hasn't it?

M. COMBES: (*Hesitation – pause.*) Yes.

CAYRE: Since when?

M. COMBES: Yesterday . . . (*Hesitation – pause.*) Some other people wanted it . . . (*Pause.*) Jean Baxter found out about it from the real estate agency, he rented it.

CAYRE: She still doesn't know about it?

M. COMBES: No. (*Pause.*) She's not ever supposed to know about it . . . (*pause*).

CAYRE: The cost of the rental either, I suppose?

M. COMBES: (*Pause.*) Right. (*Pause.*) The agent made up a price (*smile – pause*) she probably thinks it's still too expensive . . . she's always been careful about money . . .

CAYRE: (*Pause.*) What's the real price?

M. COMBES: (*Pause.*) Why do you want to know?

CAYRE: (*Pause.*) So I can see just how far Jean Baxter would go to . . . just out of curiosity.

M. COMBES: I didn't ask what the price was. (*Pause.*) Very high, I think.

CAYRE: (*Pause.*) What if she doesn't want that house?

M. COMBES: Oh . . . you know, it's just a question of money . . . the house would stay empty . . . rented, but empty . . . that's all. (*Gusts of TURBULENCE in the bar, coming and going, as if trying to enter, to find a place somewhere: a strange threatening presence, a potential contradiction. Silence.*)

CAYRE: Just like . . . from Jean Baxter's point of view . . . she's supposed to have come to Thionville alone to rent a house for the summer, right?

M. COMBES: (*Pause.*) Yes. (*Pause.*) That's what she's supposed to think . . . well, I mean, she's supposed to go on thinking that her husband doesn't know anything about your being here in Thionville. (*Silence.*)

CAYRE: How does he know that I'm here?

M. COMBES: (*Pause. Controlled arrogance.*) I saw you coming out of the Hôtel de Paris yesterday . . . It's so deserted here in the winter, you can't help but notice everyone. (*Pause.*) I'm a friend of Jean Baxter's.

CAYRE: (*Pause.*) He already knew about it.

M. COMBES: (*Pause.*) He suspected it, yes . . . (*Alluding to an unknown aspect of the story. Silence.*)

CAYRE: (*Pause.*) Of course.

M. COMBES: Yes . . . (*Silence.*)

CAYRE: Why did you come?

M. COMBES: In case you were going to go get her . . . (*No response.*). So that you'd be . . . (*Hesitation—stop.*) So that you'd respect the agreement . . . I mean . . .

CAYRE: (*Finishes her sentence.*) You mean: the series of lies surrounding Véra Baxter.

M. COMBES: (*Frank.*) Yes. (*Pause.*)

CAYRE: Who wants to know?

M. COMBES: No one . . . if that's what matters to you. Will you go?

CAYRE: You'll tell him I don't know. (*Silence. The customer is looking at them. They are looking at each other.*)

CAYRE: (*To the customer with a mixture of pain and anger.*) Can you follow what we're talking about?

CUSTOMER: (*Pause.*) Not too well . . .

M. COMBES: (*Pause.*) Sorry . . .

CUSTOMER: (*Apologizing with a gesture.*) No . . . I'm the one who should apologize . . . (*Silence. The connection has been made with the customer: the privileged observer of the story. It's happened: they've spoken to each other.*)

CAYRE: (*To the customer.*) What do you think about it?

CUSTOMER: (*Pause.*) That the illusion should remain total . . .

CAYRE: (*Pause.*) What illusion . . . ?

CUSTOMER: Of choice . . . of freedom . . .

M. COMBES: (*Pause.*) That's right . . . yes.

CUSTOMER: They wouldn't have gone to so much trouble (*smile*) to lie if it weren't to protect . . . something else . . . for example . . . some sort of . . . truth . . . some feeling . . . No . . . ? (*All three fall silent. The OUTSIDE TURBULENCE grows more audible, harsh, ironic. It is commenting ironically on the "truth" in question.*)

CUSTOMER: Or so it seems from the outside . . .

(*Blackout.*)

II. THE BAR. EMPTY NOW.

(Michel Cayre and Monique Combès are at the entrance to the bar. Their voices are low, as if overwhelmed. It seems as if Combès is also speaking for herself.)

CAYRE: When I met Jean Baxter, here, I thought that you were his wife. Then I learned that . . . *(pause)* . . . it was someone else . . . *(Long silence.)*

M. COMBES: Did you see her again . . . in Paris . . . ?

CAYRE: . . . Yes, that's right . . . I met her one afternoon . . . she wasn't with him . . . *(Long pause.)* You notice her when she's not with him . . .

M. COMBES: *(Pause.)* But after . . . you've seen her with him . . . Don't you think so?

CAYRE: Maybe *(pause)* I don't know any more. *(Silence.)*

M. COMBES: Jean Baxter still interests you a lot.

CAYRE: *(Pause.)* In a different way, I think. I don't know that any more, either . . . *(Stop. Pause.)*

M. COMBES: What are you going to do?

CAYRE: *(Pause.)* I had decided to wait until six o'clock, if she hasn't come back by then, I'll go back to Paris . . . I like to drive at night . . . *(Silence.)* Couldn't you at least let her know that . . . that I'm leaving?

M. COMBES: No. I don't know her very well . . . we don't know each other very well. *(Alluding to her affair with Jean Baxter. Silence. No response.)* I'm going to go over to the "Colonnades" as I promised I would. *(Pause. The room is empty except for the customer. Then, Michel Cayre comes into the bar. Time goes by. No movement at all.)*

CAYRE: The wind's died down. *(Pause.)* It often does here in the afternoon . . . but there's always a little.

CUSTOMER: . . . The Atlantic Ocean . . .

CAYRE: *(In a low voice.)* Yes . . . *(Michel Cayre goes over and with an inadvertent gesture sits down in front of the customer as if the latter didn't exist at all. He looks out the window.)* It's high tide. It makes you feel like swimming. *(No response. Sudden realization: Michel Cayre makes a gesture, indicating extreme fatigue. Incoherent phrases.)* I'll leave her . . . *(Pause.)* I need time to . . . I've reached the point where . . . I can't touch another woman . . . *(Pause.)* After the summer, maybe . . . *(Pause.)* I'm a person who . . . I don't want to suffer. *(Silence. Nothing moves. Michel Cayre notices the customer.)* I drink too much . . . I'm sorry . . . *(No response.)* Do you come to Thionville often?

CUSTOMER: No.

CAYRE: Doesn't the name Baxter mean anything to you?

CUSTOMER: *(Making a gesture indicating no.)* No, nothing. *(Silence.)*

CAYRE: *Nouveau riche*, you know . . . it's frightening . . . no real social standing . . . *(pause)* it makes you sick . . . and then, look what happens . . . He's a gambler, a womanizer, almost always away from home. *(Pause.)* She's always tagging along with her three children . . . and faithful on top of everything else . . . a sorry couple, I mean, non-existent and . . . and yet . . . (*Stop.*) He . . . he's a money chaser . . . tragic . . . She's . . . a kind of Catholic . . . (*pause*) . . . at heart . . . He's gone bankrupt three times . . . She's still with him. The money starts coming in again, she's still there, tagging along . . . They've been everywhere. (*Pause.*) She follows him. She would have followed anyone in the same way . . . anywhere. He goes away for six months. He comes back. She's there . . . (*Silence. He comes out of his solitary discourse; speaks to the customer.*) I've lost her. I don't know when it happened. I can't seem to figure it out. (*Pause.*) . . . I don't know why I want to know . . . Their wives are usually beautiful . . . *this* one isn't even beautiful . . . (*Silence. No response.*) The money? Do you think so . . . ? (*Silence. No response.*)

CUSTOMER: (*Unambiguous all of a sudden.*) You met her by chance . . .

CAYRE: Well . . . yes . . . a series of circumstances which led to . . . it amounts to the same thing . . . (*Stop.*) Anyway . . . that first time didn't count . . . I didn't think we'd ever see each other again (*Pause.*) It was the next day . . . desire catches up with you, you know, it takes over . . . suddenly you want to see her again, so badly . . . that had never happened to me before . . . it's as if . . . (*Stop.*).

CUSTOMER: (*Still unambiguous.*) She shared this desire . . . ?

CAYRE: (*Looks at him, with sincerity.*) I don't know. (*Long pause. Silence.*)

CUSTOMER: You were saying that you don't know when you lost her . . .

CAYRE: Oh . . . probably the first day. After that, I must have tried to make up for it . . . that's probably what I take for love, I'm no fool . . . that kind of . . . attempt to save . . . to . . .

CUSTOMER: (*Finishes his sentence.*) Get power . . . ?

CAYRE: (*Pained smile.*) Yes, of course . . . that too . . . (*He becomes quiet.*)

CUSTOMER: Did something new happen on this trip?

CAYRE: (*Thinks about it then gives up.*) Yes . . . I think so . . .

CUSTOMER: (*Pause.*) The fact that she stays shut up in that house?

CAYRE: (*Pause.*) Not just that . . . no . . . like a kind of . . . docility, yes, that's it . . . for some time now . . . that she hides behind . . . do you know what I mean?

CUSTOMER: Sort of, yes . . . (*pause*) a kind of conviction . . . ?

CAYRE: (*With a slight start.*) Perhaps. (*Pause.*) I don't know. (*Long pause. The customer looks at Michel Cayre who isn't looking at anything. The telephone rings again. Voice of the bartender from very far away. He's reiterating that Véra Baxter hasn't come back yet. Michel Cayre is suddenly afraid. The customer notices it. His voice is gentle.*)

CUSTOMER: What are you afraid of . . . ?

CAYRE: (*Pause.*) It's hard to say. It's like a threat . . . ever since noon. (*Pause.*) That's when he started to call every fifteen minutes to find out how his wife's doing. (*Silence.*) I'm a person who doesn't want to suffer.

CUSTOMER: (*As if he had guessed that.*) Yes. (*Silence.*)

(*Blackout.*)

III. THE COLONNADES

(*Later. The living room, dark, large. A sofa with a white slipcover on it. Two chairs, the telephone. The large open French windows let in a white light which will grow dimmer. Offstage we hear people talking and walking around somewhere. Far away at first, then coming closer. Women's voices.*)

M. COMBES: (*Off.*) Do you like it?

VERA BAXTER: (*Off.*) All the land in front belongs to the house. It goes all the way down to the sea (*pause*). There's a private beach. It's big. This one would be Christine's . . . This one, Marc's . . . If friends come, Irène and Christine can sleep in the same room . . . I really don't know if Christine will be coming . . . (*During this last monologue her words are spaced far apart. They come into the living room.*) She was supposed to go to England this year. (*Silence. They walk toward the terrace.*) The terrace is what makes it so expensive. Somehow I imagined it differently . . . Two million francs for the month of August is a lot, I think. (*They go over to the railing.*) "Clair Bois" was more protected from the wind . . . farther away from the sea . . . but . . . anyway, it's already rented . . . it's too late . . . (*Silence. Far away, the sounds of the TURBULENCE have started up again. Dancing, laughter and screams.*) Vandals who've broken in, perhaps. (*Pause.*) Apparently, the houses here are raided during the winter, people break in . . . (*Silence.*)

M. COMBES: (*Pause.*) There seems to be a party. (*Silence.*)

VERA BAXTER: It's so isolated here . . . you'd think you were in California . . . if you screamed . . . no one would hear you. "Clair Bois" was smaller . . . it didn't have this view . . . these grounds . . . it only had a garden. (*Pause.*) We went there too long, I think . . . ten years . . . ever since Irène was born. (*Silence. Again no response.*) I'm the one who wanted the change . . . (*Pause.*) Jean's never here during the summer, what difference does it make to him? He only comes home to sleep . . . This house or another one as far as he's concerned . . . We had seen this one before. We used to notice it from our boat . . . I remember I said to him maybe we could rent it some day . . . just once, for one summer . . . Of course there were other houses we liked too . . . (*Pause.*) He used to say, "Oh, to live love again there . . . a new love" . . . You know how he talks . . .

M. COMBES: (*Pause.*) Yes. (*They come back into the living room.*) I'd never been inside this one before. (*No response.*) The location's lovely. (*Pause.*) Will you take it?

VERA BAXTER: It's expensive, I think. I have to talk to Jean about it.

M. COMBES: (*Hypocritically.*) Hadn't you both agreed on a price?

VERA BAXTER: We haven't discussed money. (*Pause.*) I called Paris, I left this number with Marie-Louise.

M. COMBES: He wasn't there?

VERA BAXTER: No. (*Pause.*) He was supposed to call around five o'clock to find out how our youngest daughter's doing. (*Pause.*)

M. COMBES: You don't know where he's going?

VERA BAXTER: (*Pause.*) Various places ... to Chantilly, I think. (*Pause.*) To stay at a model's place. (*Silence.*)

M. COMBES: (*Pause.*) It seems he's going to spend the summer in the Balearic Islands.

VERA BAXTER: (*Pause.*) I don't know.

M. COMBES: How've you been, Véra? And the children?

VERA BAXTER: Fine.

M. COMBES: (*Pause.*) You're staying at the Hôtel de Paris.

VERA BAXTER: That's right ... (*Silence.*)

M. COMBES: Jean called me, he asked me to help you decide if you couldn't make up your mind between several houses.

VERA BAXTER: This was the one I wanted. (*Pause.*) To see the inside. (*Silence.*)

M. COMBES: You could go back to the hotel ... call from the hotel ...

VERA BAXTER: No. (*Silence.*)

M. COMBES: We haven't seen each other in a long time ... I went to Paris in October, you were in Bordeaux and ... (*Véra Baxter stares at her. Her sentence hangs in mid-air.*)

VERA BAXTER: We went to Bordeaux in October, yes ... (*Pause.*) Sometimes we travel together, he takes me along when he's alone, two or three days ... We didn't tell ... (*Long pause.*) After Bordeaux, the weather was beautiful, we went to the seashore, you know ... the place where we met ... Arcangues. (*Pause.*) We'd never been back there.

M. COMBES: (*Pause.*) He's the one who wanted to go there ...

VERA BAXTER: Yes.

M. COMBES: (*Mechanically.*) ... in October ...

VERA BAXTER: Yes.

M. COMBES: He said to me: "This year, I'll go abroad, I want to leave her alone ... one time ... without me."

VERA BAXTER: He's been talking about changing his life ... his wife ... his job ... for ten years now. You shouldn't pay any attention to what he says ...

M. COMBES: Yes. (*Silence. They are in front of the French windows. They comment.*) Fortunately there's some life around the dock over the winter ... It's so dead ...

VERA BAXTER: Yes ... You wonder how life can return ... in the summer.

M. COMBES: You didn't come to Thionville alone ... People saw you last night at the dock with a man who wasn't Jean Baxter. (*Silence.*) It's so unexpected ... I can't begin to believe it.

VERA BAXTER: It just happened; one day, then another. I didn't want anything like that to happen.

M. COMBES: (*Pause. In a low voice.*) How old is Christine?

VERA BAXTER: (*Pause.*) Seventeen.

M. COMBES: She was born very soon after you were married ...

VERA BAXTER: (*Trying to remember.*) Fifteen months. (*Long pause.*) It was after Christine's birth that money started coming into the house. (*Pause.*) Then ... he lost everything ... right before Marc was born. (*Pause.*) And then ... things began to get better ... He'd drag me along with him everywhere ... We lived everywhere in Paris ... in two rooms, in ten rooms ... it went on for a long time ... (*Silence.*) He's going to call me, I'm going to wait. (*Long pause.*) I have to speak to him about Michel Cayre.

M. COMBES: Michel Cayre ... (*Long pause.*) Is he a reporter for a Sunday newspaper?

VERA BAXTER: (*Not fooled by this.*) That's right.

M. COMBES: Jean doesn't know anything?

VERA BAXTER: (*Pause.*) No.

M. COMBES: (*Long pause.*) Are you certain, Véra?

VERA BAXTER: Yes. (*Pause.*) He can only know about it from me. (*Silence.*)

M. COMBES: But ... you've both talked about this possibility ...

VERA BAXTER: (*Long pause.*) Sometimes ... when ... (*Silence.*)

M. COMBES: My affairs are short-lived. (*Pause.*) I don't know anything about what can happen between people after a long time ...

VERA BAXTER: It's hard to say ... it's impossible ... (*Pause.*) Otherwise we don't talk much, we talk about the house, the children. Sometimes we talk about his business. (*Long pause.*) What time is it?

M. COMBES: Ten minutes after five ... how long has this been going on?

VERA BAXTER: Since October. (*Pause.*) Before the trip to Bordeaux. (*Longer pause.*) I met him at a sidewalk café, I remember now, it was raining, it was near Alma ... He had hardly noticed me here, I think ... I was sitting on the terrace, waiting for the rain to stop ... He ran in ... He didn't recognize me at first ... We watched the rain and then ... It was so sudden ... We were surprised. (*Silence.*)

M. COMBES: Véra, you're not telling the truth, are you?

VERA BAXTER: (*Pause.*) No.

M. COMBES: Both you and I lie a lot.

VERA BAXTER: A lot. Yes. (*Silence. They smile at each other, look at each other.*) I woke up early this morning to come here ... We drink all night long. (*Pause.*) He likes me to drink. (*Long pause.*) I'm so tired.

M. COMBES: They know each other.

VERA BAXTER: Who? They've played poker together. And then they've gone sailing.

M. COMBES: Then I've met him ...

VERA BAXTER: It was last year.

M. COMBES: (*Pause.*) That's true ... I avoided coming. Did Jean have any affairs here last summer?

VERA BAXTER: No. (*Pause.*) Or else they were very brief. (*Pause.*) No, last summer I was the only one ...

M. COMBES: (*Pause.*) There were times when you were the only one ...

VERA BAXTER: Yes. (*Silence.*)

M. COMBES: We've never spoken about Jean Baxter before. (*Pause.*) It's the first time.

VERA BAXTER: (*Pause.*) Yes.

M. COMBES: He never took it seriously . . . you knew that . . .

VERA BAXTER: (*Pause.*) The same as everybody else . . . no differently . . .

M. COMBES: What didn't you know?

VERA BAXTER: If you had been unhappy.

M. COMBES: Yes. (*Pause.*) He doesn't know it.

VERA BAXTER: No. (*Silence.*)

M. COMBES: You were never afraid of that affair . . .

VERA BAXTER: No.

M. COMBES: You were right.

VERA BAXTER: (*Long pause.*) He was always leaving forever.

M. COMBES: (*Pause.*) Did you believe him?

VERA BAXTER: (*Long pause.*) I don't know any more . . . all of a sudden . . . (*Silence. The TURBULENCE, far away, is starting up again.*) All of this is possible because of the money.

M. COMBES: What?

VERA BAXTER: Our marriage. (*Pause.*) When he goes away with a woman, he sends me checks. (*Pause.*) When the affair goes on for a while, he sends a lot of money. (*Pause.*) He's never forgotten to send it. Sometimes he makes a mistake and sends it twice. (*Long pause.*) When he goes away, he doesn't call for a few days. (*Pause.*) Sometimes three days, sometimes four. And then, he begins to call again.

M. COMBES: (*Pause.*) When we went to Venice . . .

VERA BAXTER: Then, too. (*Long pause.*) Afterwards . . . when he comes back . . . he sees that the children and I are still here. (*Silence.*)

M. COMBES: He talked a lot about you.

VERA BAXTER: About his wife . . .

M. COMBES: Yes. Wait a minute . . . yes . . . he'd say that she could only be known through desire. (*Pause.*) That he would have liked to . . . find her again some place else, outside of marriage . . . (*Silence.*)

VERA BAXTER: That wouldn't have been possible . . . I recognize your perfume . . . it's the same as two years ago.

M. COMBES: (*Pause.*) Yes.

VERA BAXTER: When he'd come back after seeing you . . .

M. COMBES: When you meet Jean Baxter for the first time, you think he's a lonely man. (*Pause.*) You feel sorry for him for having the wife he has. (*Pause.*) Then, gradually you forget that woman . . . (*Pause.*) You forget she even exists . . . (*Long pause.*) It's only later on . . . that you discover in Jean Baxter a kind of . . . impossibility . . . to love . . . yes . . . You wonder if Jean Baxter doesn't believe in God without admitting it. (*Long pause.*) Sometimes, you discover the truth.

VERA BAXTER: When?

M. COMBES: Yesterday, when he called to find out where you were.

VERA BAXTER: I thought it would last forever. (*Long pause.*) That wouldn't have been possible. (*The TURBULENCE starts up again.*)

M. COMBES: I forgot to tell you . . . You remember Bernard Fontaine . . . He was killed in an automobile accident day before yesterday. (*Pause.*) You didn't want to admit it, but you found him attractive.

VERA BAXTER: Maybe . . . Now that . . . you mention it . . .

(*A few seconds go by before the blackout.*)

IV. THE COLONNADES

(*The TURBULENCE. No shouts, no laughter. As if quieted down, lulled, with the coming of evening. Gradually the voice of Jean Baxter is heard, emerging from a kind of thick silence reminiscent of the thick silence of a soundproof room. Véra Baxter, seated on the sofa, in the dark, is talking on the phone.*)

JEAN BAXTER: (*Off.*) Véra . . . Hello . . . Véra?

VERA BAXTER: I'm here . . . Where are you?

JEAN BAXTER: (*Off.*) Chantilly.

VERA BAXTER: (*Silence.*) You're alone . . .

JEAN BAXTER: (*Off.*) She went for a walk in the forest. (*Pause.*) It's foggy out.

VERA BAXTER: It was windy here this morning . . . now . . . (*Long silence.*)

JEAN BAXTER: (*Off.*) Véra . . . Véra . . .

VERA BAXTER: (*Pause.*) Yes . . .

JEAN BAXTER: (*Off.*) Where are you?

VERA BAXTER: I don't know any more . . . I was calling you about the house, it's expensive . . . two million francs . . . I wanted to talk to you about it before renting it . . . It seems like a lot of money.

JEAN BAXTER: (*Off.*) What difference does it make . . . ? (*Silence.*)

VERA BAXTER: It's big. Eight rooms. (*Pause.*) There's a beach down below . . .

JEAN BAXTER: (*Off.*) Yes . . . (*Long silence. Far off, the TURBULENCE, very gentle, like a lullaby. The silence continues: "These people who don't know how to talk about their love."*)

VERA BAXTER: "Clair Bois" is already rented . . . we'd been going there for too long . . . too . . . but (*stop*) . . . the grounds here . . . it's terrible . . . terrible, I think . . . (*Long silence.*) Maybe we should have changed towns . . . everything . . . everything.

JEAN BAXTER: (*Off.*) We've tried that too.

VERA BAXTER: (*Scream.*) Jean . . .

JEAN BAXTER: (*Pause—off.*) I'm here. (*Silence on both sides.*)

VERA BAXTER: It's desolate here in the winter, it's as if no one had come here in ten years . . . (*Silence. No response from Jean Baxter.*) We could have gone away. Changed countries . . . left France . . . (*Silence. Idem.*) Seventeen years . . . and all those children besides . . . (*Silence. Idem.*) We should have separated . . . divorced . . . stopped living together . . . lost ourselves . . . and then . . . (*Long silence.*) I ran into Monique Combès . . . I talked a lot . . . a lot . . . I lied . . . about everything . . . a lot. I lie all the time . . . to everybody.

JEAN BAXTER: (*Off—pause.*) You're the only one who tells the truth . . . (*Silence. Véra Baxter screams. Muffled. Terrible. TURBULENCE. Silence.*)

VERA BAXTER: (*Scream.*) Jean . . . it's over . . . it's over . . . over . . . Jean . . . You knew it . . . (*The receiver is dropped and falls on the sofa. Silence.*)

JEAN BAXTER: (*Off.*) I don't know anything any more. (*Véra Baxter picks up the receiver again.*)

VERA BAXTER: Jean . . . Jean . . . (*Silence.*)

JEAN BAXTER: (*Off.*) I'm going to take a plane, I'll be at Thionville at eight o'clock.

VERA BAXTER: I won't be here any more. (*Pause.*) I'll have gone to join him, we'll have left Thionville. (*Silence on Jean Baxter's end.*) I've shut myself up in here to kill myself, I think . . . (*Pause.*) But . . .

JEAN BAXTER: (*Off.*) Why do you want to die? (*Silence.*)

VERA BAXTER: I don't want anything any more. I don't love anybody any more. I didn't know that . . . (*Stop. Silence on Jean Baxter's end.*) Then there's . . . I drink a lot right now . . . I wasn't used to that . . . I drink during the night . . . I enjoy it . . . and then . . . the idea of summer . . . again . . . it comes back too fast, I think . . . and then the grounds . . . so deserted . . . you'd think you were in California . . . if you screamed . . . no one would come . . . (*Silence. Then, imperceptible, far off, the TURBULENCE starting up again: it interrupts Véra Baxter's sentence.*) There's a party in one of the houses on the estate . . . Maybe that's what made me . . . Listen . . . (*She holds the receiver out toward the outside, the French windows. She stays like that, her arm out, while the TURBULENCE gradually invades the room.*)

V. THE COLONNADES

(*The TURBULENCE recedes. Véra Baxter is standing motionless, in front of the terrace. The French windows are wide open. Dusky colors already. Far off, the brightly lit house where the TURBULENCE is heard. In the dark, a man is watching. It's the customer from the Hôtel de Paris [here, the "Stranger" as far as Véra Baxter is concerned]. Véra Baxter being watched. Still. Facing out toward the sea. A sense of violation, of absolute indiscretion. Véra Baxter turns her head around slowly and sees him. They look at each other. There is no fear in Véra Baxter's look.*)

THE STRANGER: Are you Véra Baxter?

VERA BAXTER: Yes.

THE STRANGER: I've come on Michel Cayre's behalf. He asked me to come get you. (*Silence.*)

VERA BAXTER: Who are you?

THE STRANGER: A guest at the Hôtel de Paris.

VERA BAXTER: Have you been standing there for long?

THE STRANGER: (*Pause.*) You were talking about summer . . . you were finding it . . . painful to imagine . . .

VERA BAXTER: Where is Michel Cayre?

THE STRANGER: At the hotel, I believe. He said it might be easier for someone else to get you to leave this Colonnades' fortress.

VERA BAXTER: (*Mechanically.*) I was going to meet him. (*Silence.*)

THE STRANGER: You're quite a distance away here and you haven't got a car . . .

VERA BAXTER: I would have called the agency and asked them to come get me . . . or I would have walked . . . (*Silence. He doesn't answer.*) What time is it?

THE STRANGER: I don't have a watch. (*Silence.*) It's not late. The sun's still high in the sky, look . . .

VERA BAXTER: (*Pause.*) Has he been drinking?

THE STRANGER: (*Pause. Simply.*) Yes. Enough to kill you on the road . . . what with all those children you both have.

VERA BAXTER: (*In a low voice, mechanically.*) Oh . . . he told you . . .

THE STRANGER: Yes. (*Silence.*)

VERA BAXTER: You hadn't met him before?

THE STRANGER: No, never. We spent two hours together at the hotel bar . . . We talked for a long time . . . You know how it happens sometimes . . . (*Silence.*) We can leave whenever you like. The car's downstairs. (*No answer. Silence.*)

VERA BAXTER: (*Distractedly.*) It's strange, I didn't hear you come into the house . . . (*Silence.*)

THE STRANGER: That was your husband on the phone.

VERA BAXTER: Yes. (*Pause.*) About the house . . .

THE STRANGER: I know. (*Silence.*)

VERA BAXTER: (*Pause.*) I'm going to take it.

THE STRANGER: It looks like there are *some* people around. (*TURBULENCE.*) A party . . . it seems.

VERA BAXTER: Yes.

THE STRANGER: It's over there near the woods, one of the last houses on the estate . . . (*Silence.*) Two women ran into each other here a little while ago (*Long pause.*) They talked for some time. (*Long silence.*)

VERA BAXTER: Did you know them?

THE STRANGER: Not yet, no. (*Silence.*) Michel Cayre and I were walking near here. (*Pause.*) We noticed them.

VERA BAXTER: (*Pause.*) So he didn't stay in the room like he said he would.

THE STRANGER: No. (*Pause.*) He couldn't, I think. (*Pause.*) He couldn't stand waiting any more. (*Silence.*)

VERA BAXTER: Is he still at the hotel? (*He looks at her. Doesn't answer.*) What do you think?

THE STRANGER: (*Pause.*) Maybe, yes. (*Silence.*)

VERA BAXTER: (*Brutally.*) He was supposed to leave me.

THE STRANGER: He says he's reached the point where he can't touch another woman. (*Pause.*) Not yet. (*Pause.*) But . . . (*Stop.*)

VERA BAXTER: Did you watch those women a long time?

THE STRANGER: Yes. The whole time they were talking.

VERA BAXTER: (*Long pause.*) Why?

THE STRANGER: (*Slowly.*) Watching them from a distance, we almost believed we could hear their conversation. (*Silence.*) What were they talking about?

VERA BAXTER: They were talking about a writer. He was killed in an automobile accident last week. (*Pause.*) *Bernard Fontaine* . . . does that name mean anything to you?

THE STRANGER: (*Thinking.*) No . . .

VERA BAXTER: I met him here, two years ago. (*Pause.*) I had met him once before in Paris. (*Pause.*) I remember he asked me to meet him . . . near Alma.

THE STRANGER: (*Pause.*) You didn't go.

VERA BAXTER: No. (*Pause. Silence. The TURBULENCE continues.*)

THE STRANGER: There are two creeks down below. I hadn't noticed them. (*Pause.*) There's a little sand beach too. That'll be convenient for the children. You'll be able to see them from here.

VERA BAXTER: (*Pause.*) Oh . . . they're grown up now. (*Pause.*) Except for the youngest. (*Pause.*) She came along . . . We weren't expecting her . . . .(*Silence. She looks out at the surroundings, the house.*) I just wanted to see it, I think. That's all. (*Pause.*) It's as if I've got nothing more to do with it now. (*Pause.*) Maybe that's the way it always is when you rent, when you buy . . . no?

THE STRANGER: Maybe. I don't know. (*Silence.*)

VERA BAXTER: Would you like to see it . . . ?

THE STRANGER: (*Pause.*) Why not? (*They leave the stage. Silence. Véra Baxter's and the Stranger's steps can be heard. Feeling of great slowness.*)

VERA BAXTER: (*Off.*) People must break in during the winter . . . sleep here. There's bread, leftovers, in the kitchen . . . (*Stop. Silence. Then they start walking again. Sea. Stop. Silence.*)

THE STRANGER: (*Off.*) Do you like it?

VERA BAXTER: (*Off.*) It's big . . . well located . . . but . . . ugly.

THE STRANGER: (*Off. Smiling.*) Yes.

VERA BAXTER: (*Off.*) I don't know when it's ugly . . . (*They come back onstage. They stop. He looks at her. She looks outside. She goes toward the terrace and disappears from view. Silence.*)

VERA BAXTER: (*Off.*) What's the matter?

THE STRANGER: I'm looking at you. (*Silence. Nothing moves.*) Michel Cayre said: "At first, she's not beautiful. (*Pause.*) Then she is." (*Silence. Nothing moves.*

Then she comes back in.)

VERA BAXTER: We'll go by the agency and then we'll leave, if you want to . . . I'll tell him I'm renting it, we'll go back to the hotel. I'll go to bed right away. I'll have dinner in the room. (*Pause.*) I'm so tired . . . (*He doesn't answer.*) Don't you want to?

THE STRANGER: I don't think you want to go back to the hotel. (*Long silence.*)

VERA BAXTER: (*Slowly.*) What do I want?

THE STRANGER: (*Slowly.*) Nothing, I think. It's one of those times . . . you have to wait . . . (*Long silence.*)

VERA BAXTER: I'd like you to leave. I want to go to sleep.

THE STRANGER: (*Pause. Slowness.*) I'd like to be able to leave you. (*Pause.*) But I can't. (*Pause.*) You're in danger . . . I think . . . (*Silence.*)

VERA BAXTER: This morning's when I wanted to die. Then I heard that party over there . . . But this evening . . . (*Silence.*)

THE STRANGER: (*Pause.*) No . . . (*Pause.*) I think you're wrong. (*Pause.*) This morning you were expecting something . . . that call from Jean Baxter. This evening, nothing, I think. Nothing any more. (*She doesn't say anything.*) In a half hour it will be dark. (*Silence.*)

VERA BAXTER: Did you hear the whole phone coversation?

THE STRANGER: (*Pause.*) Yes. (*Silence.*) Were you very young when you got married?

VERA BAXTER: (*Distracted.*) Twenty. (*Pause.*) He was one of my brother's friends. (*Pause.*) I'd always known him. (*Silence.*) I don't know what happened.

THE STRANGER: When . . . ?

VERA BAXTER: This morning . . .

THE STRANGER: And now . . . ? (*She wonders.*)

VERA BAXTER: I've already seen you, haven't I?

THE STRANGER: I don't think so. (*Pause.*) My name wouldn't mean anything to you. (*Pause.*) I too could have met you in the Thionville bars. When you used to wait for Jean Baxter to finish his poker games. (*Pause.*) But it turns out we didn't. It didn't happen. (*Pause.*) Was he at Chantilly?

VERA BAXTER: (*Mechanically.*) Yes. At some model's place. He still goes there quite often. (*Pause.*) She had gone out for a walk. He was alone in the house. (*Pause.*) She's very beautiful . . . very young . . . She's not there all the time . . . you know, she goes on trips.

THE STRANGER: I see. (*Long silence.*)

VERA BAXTER: He told me I was telling the truth.

THE STRANGER: Jean Baxter, your husband?

VERA BAXTER: Yes. (*Pause.*)

THE STRANGER: Michel Cayre says you're a liar.

VERA BAXTER: I do lie, to him.

THE STRANGER: And to Jean Baxter?

VERA BAXTER: He never asks me any questions.

THE STRANGER: I'm only passing through, crossing through your life . . . so if a certain truth were told here this evening, it wouldn't have any future . . . there wouldn't be any consequences. (*The TURBULENCE becomes very loud all of a sudden.*) Outsiders, it seems. (*Pause.*) A party. We heard it from all over Thionville and didn't know where it was coming from. (*Pause.*) Then we saw it, a little while ago when Michel Cayre and I came here. (*Pause.*) We named it: the outside turbulence. Just like you name a storm or the wind. Probably because it invaded all of Thionville, you couldn't help but hear it!

VERA BAXTER: (*Pause.*) At one point, they waved at me . . . this afternoon . . . to come over, I think.

THE STRANGER: (*Pause.*) You didn't go.

VERA BAXTER: No. (*Silence.*) It was after that that I thought about going out . . . and that I'd meet Monique Combès over near the boat dock . . . and then she showed up.

THE STRANGER: (*Pause.*) Was she a friend?

VERA BAXTER: (*Pause.*) She used to come over to our house. (*Silence.*)

THE STRANGER: Did he say it was expensive?

VERA BAXTER: (*Pause.*) As far as he's concerned, it's not terribly expensive. (*Pause.*) It's not a lot of money. (*Pause.*) No.

THE STRANGER: Wouldn't he have given a lot more to lose you?

VERA BAXTER: (*Pause.*) He makes a lot of money. (*Silence.*)

THE STRANGER: That must be what people say about him when they've just met him, right? That he makes a lot of money.

VERA BAXTER: Yes, that's right . . .

THE STRANGER: And that he's always made money quite easily?

VERA BAXTER: Yes.

THE STRANGER: . . . And that he also spends everything he makes . . . (*pause*) on women . . . gambling . . .

VERA BAXTER: Everything he steals is what people say . . .

THE STRANGER: Yes.

VERA BAXTER: He paid Michel Cayre. Two million francs. The same price as the house.

THE STRANGER: (*Pause.*) He wanted it that way.

VERA BAXTER: (*With difficulty.*) Yes.

THE STRANGER: (*Very slowly.*) That sort of thing shouldn't have been said?

VERA BAXTER: No. (*Pause.*) I looked at the checkbook, in his office during the night.

THE STRANGER: (*Pause.*) It was probably necessary to reach that stage . . .

VERA BAXTER: (*Pause.*) I had become unapproachable, except by him, Jean Baxter. (*Very long silence.*)

THE STRANGER: You mean you've been unfaithful to Jean Baxter. (*Abnormally long silence.*)

VERA BAXTER: Yes . . . (*Another very long silence.*) I went to Michel Cayre's

place because it had been paid for. (*Pause.*) Money's what allowed . . . well
. . .

THE STRANGER: (*Still softly.*) . . . What . . . ?

VERA BAXTER: (*Softly.*) . . . The affair . . .

THE STRANGER: (*Long pause.*) Two million francs, you said?

VERA BAXTER: . . . Yes . . . They met in a baccarat club. (*Pause.*) He must have
told you? (*No answer. As if recited:*) Michel Cayre called me up, he said: "I
met Jean Baxter last week. He asked me to call you. You must know what it's
about." (*Pause.*) I said yes. (*Pause.*) I went to his place in the afternoon.
(*Pause.*) He opened the door. The apartment was dark, filled with the other
woman's things. (*Pause.*) He told me that at first he'd decided to keep Jean
Baxter's check without calling me and then . . . he'd felt like meeting me
because of the amount I was worth: two million francs. (*Silence.*) I asked him
if Jean Baxter knew what time it was supposed to happen. He said he didn't
know. In the afternoon, at Michel Cayre's, there was a phone call. (*Pause.*) I
heard a scream . . . The person on the phone, then they hung up . . . a man
. . . (*Silence. She concludes:*) Michel Cayre and I weren't supposed to go on
seeing each other. (*Pause.*) Then he called me again. (*Pause.*) As if that two
million francs were never going to run out. (*Silence. He falls silent.*) You
weren't listening. (*No answer from the Stranger. Silence.*)

VERA BAXTER: You didn't hear, perhaps . . .

THE STRANGER: (*Pause.*) I was looking at those people. The house, over there.

VERA BAXTER: Michel Cayre told you? (*Silence. Delayed answer from The
Stranger.*)

THE STRANGER: Michel Cayre told me about a gambling debt. (*Pause.*) But the
amount is the same: two million francs. (*Pause.*) I heard what you said. (*The
TURBULENCE completely lit up. Music and dancing. Sounds of voices.*) You
didn't tell Jean Baxter about that afternoon at Michel Cayre's?

VERA BAXTER: (*Pause.*) No. (*Silence.*)

THE STRANGER: But you should have? You should have brought home your in-
fidelity to Jean Baxter, isn't that so?

VERA BAXTER: Yes. (*Silence.*) He didn't ask me any questions, I expected him to
but he didn't. (*Long pause.*) That evening . . . when he came home . . . he
said he was very tired from work, he went to his room, he didn't eat any dinner. I remember. I was watching television. He was afraid we might talk to
each other. (*Pause.*) Afraid of seeing me. When the children had been put to
bed, he went out, I heard him in the hall. (*Pause.*) He must have gone out to
play cards in one of his clubs . . . (*Pause.*) For several days, we avoided each
other, tried not to run into each other in the house. (*Ellipse.*) Then I came to
Thionville to rent the house.

THE STRANGER: (*Pause.*) I'd understood that more time had gone by, the whole
winter, almost. (*Silence. No answer from Véra Baxter.*) And there'd been a trip
to Bordeaux, in October, I believe. (*Silence.*)

VERA BAXTER: Don't pay any attention to what I say.

THE STRANGER: (*Pause – kindness.*) No ... (*Long silence. Sound of the wind.*) The wind's starting up again along with night time.

VERA BAXTER: (*Slowly.*) It never stops.

THE STRANGER: Except maybe in August? ...

VERA BAXTER: (*Slowly, absently.*) Oh, three days ... He goes to Chantilly a lot since it happened, to stay out of my way, you see ...

THE STRANGER: (*Gently.*) Yes. (*Silence.*) I can see Jean Baxter. I look at you and I see him. (*Silence. She listens – as if far away. His voice is soft and low:*) Michel Cayre says: "Jean Baxter has the kind of grace that goes with money." (*Silence.*)

VERA BAXTER: Michel Cayre doesn't know how to make money.

THE STRANGER: I don't know. I don't know him.

VERA BAXTER: (*Agrees.*) No, he doesn't know how. (*Long pause.*) It's terrible ... there's never enough. (*Pause.*) Terrible.

THE STRANGER: (*Pause.*) Yes. (*Pause.*) Michel Cayre is incapable of knowing how.

VERA BAXTER: Yes.

THE STRANGER: (*Pause.*) He says: "I've never refused money no matter where it comes from. (*Hesitates.*) I'd never refuse. (*Hesitates.*) No matter what."

VERA BAXTER: Yes. (*Pause.*) He's right, I think.

THE STRANGER: (*Unambiguously.*) Yes. (*Silence. They look outside. Look at each other.*) Will Jean Baxter come this summer?

VERA BAXTER: I don't know.

THE STRANGER: All you have to do is ask him?

VERA BAXTER: He'll come for a couple of days ... to see the children. The rest of the time ...

THE STRANGER: He'll go to the Balearic Islands, with a woman from Chantilly?

VERA BAXTER: That's possible. (*Pause.*) You know ... he does whatever other people do, he does whatever his colleagues do. He goes wherever they go ... to Cannes ... to the Balearic Islands. Except for money matters ... he doesn't have much imagination, you know ... He's a rather ordinary person. (*Silence.*)

THE STRANGER: (*Softly.*) The grounds are dark now. (*Pause.*) But the beach is still lit up; so is the sea ...

VERA BAXTER: (*Continues as if she hadn't heard.*) He has no idea what the word intelligence means ... He doesn't think at all ... as if it weren't worth the trouble. As for me, I didn't care, you know, and I even preferred ... (*Stops short.*)

THE STRANGER: (*Softly.*) Yes, I know. (*Silence.*)

VERA BAXTER: He doesn't have anything, but that ... money ... he's not even rich ... he has some money ... that's all.

THE STRANGER: (*Unambiguous all of a sudden.*) And Jean Baxter knows that himself.

VERA BAXTER: Yes. That's right.

THE STRANGER: You should come over here and see . . . (*No answer. She comes over near the Stranger to see. They are seen from the back.*)

VERA BAXTER: He was crying.

THE STRANGER: This evening? . . .

VERA BAXTER: Yes.

THE STRANGER: (*Pause.*) He said that it had to be done, that it was a crime? . . . That you were . . . (*Stop.*) That one day, he would give you away?

VERA BAXTER: Yes. (*Pause.*) It wasn't serving any purpose.

THE STRANGER: He had made bets on it too. Twice, I think . . . Wasn't it? With friends of his.

VERA BAXTER: I don't know.

THE STRANGER: Three years ago.

VERA BAXTER: I didn't know that. (*Pause.*) It was only last summer when he met Michel Cayre that he discovered what needed to be done. (*Silence.*)

THE STRANGER: Jean Baxter was always having affairs? . . . (*No answer.*) He was never without one? . . . (*No answer.*) And your affairs were Jean Baxter's affairs?

VERA BAXTER: (*In a low voice.*) Maybe . . . I don't know any more . . . yes. (*Silence.*)

THE STRANGER: You understood that it had to happen?

VERA BAXTER: (*Long pause.*) Sometimes . . . in the summertime . . . he would go away for a long time sometimes. I lied. (*He doesn't move.*) It was . . . (*Stop.*)

THE STRANGER: (*Softly.*) It didn't happen in October.

VERA BAXTER: No. (*With difficulty.*) It was three days ago . . . (*Stop.*) In Paris. Near Alma, I think . . . it was raining . . . (*Stop.*) I went into a café . . . on the terrace . . . and . . . (*Stop – silence.*)

THE STRANGER: (*Continues, slowly.*) Was it Bernard Fontaine?

VERA BAXTER: No. (*Pause.*) Someone else. (*Pause.*) Someone I'd never seen before . . . (*Long silence.*)

THE STRANGER: He wasn't like anyone you knew . . .

VERA BAXTER: No. (*Pause.*) I don't know his name. As soon as he came over . . . (*With great difficulty. Stop.*) We went to a hotel . . . (*Stop – very slowly.*) That's when . . .

THE STRANGER: (*Slowly.*) Did you see him again?

VERA BAXTER: No.

THE STRANGER: You mean it wasn't worth the trouble . . .

VERA BAXTER: (*Pause.*) That's right, yes . . . (*Pause.*) That time . . . Jean sensed it, I think. That evening . . . (*Stop.*)

THE STRANGER: (*Pause.*) And Michel Cayre?

VERA BAXTER: No. (*Pause.*) That was three days ago. The night before I came here.

THE STRANGER: It's strange . . . that pain . . . when you were talking . . . "there." (*He puts his hand on his chest. She says nothing.*) As if I too had just lost you. (*She doesn't answer. Silence everywhere. Silence as if it were an event. Then an outside "incident"—a boat going by, shouts, song of the TURBULENCE—then everything falls silent. He is in pain:*) The light's getting dimmer. Look at the sea.

VERA BAXTER: Almost black. (*Silence once again. Véra Baxter leaves the terrace. He doesn't move.*)

THE STRANGER: (*Softly.*) He's stayed quite young, hasn't he, Jean Baxter? . . . He doesn't know how to suffer . . . Isn't that right? (*Silence. No response.*) In the same way that he has to be happy no matter what . . . doesn't he? (*No answer.*) You were right. (*Pause.*) He was mistaken. We've all been mistaken. He didn't know anything before this evening. (*Silence. No response. Softly.*) The pain must have been hovering there for days now . . . and then you "spoke" . . . (*Silence. No response.*) Jean Baxter will probably never be the same again . . . less childlike, perhaps . . . less innocent . . . (*No response. Silence.*) It's strange, yes, I see him better than that man at the hotel . . . (*Pause.*) Jean Baxter, the money man. A lost man, a clown. (*Pause. Silence.*) You ought to come over here and see. The sun's going down into the sea. The dock's the only thing left with light on it.

VERA BAXTER: Sometimes, in the summer, it's as if it were on fire . . .

THE STRANGER: You can tell it's still winter by the colors . . . (*Long pause.*) No matter what the weather's like things always calm down around this time.

VERA BAXTER: (*Pause.*) I think so. (*Far off, a siren.*)

THE STRANGER: It's the siren at the gun powder factory. (*Pause.*) It's six o'clock. (*Silence.*)

VERA BAXTER: The agent was supposed to call . . . I don't understand. (*Pause.*) He probably couldn't reach the owners . . . It takes so long. (*No response. Silence.*) Let's go. We'll go over to the agent's, if you don't mind . . .

THE STRANGER: (*Pause, frank.*) There's no need to. (*Pause.*) The house is already rented. It's been taken care of. (*Silence. No response.*)

THE STRANGER: Jean Baxter rented it, yesterday morning. (*Pause.*) The agent knows about it. (*Pause.*) The check's been made out and sent. (*Pause.*) Michel Cayre met Monique Combès today at the Hôtel de Paris, she told him. (*Long silence.*)

VERA BAXTER: Did they say what the rent was?

THE STRANGER: Enormous, it would seem. That's the word Monique Combès used.

VERA BAXTER: (*Pause.*) How much?

THE STRANGER: She didn't know. (*Silence.*)

VERA BAXTER: This house. . . . it's the time of day that makes it seem so sad, don't you think? (*Pause.*) The grounds are frightening. (*Pause.*) The sunset's sad on this part of the coast . . . and you can see all of it from here . . . (*Gesture.*)

THE STRANGER: (*Pause.*) It's a difficult time of day everywhere . . .

VERA BAXTER: Yes. (*Pause.*) It belongs to some people from Rouen. The Jacquements. They're more or less separated. They had it built and then . . . (*Rather long silence.*) Something must have happened here, a few years ago . . . I can't remember too well . . . the wife tried to kill herself, or else someone tried to kill her . . . (*Stop. She falls silent. Silence.*) It's as if I'd lived here for months . . . (*No answer from the Stranger.*) I could just leave things as they are . . . (*Pause.*) If ever . . . (*Stop.*) It would stay empty but rented? (*He doesn't respond.*) I could still call the whole thing off. (*Stop.*) Go over to the agency and tell them I've changed my mind? But then, what about the children? Where would they go? (*Pause.*) Christine was supposed to go to England . . . that just leaves Irène . . .

THE STRANGER: Your youngest? . . .

VERA BAXTER: Yes. (*Pause—violently.*) It's still hard for me to let her go. (*Long pause.*) She's a difficult child, stubborn . . . often sad, too . . . she's a liar . . . little white lies, you know, but you wonder why . . . Jean says it's not important . . . it frightens me though . . . (*Stop. The Stranger looks at her. Fear, like the darkness, slowly takes over the place.*) Michel Cayre left, didn't he?

THE STRANGER: Yes. (*Silence. They look at each other.*)

VERA BAXTER: He'd already left when you came?

THE STRANGER: Yes. (*Pause.*) I decided to come after he left.

VERA BAXTER: Why?

THE STRANGER: Because of your name I think. As soon as I'd heard it, back there at the Hôtel de Paris, for the first time, I wanted to see the person who had that name. (*Pause.*) Just because of those two words. (*Pause*) Véra (*pause*) Baxter. (*Pause.*) That name.

VERA BAXTER: Véra Baxter.

THE STRANGER: Yes. (*Pause.*) I recognized it. (*Pause.*) Do you remember?

VERA BAXTER: No.

THE STRANGER: It was a thousand years ago, not here but in the forest on the Atlantic Coast, there were some women . . . their husbands were almost never there, fighting in the holy wars during the Crusades and sometimes they'd stay for months in their huts all alone in the middle of the forest, waiting for them. (*Pause.*) And that's why they began talking to the trees, to the sea, to the animals in the forest . . .

VERA BAXTER: Were they burned? . . .

THE STRANGER: That's right, yes. (*Pause.*) One of them was called Véra Baxter. (*Increasing darkness. The TURBULENCE continues.*)

VERA BAXTER: (*With muted violence.*) I don't know how to want anything any more.

THE STRANGER: (*Pause.*) You knew how to want to die. (*Long pause.*) But then that's the easiest of all desires.

VERA BAXTER: You knew how to once yourself. (*No response from the Stranger.*)

As soon as you began talking (*stop*) I guessed that you too . . . at one point . . . had wanted to die.

THE STRANGER: That's one possible identity (*pause*) I might hold on to, for you. (*No response from Véra Baxter. Sounds of voices on the road: coming from the house — the house of the TURBULENCE — where, one by one, the young people are leaving. We wait until they disappear: until the OUTSIDE TURBULENCE has completely waned: both disappearances are equally painful. Silence. It's over: the TURBULENCE has faded away.*)

VERA BAXTER: It's going to get dark very quickly now. The electricity's been turned off. (*No response from the Stranger.*) We'll close up . . .

THE STRANGER: (*Gently.*) Why? . . .

VERA BAXTER: (*Stop.*) It'll be dark soon . . .

THE STRANGER: There's no need to, I think.

VERA BAXTER: But . . .

THE STRANGER: Whatever you like. (*She comes back in. Her gestures are slow. She goes to pick up her coat, her handbag. He starts to move as well. They speak slowly like people who've just been afraid.*) The weather was nice in Paris today too.

VERA BAXTER: I think it rained this morning. (*It's over: she goes toward the door. He is next to her. Silence. Then she speaks.*) We always used to go to the Atlantic beaches.

THE STRANGER: A habit.

VERA BAXTER: Yes. It would have gone on, I think . . . always around here . . . He only liked the Atlantic coast . . .

THE STRANGER: And you?

VERA BAXTER: I had no opinion. (*Slight pause, last look, as if she had forgotten something. Then she leaves. The Stranger follows her. It's over. They go out. It's happened imperceptibly, she can't have noticed that she "was going out." We can hear their voices, outside already, far off.*)

VERA BAXTER: (*Off.*) The Balearic Islands are beautiful, I think.

THE STRANGER: I've never been there. (*The stage remains empty. Focus on the open French windows. In the distance, like a fire amid the dark masses of the grounds, the House of the OUTSIDE TURBULENCE is brightly lit up.*)

END

Over Nothing At All

Nathalie Sarraute

OVER NOTHING AT ALL
(France)
Directed by Simone BenMussa

CHARACTERS:

M. 1
M. 2
M. 3
W

M. 1: Listen, I've been meaning to ask you . . . That's sort of why I came by . . . I'd like to know . . . what's happened? Have I done something wrong?

M. 2: Absolutely nothing . . . Why?

M. 1: Oh, I don't know . . . It feels like you've become a little distant . . . You never call . . . I'm the one who has to . . .

M. 2: You know very well: I never take the initiative, I'm afraid I'll disturb people.

M. 1: Not me, though? You know that I'd say something to you . . . We haven't reached that stage, have we . . . No, I feel that something's . . .

M. 2: What can you possibly be thinking of?

M. 1: That's exactly what I've been asking myself. I've tried to figure it out . . . never . . . in all these years . . . nothing's ever come between us . . . nothing I can remember . . .

M. 2: There are certain things I never forget. You've always been terrific . . . there were times when . . .

M. 1: When what? You've always been perfect too . . . a real friend . . . Do you remember how moved your mother used to get by us?

M. 2: Yes, poor, dear Mother . . . She liked you a lot . . . she used to say: "At least he's a real friend, you'll always be able to depend on him." And that's exactly what I've done.

M. 1: So?

M. 2: (Shrugs his shoulders.) . . . So . . . what do you want me to say?

M. 1: Well, . . . I know you too well: something's changed . . . You've always kept your distance with everybody . . . but now it's my turn . . . just the other day, on the phone . . . you were miles away . . . that hurts me, you know . . .

M. 2: (With a burst of feeling.) Well, me too, just imagine . . .

M. 1: Oh, you see, I am right . . .

M. 2: I can't help it . . . I like you just as much as ever, you know . . . don't think anything different . . . but I can't help it . . .

M. 1: Can't help what? Why don't you want to tell me? Something really has happened . . .

M. 2: No . . . nothing really . . . Nothing you can talk about . . .

M. 1: Try anyway . . .

M. 2: Oh no . . . I don't want to . . .

M. 1: Why not? Tell me . . .

M. 2: No, don't force me to . . .

M. 1: Is it as terrible as all that?

M. 2: No, it's not terrible . . . it's not that . . .

M. 1: So what is it then?

M. 2: It's . . . It's really not much of anything . . . Nothing at all, really . . . what you'd call nothing . . . just talking about it, bringing it up even . . . could lead to . . . what would people think? Nobody ever . . . nobody would dare . . . you never hear people talk about . . .

M. 1: Well then, I ask you in the name of everything you claim I've meant to you . . . in the name of your mother . . . of our parents . . . I beg of you, solemnly, you can't back down now . . . What's happened? Tell me . . . you owe me that . . .

M. 2: (*Woefully*.) I've told you: it's nothing you can tell . . . nothing people are allowed to talk about . . .

M. 1: Oh, come now, out with it . . .

M. 2: Well, it's just some words . . .

M. 1: Words? Between us? Don't tell me we've had words . . . that's not possible . . . I would have remembered that . . .

M. 2: No, not those kinds of words . . . other kinds . . . not the kind you say you've "had" . . . But words we didn't "have" . . . You never know how they get started . . .

M. 1: Which ones? What words? You're holding out on me . . . You're teasing me . . .

M. 2: Not at all, I'm not teasing you . . . Still if I tell you . . .

M. 1: Then what? What will happen? You've said it was nothing . . .

M. 2: Precisely, it's nothing . . . and because of that nothing . . .

M. 1: Ah, at last we're getting somewhere . . . so it's because of that "nothing" you've become distant? You've wanted to break off our relationship?

M. 2: (*Sighs*.) Yes . . . that is the reason . . . You'd never understand . . . Anyway, nobody could ever understand . . .

M. 1: Try me, why don't you? I'm not so dense . . .

M. 2: Oh yes you are . . . about such things you are. Anyway, you all are . . .

M. 1: Then I dare you . . . we'll see what happens . . .

M. 2: All right . . . a little while ago you said . . . you said . . . when I'd boasted about who knows what . . . about some minor accomplishment or other . . . yes . . . minor . . . when I spoke to you about it . . . you said: "Oh, that's . . . nice . . ."

M. 1: Tell me again, please . . . I must have misunderstood.

M. 2: (*Gathering courage.*) You said: "Oh, tha-at's . . . nice . . ." With exactly that same intonation . . . that same accentuation . . .

M. 1: That's not true. It can't be that . . . that's not possible . . .

M. 2: You see, I told you so . . . what's the use? . . .

M. 1: Oh, my God, you're not joking? You're really serious?

M. 2: Yes. Very. Very serious.

M. 1: Listen, tell me if I'm crazy . . . if I'm wrong . . . you told me about some accomplishment of yours . . . which one, by the way? . . .

M. 2: Oh, it doesn't matter . . . just some old accomplishment or other . . .

M. 1: And then I supposedly said: "Oh, that's nice?"

M. 2: (*Sighs.*) Not quite like that . . . there was more of a space in between "Oh" and "that's nice." "Oh . . . tha-at's . . . nice . . ." With emphasis on the "that," drawing it out and then a pause before getting to the "nice." That's not so unimportant.

M. 1: And *that's* what . . . no pun intended . . ."nice" preceded by a pause . . . has made you decide to break off . . .

M. 2: Oh, break off . . . no, I haven't broken off . . . at least not for good . . . just maintaining a little distance.

M. 1: But it was such a great opportunity to drop me, to stop seeing your lifelong friend . . . a brother . . . I wonder what ever kept you from . . .

M. 2: Oh, but it's not allowed. I didn't get permission.

M. 1: Oh? Did you ask for it?

M. 2: Well, I made some inquiries . . .

M. 1: Who did you ask?

M. 2: Well, the people who've got the authority to give such permission. Normal people, people with common sense, like people on jury duty, citizens whose respectability can be vouched for . . .

M. 1: Well? What did they say?

M. 2: Well . . . as might be expected . . . My case wasn't the only one, by the way. There were other similar ones: between parents and children, brothers and sisters, husbands and wives, friends . . .

M. 1: Who'd allowed themselves to say "Oh . . . tha-at's nice" with a pr-regnant pause?

M. 2: No, not those words . . . but others, more obvious even . . . and there wasn't anything that could be done to . . . every single one was found guilty. Ordered to pay a fine . . . And some, like me, were even prosecuted . . .

M. 1: Prosecuted? You?

M. 2: Oh yes. Once I'd made my inquiries, they started investigating me and they discovered that . . .

M. 1: Oh? What? What am I going to find out now?

M. 2: They found out that I've already broken off for good with some very close friends . . . for reasons that nobody could understand . . . I had been found guilty . . . at their request . . . *in absentia* . . . I didn't even know about it . . .

I found out that I have a police record in which I'm labeled as "the one who breaks off relations over nothing at all." That gave me something to think about . . .

M. 1: So that's why you've been so cautious with me . . . nothing frank. Nothing open . . .

M. 2: Well, that's understandable . . . "Breaks off over nothing at all . . ." Do you realize the implications?

M. 1: Now I remember: it must be common knowledge . . . I'd already heard about it. Someone told me: "You know, you have to watch out for him. He seems very friendly, affectionate . . . and then, bang! over nothing at all . . . he disappears." I was outraged, I tried to defend you . . . But now, even with me. If someone had ever even suggested that . . . really, that is an appropriate expression: over nothing at all . . . Just because I said: "Oh, that's nice" . . . Excuse me, I didn't say it the right way: "Oh, . . . tha-at's . . . nice . . ."

M. 2: Yes. That's the way . . . exactly . . . with that same emphasis on "that" . . . drawing it out that very same way . . . that's it, I can just hear you, I can even see you . . . "Oh, . . . tha-at's . . . nice." And I didn't say a word and I'll never be able to talk about it.

M. 1: Oh yes you can . . . just between us . . . Come on now . . . tell me, let it out . . . maybe I can understand . . . it can only do us both some good.

M. 2: You mean you don't understand?

M. 1: No, I swear I don't . . . I said those words in complete innocence. And furthermore may I be hung if I remember them . . . When did I say them? What were we talking about?

M. 2: You took advantage of a moment of weakness . . . I admit that I asked for it.

M. 1: What on earth are you talking about?

M. 2: Yes. I asked for it. Just like that. Unsuspecting. Vulnerable. I had this glorious idea of bragging about myself . . . I wanted to grow in your esteem . . . I boasted . . . to you . . . about some insignificant accomplishment . . . I tried to climb up to your place . . . I wanted to raise myself up to those heights you live in . . . and you picked me up by the scruff of my neck, you held me in your hand, you turned me this way and that . . . and you let me drop, saying "Oh . . . tha-at's . . . nice."

M. 1: Tell me, is that what you told them in your petition?

M. 2: Yes, more or less . . . I don't remember very well . . .

M. 1: Yet you're surprised they dismissed your case?

M. 2: Not really, you know . . . that sort of thing hasn't surprised me for some time now.

M. 1: Still you tried . . .

M. 2: Well, yes . . . I thought it was an open and shut case.

M. 1: Do you want me to tell you something? It's too bad you didn't consult me,

I could have helped you write your petition. There's one particular term you should have used . . .

M. 2: Oh? What?

M. 1: Well, the word "condescending." That's what you felt about the emphasis on "that's . . ." and the pause . . . that's called condescending. I'm not saying that you'd have gotten permission to stop seeing me because of that but maybe you could have avoided being found guilty. A condescending tone might have been extenuating circumstances. "We agree, he wanted to break off relations with such a friend . . . but still we could mention that impression he had of a certain condescending tone . . ."

M. 2: Oh? So you do admit it? You acknowledge it?

M. 1: I'm not admitting anything. Besides, I don't see why . . . how I could have . . . with you . . . no, really, you must be . . .

M. 2: No, stop right there . . . not that . . . don't say I'm maybe this or that . . . no, no, please don't, if you want us to come to an understanding . . . you still want that, don't you?

M. 1: Of course I do, I told you already, I came here for that very reason.

M. 2: Good, so if it's all right with you, let's use that word . . .

M. 1: What word?

M. 2: The word "condescending." Even if you don't believe it, please admit that there was some, yes . . . some condescension . . . I hadn't thought of that term. I never find those words when I need them . . . but, now that I've got it, allow me . . . I'll begin again . . .

M. 1: Are you going to submit another petition?

M. 2: Yes. Just to see. In your presence. You know, it might be fun . . .

M. 1: Maybe . . . but who should we ask?

M. 2: Oh, you don't have to look very far for . . . You can find them anywhere at all. Right here, for example . . . my neighbors . . . very helpful people . . . just the kind you'd choose for jury duty . . . Honest. Solid. Full of good common sense. I'll go get them. (*He goes out and comes back with a couple.*) Here they are . . . I'll introduce you . . . no, please, it won't take long . . . we've had a disagreement . . .

THEY: Oh. but, you know, we're not competent enough . . .

M. 2: Oh, but of course you are . . . More than most . . . Here's what it's all about. My friend here, a lifelong friend . . .

W.: He's the one you've so often told me about? I remember . . . when he was sick . . . you were so worried . . .

M. 2: He's the one all right . . . that's exactly why it hurts me so deeply . . .

W.: Don't tell me that the two of you . . . after years of friendship . . . you always told me that he had treated you . . .

M. 2: Perfectly, yes . . . I'm grateful to him for that . . .

W.: Well then, why?

M. 1: Well, I'm going to tell you: it seems that I spoke to him in a condescending manner . . .

M. 2: Why do you say it like that? With that ironic tone? Don't you want us to give it a try?

M. 1: Yes, yes of course. I said that seriously. I upset him. He felt belittled . . . so ever since then, he's been avoiding me . . . (*They, silent . . . ambivalent . . . nodding their heads . . .*)

W.: Indeed . . . it does seem . . . a bit excessive . . . over just a slightly condescending tone . . .

M. 3: But condescension, sometimes, you know . . .

M. 2: Ah? So you do understand?

M. 3: Well, . . . I wouldn't go so far as to stop seeing someone, but . . .

M. 2: But, but, but . . . Oh, you see, you *can* understand me.

M. 3: I wouldn't go so far as to say that . . .

M. 2: Yes, of course you would . . . you'll see . . . allow me to explain . . . it's like this . . . First of all, I have to tell you that I never, truly never, agreed to go over to his place . . .

W.: You never go over to his place?

M. 1: Of course he does, now really . . . what *is* he talking about?

M. 2: That's not what I'm saying. I used to go to see him . . . see him, that's true. But never, ever did I try to settle down in his territory . . . in those spheres he lives in . . . I don't play that game, you see.

M. 1: Oh, so that's what you meant . . . Yes, that's true; you've always kept yourself outside of things . . .

M. 3: He's an outsider?

M. 1: Yes, if you like. But I must say he's always earned his living . . . he never asked anybody for anything.

M. 2: Thanks, that's nice of you . . . but where were we? Oh, yes, that's right; he told you that I stay on the sidelines. He stays in his place. I stay in mine.

W.: That's perfectly normal. Everyone leads his own life, right?

M. 2: Well, you can believe it, he can't stand that. He desperately wants to pull me over . . . into his space, over there . . . I have to be there, with him, I can't get away . . . So, he set a trap for me . . . he set a mousetrap.

EVERYBODY: A mousetrap?

M. 2: He used me to . . .

W.: (*Laughs.*) A used mousetrap?

M. 1: No, don't laugh. He's quite serious, I assure you . . . What mousetrap, tell us . . .

M. 2: Well, I had congratulated him on his promotion . . . and he said that, among other things, it gave him the opportunity to take some very exciting trips . . .

M. 1: Go on. This is getting interesting . . .

M. 2: Yes. Some exciting trips . . . and I ventured further than I usually do . . . I expressed something like longing . . . so . . . he offered to . . . use his contacts . . . I'd done some small jobs . . . he said that maybe he could ask someone influential to put my name on the lecture circuit . . .

W., M. 3: Well, I think that's quite good of him . . .

M. 2: (*Groans.*) Oh!

W., M. 3: Don't you think that's good of him? If someone offered me that . . .

M. 2: What's the use of going on? I'll never finish.

M. 1: Oh yes you will. I insist. Please go on. Wasn't it good of me?

M. 2: I'll have to start all over again . . .

M. 1: No. To sum it up: you like to travel. I offered to get you on the lecture circuit . . .

M. 2: Yes. So, you see, I had a choice. I could . . . and that's what I usually do, without even thinking . . . I could have backed off and said: "No, you see, travel . . . and especially under those circumstances . . . just isn't my thing." That way, I would have stayed outside. Or, I could have let myself be tempted, take the bait, swallow it whole and say: "Well, thank you very much, I'd love to . . ." and I would have been hooked and led to my designated place, over there, in his space . . . my rightful place. That wouldn't have been so bad. But I went even further . . .

M. 1: Oh? You went even further?

M. 2: Yes. I said . . . but how could I have done such a thing? . . . just thinking about it . . .

M. 1: Now I remember: you said that if you wanted to, you could . . . that someone had made you an offer, with the best possible conditions.

M. 2: Yes, that's right . . . I feel so ashamed . . . I settled right into the back of the cage. Just as if I'd always lived there. I played the game the way they all play it. According to all the rules. I wanted to promote myself . . . just like everybody else, over there . . . I didn't need his protection, hell no; I had my own position here, with these people . . . an excellent position . . . I was proud of it. I played their game to the hilt. You would have thought I'd never done anything else. So, all he had to do was trap me . . . he held me in the palm of his hand, he examined me: Just look at that, just take a look at this guy, he says that he too has been asked to . . . and in the most enviable conditions imaginable . . . and oh, how proud he is . . . look at how he draws himself up . . . well, now, he's not as small as we thought . . . he managed to be deserving, after all, just like a big person . . . Oh, . . . tha-a-at's . . . nice . . . tha-a-at's . . . nice . . . Oh, what could you possibly understand . . .

M. 3: Not much, I must say.

W.: Same here, I can't follow you at all . . . anyway, I haven't got the time . . . I have to leave . . . But it seems to me that all this agitation . . . he looks so upset . . . and all these ideas about mousetraps and lures . . . Wouldn't it be better? . . .

M. 1: No, don't worry about a thing. Leave us alone, I'll handle this. (*M. 3 and*

W. exit. Long silence.)

M. 1: (*Gently.*) So you really believe that when I talked about recommending you, I was trying to trap you?

M. 2: Well, you're certainly trying to this very minute, in any case . . . You could see they think I'm crazy . . . and you want me to prove it to you even more clearly.

M. 1: No, of course not. You know very well that between us . . . do you remember our diving together? When you'd got me to go along with you . . . I really liked that, it was very exciting . . . Have I ever called you crazy? Hypersensitive, maybe, for sure. A bit of a persecution complex . . . but that's part of your charm . . . Come on, now, tell me, do you really believe that I was trying to trap you?

M. 2: Oh, consciously, no, . . . that's going a bit far. You probably weren't consciously trying to trap me in the beginning, when you started talking about your trips . . . But afterwards, when you felt that slight quiver in me . . . something like longing . . . a kind of yearning . . . then you began to strut, to show off . . . like you always do when you show off in front of me . . .

M. 1: Show off? Me? How do I show off? Have I ever bragged about anything at all?

M. 2: Bragged, no . . . how stupid of me . . . there I go again, I'm the one who was bragging. I'm the one who's awkward around you.

M. 1: Oh, I'm flattered. I thought that as far as subtleties go . . .

M. 2: Oh, come now, you're much more subtle than I am.

M. 1: How can you say that? Much more subtle? How can you . . . ?

M. 2: Exactly, when you display your advantages. The finest imaginable. And what's brilliant about it, is that *it* never seems to be there to be looked at. It's just something that's naturally there. It exists, that's all. Like a lake. Like a mountain. It's equally self-evident.

M. 1: What do you mean by *it*? Quit using metaphors. What's self-evident?

M. 2: Happiness. Yes. Happiness, in all of its guises. And what happiness. The kind that's most valued. Most highly prized. The kind of happiness that all the poor guys contemplate with their noses pressed up against the windowpane.

M. 1: Give me an example, please.

M. 2: Oh, the choices are too numerous . . . but wait, if you want one, here's one of the most striking . . . when you were sitting there in front of me . . . comfortably settled down in your armchair, your first-born standing there between your knees . . . the very image of fulfilled fatherhood . . . that's how you imagined it, how you presented it . . .

M. 1: Why don't you just say that I was posturing . . .

M. 2: I didn't say that.

M. 1: I hope not. I was happy . . . I can be happy, you know . . . and it shows, that's all.

M. 2: No, that's not all. Absolutely not. You felt happy, that's true . . . just like when you and Janine probably felt happy when you stood there in front of me: a perfect couple, arm in arm, laughing blissfully, or gazing into each other's eyes . . . but a little corner of your eye was turned towards me, a little glance in my direction to see if I'm contemplating . . . if I'm leaning towards that, as I should be, as everybody should be . . . and I . . .

M. 1: Ah, now I get it. I understand. And you . . .

M. 2: What about me? What was I?

M. 1: You . . . you were . . .

M. 2: Go ahead, say it, I was what?

M. 1: You were jealous.

M. 2: So now the truth's out. Yes. That's what you wanted, that's what you were getting at; you wanted me to be jealous . . . That's the whole point. The whole point. You needed me to be jealous and I wasn't. I was happy for you. For you . . . Yes, but only for you. I didn't want any part of that happiness. Neither cooked nor raw . . . I was not jealous! Not, not, not jealous. No, I wasn't envious . . . But how is that possible? That wasn't Happiness, then? *The true* Happiness, universally recognized? Desired by all? The kind of Happiness worth all the struggle and all the sacrifice? No? Really? There really was a little princess, hidden deep in the forest . . .

M. 1: What forest? What princess? You're raving mad . . .

M. 2: Of course, I'm raving mad . . . What are you waiting for to call the neighbors back in? "Listen to him, he's a raving maniac . . . what forest?" Ah, yes, my good people, the forest of that fairy tale in which the queen asks her mirror: "Who is the fairest of them all . . ." And the mirror answers: "You are fair, most fair, but over there, in a cabin deep in the forest, there's a little princess who is even fairer than you . . ." And you are like that queen, you can't stand it that somewhere, there just might be . . .

M. 1: Another kind of happiness . . . a greater happiness?

M. 2: No, it's even worse than that. You could admit that there might be another kind of happiness.

M. 1: Really, you amaze me . . . I could be as generous as that?

M. 2: Yes. Another kind of happiness, even greater than yours, perhaps. If, and only if, it can be identified, classified, and if you can find it on your lists . . . It would have to be in the catalogue of happinesses. If mine were the happiness of a monk living in a cell or of a hermit high on his pole . . . classified among the beatitudes of mystics and saints . . .

M. 1: You're absolutely right about that, there's not the slightest chance I could join you there . . .

M. 2: No. Neither there nor elsewhere. My happiness isn't classified anywhere at all.

M. 1: A nameless happiness?

M. 2: Neither with a name nor without one. Not happiness at all.

M. 1: So, what is it?

M. 2: It's nothing that's called happiness. Nobody's present to see it, to give it a name . . . We're someplace else . . . outside . . . far away from all that . . . we don't know where we are, but we're not on your lists in any case . . . And that's what you can't stand . . .

M. 1: Who's "you?" Why do you insist on including me in? . . . If that's how you see me . . . If I had known I was going to hear such things . . . I wouldn't have come over.

M. 2: Ah, but you absolutely have to come over, don't you? To see . . . You feel attracted . . . you feel drawn, don't you? What is that thing? Has it always been there, somewhere, outside of our borders? And it's still there, that kind of . . . contentment . . . just like that . . . for no good reason . . . a reward for nothing, nothing, nothing . . .

M. 1: This time I think it'd be better if I left . . . (*Goes toward the door. Stops in front of the window. Looks out.*)

M. 2: (*Watches him for a minute. Goes over to him, puts his hand on his shoulder.*) Forgive me, won't you? . . . You see, I was right: that's what happens when you start trying to explain things . . . You say all the wrong things . . . You say more than you really think . . . But I like you a lot, you know that . . . I feel it really strongly in moments like these . . .

M. 1: Like these?

M. 2: Yes, like right now, when you stopped in front of the window . . . to look out . . . with that look of yours . . . sometimes, you kind of let go, it's as if you blend right in with what you see, you lose yourself completely in it . . . if only for that reason . . . yes, if only for that . . . I feel suddenly so close to you . . . You understand why I'm so fond of this place? It may seem a little shabby . . . but it would be hard for me to move . . . there's something here . . . it's difficult to put your finger on . . . but you feel it, don't you? Like some kind of energy coming from . . . from . . . from that alley, from that little wall, over there, to the right, of that roof . . . it's reassuring, invigorating . . .

M. 1: Yes . . . I understand . . .

M. 2: If ever something kept me from seeing that . . . it would be like . . . I don't know . . . Yes, for me, you see . . . life is here . . . Oh, what's wrong with you?

M. 1: "Life is here . . . simple and calm . . ." "Life is here, simple and calm . . ." That's Verlaine, isn't it?

M. 2: Yes, it's Verlaine. But why?

M. 1: Verlaine. That's it.

M. 2: I hadn't thought of Verlaine . . . I just said: life is here, that's all.

M. 1: But the next words just came naturally; all you had to do was keep going . . . After all, we all went to school . . .

M. 2: But I didn't keep going . . . But why am I defending myself? What's the matter? What's got hold of you all of a sudden?

M. 1: What's got hold of me? "Got hold of" are the right words. Yes, what's got hold of me? A little while ago, you weren't talking for no good reason . . . you taught me a lot, you know . . . Now even I can understand certain things. This time you're the one who put out the little piece of bacon.

M. 2: What piece of bacon?

M. 1: But it's so obvious. When you saw me standing in front of the window . . . When you said to me: "Look, life is here . . ." Life is here . . . nothing more . . . life . . . when you sensed that I was drawn towards the bait for just an instant . . .

M. 2: You're crazy.

M. 1: No. No more crazy than you were when you said I had lured you with my talk of trips in order to get you into my place, into my cage . . . that seemed crazy, but maybe you weren't as mistaken as all that . . . Now this time, you're the one who's lured me over . . .

M. 2: Lured you over where? Where did I try to lure you to?

M. 1: Oh, come now, don't play the innocent . . . "Life is here, simple and calm . . ."

M. 2: First of all, I didn't say that.

M. 1: Yes you did. You did say that. Implicitly. And it's not the first time. And you claim to be elsewhere . . . outside . . . far away from our catalogues . . . outside of our compartments . . . it's got nothing to do with mystics and saints . . .

M. 2: That's true.

M. 1: Yes, that's true, nothing to do with them. You've got a better place . . . What could be more valued than your territory, into which you so graciously let me enter so that I too might collect my thoughts in peace . . . "Life is here, simple and calm . . ." That's where you reside, far from any corrupting contact with us . . . protected by the greatest . . . Verlaine . . .

M. 2: I must reiterate that I wasn't thinking of Verlaine.

M. 1: All right. I can accept that. You weren't thinking of him, but you have to admit that with the little wall, the roof, the sky above the roof . . . we were smack in the middle . . .

M. 2: In the middle of what?

M. 1: Oh, come now, in the middle of "poetic" matters, of "poetry."

M. 2: Oh, my God! all of a sudden, everything's coming out . . . it's those quotation marks . . .

M. 1: What quotation marks?

M. 2: The ones you always put around words when you say them in my presence . . . "Poetry." "Poetic." That distance, that irony, that scorn . . .

M. 1: *I* make fun of poetry? *I* speak scornfully of the poets?

M. 2: Not the "true" poets, of course. Not the ones on pedestals, or in niches, that you visit with such admiration on holidays . . . No, quotation marks aren't ever for them . . .

M. 1: Well then who are they for?

M. 2: They're for . . . they're for . . .

M. 1: Go ahead, say it . . .

M. 2: No. I don't want to. It would get us into too much trouble . . .

M. 1: Well then, I'm going to say it. It's when I'm with you that I put those quotation marks around words . . . yes, with you . . . just as soon as I sense something in you, I can't hold myself back, those quotation marks just come out, despite myself.

M. 2: That's it. I think we're finally there. You put your finger on it. That's the whole point. The source is right here. The quotation marks are for me. As soon as I look out the window, as soon as I allow myself to say "life is here," I'm immediately placed in the section called "poets . . ." the ones who get quotation marks around their names . . . the ones who get shackles put on them . . .

M. 1: Yes, I don't know if we're finally there this time, but I get a feeling that we're getting there . . . so, as long as we're on the subject, I too have some memories . . . one, in particular . . . maybe you've forgotten it . . . it was back when we used to go mountain climbing . . . in the Dauphiné . . . we'd climbed the Barre des Ecrins, . . . remember?

M. 2: Yes. Of course.

M. 1: There were five of us: the two of us, two friends and a guide. We were coming back down . . . and all of a sudden, you stopped short. You stopped the whole rope party and you said, using a certain tone . . . : "Why don't we stop here a minute to look at the view? It's really worth it . . ."

M. 2: I said that? I dared to say such a thing?

M. 1: Yes. And everybody had to stop . . . We just stood there, waiting . . . stamping our feet, marking time . . . while you stood there "contemplating" . . .

M. 2: In front of all of you? I must have been out of my mind . . .

M. 1: Not at all. You forced us to stand still, right there, on the spot, whether we wanted to or not . . . Well, I just couldn't resist. I said: "Let's get going, we haven't got any time to waste . . . You can find some pretty postcards back at the stationery store" . . .

M. 2: Oh, yeah. I remember now . . . I wanted to kill you.

M. 1: And I wanted to kill you . . . And if the others could have opened their mouths, they would have admitted that they wanted to push you into the ravine.

M. 2: And I . . . yes . . . if only for that very reason, the postcards . . . how could I go on seeing you . . .

M. 1: Oh, there must have been a moment when you began to hope again . . .

M. 2: Hope? After that?

M. 1: Yes, you never lose hope. You must have been desperately hoping, when you tapped me on the shoulder . . . a little while ago, in front of the window

. . . "Oh, that's nice . . ."

M. 2: That's nice?

M. 1: Yes, of course, you know how to say it too . . . at least, you know how to insinuate it . . . Oh, . . . tha-a-at's . . . nice . . . there's a nice fellow who knows the value of things . . . you wouldn't believe it, but you know, no matter how thick he is, he can still . . .

M. 2: My God! just to think that I believed that . . . how could I have forgotten? Oh, but I hadn't forgotten . . . I knew it, I'd always known it . . .

M. 1: Known what? Say it.

M. 2: Known that there is no reconciliation possible between us. No truce . . . a ruthless combat. A fight to the death. Yes, a fight for survival. There is no choice. It's either you or me.

M. 1: Aren't you exaggerating a little?

M. 2: No, not at all. We've got to face up to things: we're in adversarial camps. Two soldiers in two enemy camps; confronting each other.

M. 1: What camps? They've got a name.

M. 2: Oh, names are your specialty. You're the one, you and people who put labels on everything. You're the people who put quotation marks around . . . Oh, I don't know.

M. 1: Well I do know. Everyone knows. On one side, there's my camp, the one in which men fight, devote their entire strength . . . they create life around them . . . not the kind you contemplate out the window, but "real" life, the life everybody lives. And on the other side, . . . well . . .

M. 2: Well?

M. 1: Well . . .

M. 2: Well?

M. 1: No . . .

M. 2: Yes. I'm going to say it for you . . . Well, on the other side are the "failures."

M. 1: I didn't say that. Anyway, you've got a job . . .

M. 2: Yes, a job that gives me just enough to live on. I don't give it all my energy.

M. 1: Oh! You save some?

M. 2: I see what you're up to . . . No, no, I don't "save" any . . .

M. 1: Yes you do. You do save some. What do you save your energy for?

M. 2: That's none of your business. Why do you always have to come over to my place to inspect, to dig into everything? You're afraid, aren't you? . . .

M. 1: Afraid? Afraid!

M. 2: Yes, afraid. You're afraid of the unknown, of a threatening presence, hidden somewhere in the dark . . . a mole digging its tunnel under the well-kept lawn where you're entertaining . . . You just have to make it come out, here's an unbeatable product: "He's a failure." "A failure." Can't you see it right away? Here he comes; he's all excited: "A failure? Me? Whatever am I hearing? What are you saying? Of course I'm not one of those, don't believe

to you ..." No, don't count on it. Even that, even "a failure," however power-
ful that may be, won't make me leave my hole, I'm too comfortable in it.

M. 1: Really? You're as comfortable as all that?

M. 2: More comfortable than at your place, in any case, on your lawn . . . I'd
waste away there . . . I'd want to escape . . . Life isn't worth . . .

M. 1: Life isn't worth living any more . . . that's it. That's exactly what I feel
when I try to put myself in your place.

M. 2: Who's forcing you to put yourself in my place?

M. 1: I don't know . . . I always want to understand . . .

M. 2: That's what I was saying: you're never sure, you're afraid that there really
is a little cabin over there in the forest.

M. 1: No, I want to know where that detachment comes from. It's supernatural.
I can never get over it: you must feel supported . . .

M. 2: Ah, Verlaine again, right? Poets . . . Well, no, I'm not one of them . . . and
if you really want to know, I'll never be one of them. Never. You'll never
have that opportunity.

M. 1: Me? That opportunity? If you were to become a real poet . . . it seems to
me that opportunity would probably be on your side.

M. 2: Oh, come on now, what on earth are you talking about? You couldn't
possibly be thinking of that . . . You even have a word for it: reinstated. I'd
be reinstated. Reintegrated. Put over into your place. No more quotation
marks, of course, but in my right place, under surveillance at all times. "Oh
. . .tha-at's. . . nice" will be too fine a phrase for me when I come over to present you with . . . waiting . . . hoping . . . "Oh, yes? Do you really think so?
Yes? That's nice? . . .Of course I can't claim. . .with all those famous people,
behind me, next to me . . ." You'll tap my shoulder . . . isn't that touching?
You'll smile . . . "But who knows? Right? Who can predict? . . . There've
been cases . . ." No. Don't count on it. You can look everywhere: open my
drawers, search my closets, you won't find a single piece of paper . . . not a
single sketch . . . not the slightest attempt . . . *Nothing* you can sink your
teeth into.

M. 1: Too bad. It could have been pure gold. Diamonds.

M. 2: Or lead, don't you agree, as long as you can tell what it is, as long as you
can classify it, give it a rating . . . We absolutely have to know what we're up
against. Then we can relax. We don't have to be afraid of anything . . .

M. 1: Afraid? You're back to that again . . . Afraid . . . Yes, maybe . . . Maybe
you're right in the long run . . . it's true that when I'm with you I feel kind of
apprehensive . . .

M. 2: Aha!

M. 1: Yes . . . for me, the place where you are isn't . . . I don't know how to say it
. . . quite firm or steady enough . . . quicksand that swallows you up . . . I
feel like I'm losing hold . . . everything's shaky, it's all going to fall apart . . . I
have to get out of there as fast as possible . . . I have to get back to my place

where everything is steady. Solid.

M. 2: You see . . . And when I . . . since we're on the subject . . . and when I'm at your place, you see, I feel claustrophobic . . . I'm in a completely closed building . . . compartments everywhere, partitions, levels . . . I want to get out of there . . . but when I get out, when I come back to my place, I have trouble . . .

M. 1: Yes? trouble doing what?

M. 2: Trouble coming back to life . . . even the next day sometimes I feel slightly inert . . . and the things around me too . . . I need time before it comes back, before I feel that beat again, a pulse starting up again . . . so you see . . .

M. 1: Yes. I see. (*Silence.*)

M. 1: What's the use of trying so hard?

M. 2: It would be so much more healthy . . .

M. 1: For both of us . . . so much more beneficial . . .

M. 2: The best solution . . .

M. 1: But you know only too well how we both are. Even you didn't dare take the initiative.

M. 2: No. I need someone to give me permission.

M. 1: What about me? you know how I am . . . (*Silence.*)

M. 1: What do you say . . . What if we submitted a petition . . . the two of us, this time . . . maybe we could explain better . . . maybe we'd have a better chance . . .

M. 2: No, what's the use? I can tell you everything in advance . . . I can see their look . . . "Now, what's it about this time? What? What are they talking about? What moles? What lawns? What quicksand? What enemy camps? Let's take a look at their files . . . Nothing . . . we've tried to find . . . we've examined all the usual areas of contention . . . there's nothing anywhere but evidence of a perfect friendship . . ."

M. 1: That's true.

M. 2: "And they want to break off their relationship. They don't ever want to see each other again . . . it's a disgrace . . ."

M. 1: Yes, there's no possible doubt about it, no hesitation whatsoever: both cases dismissed.

M. 2: "And furthermore, they better watch out . . . they better be very careful. Everybody knows the penalties incurred by people who have the nerve to, for no good reason, they'll be reported . . . No one will want to go near them except with the utmost caution and suspicion . . . Everyone will know what they're capable of and the reason why they might be found guilty: they might break up over nothing at all."

M. 1: Over something . . . or over nothing? (*Silence.*)

M. 1: Something or nothing? . . .

M. 2: That's right: something or nothing.

M. 1: But it's not the same thing . . .

a word of it . . . I'll tell you what I am, what I'll be . . . you'll see, I'll prove it

M. 2: It is: Yes . . . or no?

M. 1: Yes.

M. 2: No!

END

Chamber Theatre

two plays

Dissident, Goes Without Saying

and

Nina, It's Different

Michel Vinaver

AUTHOR'S NOTE

On Tuesday, 10 August 1976, I sat down and wrote scenes 1 to 6 of *Dissident, Goes Without Saying*. On Wednesday I wrote scenes 7 and 8. On Thursday I wrote scenes 9 to 12. That was it. On Friday 13 August I did nothing. On Saturday I wrote scenes 1 to 3 of *Nina, It's Different*. On Sunday I did nothing. Scenes 4 to 7 were written on Monday the 16th. I did nothing on Tuesday. I wrote scenes 8 and 9 on Wednesday, and scenes 10 to 13 on Thursday the 19th. Finished. Subsequently I reduced the number of scenes of *Nina* to 12.

The process of writing the two plays encompassed ten days. There had been no "planning" prior to that. No idea. No intention. Except that until then the plays I had written were long and complex and expensive to produce, and I decided I would try and write extremely simple and short plays that anyone could produce anywhere at any time. Having done the two plays, it did not occur to me that they constituted a unit. Well, they do and they don't. The first production, in Paris, was in the form of a double bill. Since then, they have most often been performed independently one from the other. Each stands on its own feet, yet they also form a diptych, and the title then becomes *Chamber Theatre*.

Chamber theatre, as there is chamber music, the "matter" of which surges out of the interplay of a small number of voices, of themes. Chords and dissonances. Repetitions and variations.

A theatre of little. Of lightness. Not much story. What is unsaid weighs more than what is said. Things said belong to the realm of banality. A realm truly vast, infinite, fascinating, calling for endless exploration.

"Chamber theatre" because it is fitting to play it in a chamber, the audience inside it.

M. V.

Dissident, Goes Without Saying

DISSIDENT, GOES WITHOUT SAYING
Théâtre de l'est Parisien (France)
Directed by Jacques Lassalle

CHARACTERS:

Helen
Philip

ONE

HELEN: They're in my coat pocket
PHILIP: No not on the dresser either
HELEN: You're a real help
PHILIP: Because you left it double-parked?
HELEN: Well maybe I left them in the car
PHILIP: Some day it's going to get stolen
HELEN: Didn't you go?
PHILIP: Sure
HELEN: I gave up I don't know how many times I went around the block
    it's getting harder and harder
PHILIP: I'm going to go down and park it for you
HELEN: Just a year and you can get your permit
PHILIP: Uhuh
HELEN: That a new sweater?
PHILIP: Uhuh
HELEN: Hmm where's the money come from?
PHILIP: Oh you know we trade things
HELEN: Yes but somebody bought it
PHILIP: Things get passed around
HELEN: But somebody owns it
PHILIP: You and your sense of private property
HELEN: Things belong to somebody (*Philip goes out. Helen makes a pack-
    aged soup. Philip returns.*) I wonder if you tell me the truth
PHILIP: I must have been out of it not unusual I didn't even hear it
HELEN: I set the alarm for eight
PHILIP: And you made me coffee
HELEN: The thing is you don't even care it's beyond me
PHILIP: How many times have I gone and signed up and for what?
HELEN: You like it? New kind of cream of bean I said why not give it a

try you like it? yes? all it takes is one time Philip just one lucky break your father answered a want ad and he's still there eighteen years later he's moved right up there with that company

PHILIP: Good night Mom

HELEN: Where you going?

(*Lights out.*)

TWO

HELEN: It really hurts me to see you lying around with our records that way you know not having a goal in life

PHILIP: I want to fight for the widow and the orphan come on let me I want to touch your hair

HELEN: Seriously Philip you can get along without a lot of things but if you just have some goal

PHILIP: I have a goal but it's beyond reach

HELEN: I'd like

PHILIP: That way I'm sure I'll always have it

HELEN: And get nowhere?

PHILIP: I'd like just two things first for you not to be alone

HELEN: You're here I'm not alone

PHILIP: For you to find a nice boy friend and let me

HELEN: What?

PHILIP: I don't have to say it

HELEN: You want me off your back?

PHILIP: Not exactly

HELEN: It's been a long time since I tried to interfere in your life

PHILIP: For you to let me be

HELEN: If only you made a little effort work doesn't grow on trees all the more reason it really pains me to see you hardly trying instead of really throwing yourself into it why if I were you

PHILIP: You're not

HELEN: You stood your father up again he had a table reserved

PHILIP: He *had* a table reserved *by* his secretary in one of those nice neighborhood restaurants he lists in his notebook always kept up to date I completely forgot about it

HELEN: He called me at work this afternoon he waited for you you know how punctual he is he thinks I'm the one that keeps you from seeing him you put me in a fine position

PHILIP: I have nothing to say to him

HELEN: He is your father you know

PHILIP: So?

HELEN: Have you finished?

PHILIP: Sooner or later he'll have to understand
HELEN: For him an appointment is an appointment
PHILIP: And a son is a son
HELEN: You could make me happy by picking up your records gathering dust on the floor

(*Lights out.*)

THREE

PHILIP: You look tired tonight
HELEN: No not more than usual
PHILIP: Your hair's wet the grind that's what's tiring
HELEN: It started to rain I didn't have my umbrella
PHILIP: Well you worked on the statistics?
HELEN: What do you mean?
PHILIP: As usual?
HELEN: Why sure
PHILIP: What's a statistics clerk do?
HELEN: We analyze invoices by sales districts
PHILIP: For what?
HELEN: So they can follow trends in sales up or down according to districts compared to the previous year soon it will all be done by machines
PHILIP: Which means?
HELEN: They're going to feed it all into computers
PHILIP: Why is that?
HELEN: So that it gets done faster and cheaper
PHILIP: Why you unloading all that stuff on me?
HELEN: Because you ask me
PHILIP: Me you don't ask me anything?
HELEN: You who never ask questions
PHILIP: Don't you notice anything?
HELEN: What is it? you frighten me
PHILIP: Because I ask questions?
HELEN: You should have said something to your father it's set then tomorrow night he's taking you to the movies
PHILIP: To see what?
HELEN: You know he just got back from a trip to Africa don't forget to ask him how he's feeling all this travel and with his diabetes
PHILIP: Tomorrow night I can't make it
HELEN: Oh come on now
PHILIP: Shut up and look
HELEN: But
PHILIP: It's a surprise well go ahead and open it

HELEN: Chocolate covered truffles are you crazy?

PHILIP: It's not your favorite in the whole world?

HELEN: Yes

PHILIP: The last time he took me to the movies it was a film on Chile he wants to convert me to his progressive ideas at any cost me I don't give a shit about Chile tomorrow I start as an apprentice on the night shift I found work

(*Lights out.*)

FOUR

HELEN: I'm getting back to normal now believe me I was getting all worked up not so much because of the money but being idle it's awful for a young person and seeing you worried

PHILIP: You didn't think I worried enough eh what do you want from me?

HELEN: Why nothing

PHILIP: Come on don't act dumb

HELEN: Why you yelling at me everything's fine I'm so happy

PHILIP: All you see's the good side of things as much as seeing nothing

HELEN: I'm trying you know the car's beyond repair or I mean so expensive to repair that the man in the garage said it wasn't worth fixing he made me an offer for it as is two-fifty I took it real fortune couldn't wait to spend it I bought a huge salami

PHILIP: It'll last ages

HELEN: All beef

PHILIP: What if I move out?

HELEN: When?

PHILIP: Next year

HELEN: Where to?

PHILIP: This is December

HELEN: You've just found a job

PHILIP: I'd like to find a valley

HELEN: A valley?

PHILIP: Closed at both ends

HELEN: Me who's never had an accident I don't believe in accidents anyway I'm safe and sound you can see the doctor says anybody can have a fainting spell I bought a bottle of wine too the cop was astounded sometimes I wonder where your next scheme is coming from instead of taking an interest

PHILIP: In what?

HELEN: In a hundred things look in everything that's around you but I decided not to replace it no parking is impossible and anyway the subway is as fast and then

PHILIP: But you really like to drive

HELEN: With the money you bring in after we've saved and saved at the hospital the doctor couldn't believe it not a rib cracked not a tooth broken whereas the impact not a single memory either I'll never know what went on

PHILIP: With the money I bring in

HELEN: You'll buy us a new one

PHILIP: Quiet one

(*Lights out.*)

FIVE

PHILIP: Was it Simon?

HELEN: Your friends don't say their names they come in go out they don't say hello either

PHILIP: Then who was it?

HELEN: I open the door and they don't even see me

PHILIP: You don't exactly give them the big welcome

HELEN: I've told you what I think of their way of living call that living

PHILIP: He said I could go over to Simon's that all?

HELEN: I can't understand what you see in those guys

PHILIP: That's enough

HELEN: He said at Simon's or if he isn't there Patti's

PHILIP: Patti?

HELEN: I think he said Patti and he said before noon

PHILIP: Well I'm off

HELEN: No Philip first you're going to have lunch we're going to have lunch I was waiting for you see and before you sit down listen to me

PHILIP: What?

HELEN: Take off your coat and gloves and you can wash your hands

PHILIP: I really just want to sleep

HELEN: So you're not going?

PHILIP: I don't care

HELEN: Have they put you on the regular payroll?

PHILIP: What?

HELEN: You started a month ago today

PHILIP: Oh ya

HELEN: What?

PHILIP: Uh here's my pay

HELEN: Oh

PHILIP: Go ahead take it

HELEN: I didn't ask for anything

PHILIP: It really looks funny huh?

HELEN: Now that you're on the right track I can dream a little can't I? I'd like you to find a job that's less dull where you can use your head a little

PHILIP: Not so fast

HELEN: Are you going to eat your salad with your fingers for the rest of your life? You were first in your class in composition always

PHILIP: Seen enough of that dress

HELEN: But you never look at me

PHILIP: Buy yourself another dress

HELEN: Philip

PHILIP: Get dolled up my friends will start looking at you

HELEN: Really?

PHILIP: Remember you used to have a white dress? you should go to your hairdresser have him give you bangs and cut all that off you can't see your face your neck

HELEN: Maybe I'm hiding but you

PHILIP: Show yourself

HELEN: You've gotten very thin your eyes your brow your cheekbones

PHILIP: I've never felt better Dad told me I was a sharp guy just like him

HELEN: Oh he wanted to talk to you

PHILIP: He talked to me

HELEN: Well?

PHILIP: He told me there was a place in his company for a sharp guy with a future like me how could you?

HELEN: How could I what?

PHILIP: Get interested in a guy like that

HELEN: You're hurting me

PHILIP: I want to know

(*Lights out.*)

SIX

HELEN: You know Grandma wasn't feeling at all well

PHILIP: Did she die?

HELEN: Couldn't hold on any longer

PHILIP: I'm not working tonight we're on strike I'm taking you out to eat and then to a movie

HELEN: You weren't listening you picked a fine day

PHILIP: Grandma died

HELEN: Yes after all

PHILIP: But we didn't

HELEN: You know what you're saying?

PHILIP: You look beautiful today madam

HELEN: Imagine I cried

PHILIP: All the same we can go to the movies

HELEN: I didn't love her you think you no longer love your mother no tonight I believe I'll it's stupid stay here quiet at home it's stupid

PHILIP: You're very beautiful
HELEN: You're funny sir
PHILIP: There's this fantastic movie down the street
HELEN: You've never asked me out to the movies
PHILIP: I want to go out with some classy lady
HELEN: It's time you found some nice
PHILIP: And you the right kind of man
HELEN: Sometimes I wonder if you're serious when you talk like that and
    where exactly you are with girls
PHILIP: Or maybe if I'm a homosexual
HELEN: You never say anything
PHILIP: I tell you lots of things all the time
HELEN: Sure me to figure out
PHILIP: I'm telling you to find some guy there's agencies that use compu-
    ters
HELEN: I know sooner or later everything ends up in a computer they
    just finished installing ours at work air conditioned room
PHILIP: Find yourself a neat programmer
HELEN: Maybe during the coming three months they're going to try out
    the program we'll continue doing the statistics by hand alongside the
    machine will provide the same figures as a check if everything goes as it's sup-
    posed to after three months there'll be just the computer program
PHILIP: So
HELEN: Fortunately you have your job
PHILIP: Yes fortunately
HELEN: Why you laughing?
PHILIP: Long live the stamping machines at Peugeot

(*Lights out.*)

SEVEN

HELEN: If I started wondering? why sure I started wondering I'm not used
    to having you disappear for several days without saying something
PHILIP: No I'm not hungry I think I'm going to go to bed
HELEN: But with which friends?
PHILIP: The foreman has a place out in the country he and two other guys
    said come on I went we lived it up a little when you're on strike you get to
    know the people normally you hardly ever talk you can't on account of the
    noise level and when the whistle blows everybody splits not a word next day
    back on the machines
HELEN: I thought you took over the plant?
PHILIP: Yes occupy it in shifts
HELEN: But you stayed three days in the country?

PHILIP: Yes you know uh that strike I dunno the Algerians have taken it over it's falling apart

HELEN: What's the strike for?

PHILIP: In the beginning it was against the speed of the production lines and the number of decibels then well then the foreman has this little farm down south his parents were farmers

HELEN: I got a letter from your father I'm going to read it to you "My dear Helen, I'm writing to tell you that I intend to deposit four-fifty a month instead of three-seventy-five as usual. As is only fair I'm increasing your monthly support in consequence of a promotion I have received. You are aware that I have in fact been fulfilling the functions of the position of director of exports without actually having that title. I have now been officially named to the post and have had my salary upgraded. I think it a normal thing that Philip and you should benefit from this also. I am well and hope you are too."

PHILIP: As is only fair

HELEN: He often uses that expression

PHILIP: I think it a normal thing

HELEN: Your father makes a religion of decorum

PHILIP: He used to say come here and while he beat me

HELEN: You never cried

PHILIP: I was busy breaking his skull open kneading his brain with my fingers I no longer felt the blows at all

HELEN: How stupid of me I was looking for the car keys without realizing

PHILIP: You going out?

HELEN: I'm so scatterbrained forgot what I was going to do

PHILIP: Buy bread

HELEN: Don't need the car to go buy bread

PHILIP: You never feel the need for a man?

HELEN: You're almost a man already

PHILIP: In bed

HELEN: That's something else

PHILIP: Well you going out?

HELEN: It's coming back to me now I have to go see Mrs. Tissot she's in the hospital

PHILIP: What's her problem?

HELEN: Cancer of the brain it's all over with

PHILIP For whom?

(*Lights out.*)

EIGHT

PHILIP: So you going to look for another job?

HELEN: Not right away so many things I've wanted to do for so long now keep putting them off year after year oh these phonograph records

PHILIP: I'll straighten them out

HELEN: So many things I'm not even sure I'll be able to make my dream come true six months off boy you couldn't imagine

PHILIP: You could stand being without work?

HELEN: Oh I'll eventually go back to work but first a good long vacation I'll go for walks go to the library you know what my single greatest regret is? I never see you with a book in your hands

PHILIP: I already have enough of that stuff crammed in my head

HELEN: What kind of stuff?

PHILIP: I've got a whole finished book in my head

HELEN: What's the title?

PHILIP: No title

HELEN: Write it

PHILIP: I want to live it

HELEN: What does that mean?

PHILIP: If you don't get it

HELEN: It takes more than just daydreaming when you were little you used to write all the time I'm sure that if you had just kept it up

PHILIP: Stop

HELEN: Your life you let it slip through your fingers grab hold of it make something of it

PHILIP: I'm going to show you my life look

HELEN: I'm looking

PHILIP: The part comes down the conveyor in front of you

HELEN: Yes

PHILIP: I put it like so I stick it in

HELEN: Uhuh then what?

PHILIP: There's a pedal down here you step on it the press comes down plop I pull the part out the conveyor sends me another one

HELEN: Then?

PHILIP: Plop in pedal plop

HELEN: And that's your life?

PHILIP: See you bought the white dress

HELEN: I didn't vacuum yesterday you know feel I'm changing

PHILIP: Bought yourself the white dress

HELEN: This pair of clogs too

(Lights out.)

NINE

PHILIP: You're crying listen it's no big deal I can tell them not to come anymore

HELEN: Your friends are welcome in your house I've already told you so

PHILIP: We can set up somewhere else

HELEN: What do you mean we?

PHILIP: I don't know

HELEN: There's four of them in your room one girl I made them something to eat they asked me they even say hello now I mentioned it to the big curly haired one the other day

PHILIP: Simon

HELEN: But don't they work?

PHILIP: They're not all as lucky as I was

HELEN: Two of them have been sleeping on your bed since seven they look exhausted

PHILIP: You're a fabulous mother you know?

HELEN: Are they really your friends?

PHILIP: What do you mean?

HELEN: They don't look like your kind I have to say this I'm not happy with their having a key to the house

PHILIP: Let me explain

HELEN: When I got home from the office I found them moved in there

PHILIP: Oh ya I saw Dad he gave me a lecture on socialism he told me he met you through politics

HELEN: He'd really like you to share his ideas

PHILIP: You still believe in it in socialism?

HELEN: Way back I was an activist I'm for the struggle against privileges

PHILIP: Which ones?

HELEN: Absolute power of management

PHILIP: And him isn't he a boss? while he was talking I heard nothing kept looking at his nose can't take him any more don't want to see him ever again

HELEN: You can't doubt his sincerity

PHILIP: He abandoned you

HELEN: It wasn't working out I'm happier now it's hard but I like my independence

PHILIP: But you still love him

HELEN: That's not the point aren't you going out with your friends?

PHILIP: Mrs. Tissot was by I told her I thought she was in the hospital should have seen the look she gave me

HELEN: She's out

PHILIP: She was never in she said she was in the neighborhood took the opportunity to bring you the lace she said you could pay next time and she's expecting some very pretty colors she'll show you them next time what did you have done to yourself in that hospital? what do you plan on doing with that lace?

HELEN: Sunday tablecloth for us

(*Lights out.*)

TEN

PHILIP: What a dreary dinner that was

HELEN: Because you spent the time sulking but tell me what you think of him

PHILIP: Weak

HELEN: Well I liked him pretty much what I asked for

PHILIP: His way of looking at everything like he already owned it

HELEN: He likes ideas books walks in the country

PHILIP: He's beneath your class you'll dominate him and then you'll be more bored than when you're by yourself

HELEN: Well maybe the description I gave the computer wasn't accurate

PHILIP: And you showed up more than a half hour late

HELEN: I might have done it unconsciously on purpose

PHILIP: I had to sit there and listen to the old boy's talk

HELEN: Yes on purpose

PHILIP: I was worried

HELEN: About me?

PHILIP: After your accident

HELEN: But I don't have a car anymore

PHILIP: What about your dizzy spells?

HELEN: I've always been a scatterbrain

PHILIP: I know what you're hiding from me and you're going to marry *that*?

HELEN: Philip my crazy boy you don't believe me it's all because of that story about Mrs. Tissot you know I never see anything about that strike not in the papers or on TV

PHILIP: It's just two shops not enough to shut the whole plant down believe me

HELEN: Yes but I called Peugeot too

PHILIP: They just lied to you

HELEN: I don't know Philip you've stopped eating those bags under your eyes and your father called wanted to know why you asked him for money

PHILIP: He's loaded you're out of work

HELEN: But we're not starving I'm collecting ninety percent compensation

PHILIP: That's between him and me

HELEN: After everything you said about him?

PHILIP: Makes me want to puke

HELEN: Why what sense what in God's name do you think you're doing are you crazy? don't you dare hit me

(*Lights out.*)

ELEVEN

PHILIP: You coming from the hospital?

HELEN: What do I have to do to make you believe that there's nothing the matter with me? you start imagining and it really makes me angry come home and find your room full

PHILIP: Full of what?

HELEN: Your buddies all over the floor and one girl looked asleep on her feet

PHILIP: Patti

HELEN: You in love with her?

PHILIP: Crazy about her

HELEN: She's very pretty but why one girl with all those boys?

PHILIP: They have their girls they don't bring them along

HELEN: But what do they come here for?

PHILIP: We talk

HELEN: Since you know the foreman you could talk to him ask him to have you switched to another shop

PHILIP: Yes that's a good idea

HELEN: Now that the strike is over

PHILIP: Yes

HELEN: If you just made the effort there's so many ways to show your best side only you have to

PHILIP: A goal in life any of that sausage left?

HELEN: Just the very end⁻

PHILIP: Went a long way

HELEN: That book you should try to write it

PHILIP: And it will really sell big you'll get out the tablecloth with the lace I'll buy you a sports car Dad will drop in with the socialist party I'll invite the foreman there'll be chocolate covered truffles and let's see yes TV TV

HELEN: I'll buy another sausage pure beef

PHILIP: And all your boy friends

HELEN: We'll stand them in a row

PHILIP: Patti will dance she's a super dancer

HELEN: The money

PHILIP: What?

HELEN: You know what I mean

PHILIP: No

HELEN: It's gone
PHILIP: I forgot to tell you
HELEN: What's become of it?
PHILIP: I'll pay you back
HELEN: You took it
PHILIP: No big deal
HELEN: My savings you took everything?
PHILIP: One of my friends had a problem
HELEN: Without telling me?
PHILIP: You'll have it before the end of the month

(*Lights out.*)

TWELVE

HELEN: Yes I was sleeping
PHILIP: Sorry I got you up
HELEN: Five in the morning can I make you something to eat?
PHILIP: I'm not hungry
HELEN: Were you far away?
PHILIP: It was Simon that gave us
HELEN: Your face is all hollow cheeks your eyes are sockets
PHILIP: No mail? what's this?
HELEN: Mrs. Tissot's announcement your magazines there's three of them
     I haven't seen you for almost a month
PHILIP: But you reported to the police
HELEN: Not right away first I went to personnel at the factory
PHILIP: They told you
HELEN: That you were on the employee list three weeks in all I'm going to
     make you a cup of coffee
PHILIP: Thanks how about you? everything OK?
HELEN: You can see for yourself
PHILIP: I brought you back part of the money
HELEN: I was at the funeral
PHILIP: Nobody come by for me?
HELEN: Your friends?
PHILIP: I'm cold
HELEN: Wrap yourself in this cover I'll go get you some wool socks
PHILIP: Hey this is new
HELEN: From the office going-away present the girls gave us Lillian got a
     vase I got that bedside lamp
PHILIP: They knew you like to read in bed
HELEN: Yes
PHILIP: Now you're free

HELEN: I can take care of you as long as you're going to be here

PHILIP: If I stay here they'll be by to pick me up

HELEN: They've already been here a number of times I imagine they're watching the house

PHILIP: They didn't bother you did they?

HELEN: They took me to the station to make a deposition they were actually rather nice but they did search the apartment they read all the letters I was keeping they pulled your bed apart

PHILIP: What did they tell you?

HELEN: Breaking into several drug stores and that three of your group have already been arrested

PHILIP: What else?

HELEN: Breaking and entering with theft possession and sale of drugs

PHILIP: Painful words huh?

(*Doorbell rings.*)

HELEN: Already

PHILIP: You'll be able to buy a new car

HELEN: You think?

PHILIP: It'll simplify your life at any rate

(*Doorbell and knocking.*)

HELEN: Any advice on a make or model?

PHILIP: Yes the new Renault 5 you know?

HELEN: With the double-welded frame

PHILIP: I wanted to see you one more time I knew they'd come

(*Loud knocking at the door.*)

HELEN: Don't be worried about me

PHILIP: I'll be all right don't worry

HELEN: Shall we make them wait a little longer?

PHILIP: Yes a little bit

HELEN: Like me to put on a record?

(*Lights out.*)

END

Nina, It's Different

a play in twelve parts

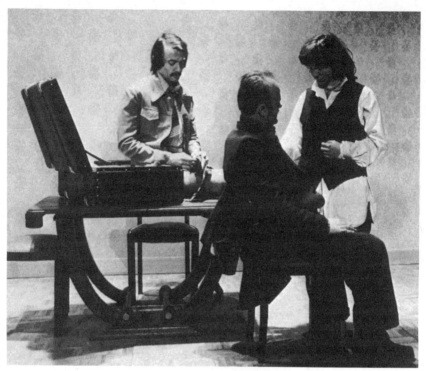

NINA, IT'S DIFFERENT
Théâtre de l'est Parisien (France)
Directed by Jacques Lassalle

CHARACTERS:

Sebastian
Charles
Nina

I. OPENING THE PACKAGE OF DATES

SEBASTIAN: Want to promote me to crew leader
CHARLES: Come on tell
SEBASTIAN: I've told you a hundred times
CHARLES: How she spread your legs
SEBASTIAN: No she spread hers it was her
CHARLES: Right she anyway a fellow doesn't refuse to get ahead
SEBASTIAN: I don't care to order people around
CHARLES: You open it here along this side
SEBASTIAN: She had little bells on her bracelets on her necklace
CHARLES: Me I'm really afraid for Nina here we have plenty of space she hardly
     takes up any room she's only five-one
SEBASTIAN: Here
CHARLES: If they put you up for crew leader it's because they think you can do
     the job
SEBASTIAN: She had this long necklace that trailed on my stomach
CHARLES: The boss you know one of these nights he's going to follow her home
     right up to her room you see her eat last night rabbit is one of her favorite
     things she loves rabbit stew she had seconds and thirds she'd be better off if
     she moved
SEBASTIAN: If I say no they'll write it down in their little black books then just
     one little slip
CHARLES: If you say yes it's a promotion all right with raise
SEBASTIAN: She told me to lie on my back she straddled me with her little bells
     under the palm tree her breasts were pointed I had one in each hand from
     time to time I took my hands from her breasts and put them on her butt or
     else I left one hand there and put the other in her crack they had this big
     earthquake in China did you see that? No big deal now if it happened in
     France or in England
CHARLES: They don't have earthquakes in England

SEBASTIAN: I know but imagine if it happened in France

CHARLES: She thinks you're sort of closed how many years does that make now?

SEBASTIAN: Well since they brought the troops back from Tunisia

CHARLES: This is '76

SEBASTIAN: It was in '54

CHARLES: Mind you she does like you besides the curry sauce she's crazy about it I told her it was ma's recipe and you'd never even cooked before that she couldn't get over she really thinks it's great for a son what do you think of her? she's actually interested in everything not a bore

SEBASTIAN: This is the twenty-second year

CHARLES: Twenty-two years she'd been sending you the box of dates for your birthday

SEBASTIAN: Don't mean anything

CHARLES: Means a hell of a lot

SEBASTIAN: It's a habit

CHARLES: And never a little note in it? Her name and address always the same on the outside? It does mean something she's persistent

SEBASTIAN: After one night only not even I went back on guard duty she bit my ear lobes till I bled I don't like dates

CHARLES: Never thought of sending for her? Maybe that's what she's waiting for down there all alone on the sand dunes I don't care for them either

SEBASTIAN: Ma loved them we could send them to China for the victims they published an official notice no foreign relief aid needed from anywhere that's what I call pride the Algerians too what I call proud people not like your Tunisians they're the other way round they're pliable

CHARLES: Well would it be all right with you?

SEBASTIAN: They work like donkeys and make no fuss

CHARLES: Suppose she moves in she really goes for dates

SEBASTIAN: No

CHARLES: So tell after that what she did to you

SEBASTIAN: What I like about Chinamen is the combination of calm and will power the English and the Chinese they both have it in 1940-41 the English didn't bend their necks if it happened in France

CHARLES: One of these days the boss

SEBASTIAN: In France you figure an earthquake right in the heart of Paris

CHARLES: He and I are going to have it out

SEBASTIAN: Incredible mess here

CHARLES: Well what do you say?

SEBASTIAN: Panic everybody for himself save your own skin

II. ROAST VEAL WITH SPINACH

CHARLES: I didn't say that never I said her voice is like a flute

SEBASTIAN: That's not what you said

CHARLES: It's not to take ma's place just a woman's voice around the house

SEBASTIAN: Too dull for you around here?

CHARLES: Ma never said we should live like in a tomb here for some time now he's been slipping his hand between her legs at work regularly well it's more or less normal practice with shampoo girls but with Nina it's different this is genuine old fashioned spinach this is Sebastian

SEBASTIAN: The first fresh spinach of the season

CHARLES: Roast veal with spinach

SEBASTIAN: Remember? we had it every Wednesday I chopped them by hand

CHARLES: Like mom

SEBASTIAN: I used to watch her do it sat there quiet she chopped 'em so fast without any hurry

CHARLES: A pretty pair of legs to look at alongside yours and mine

SEBASTIAN: And if I say no?

CHARLES: But if you say yes you move up the scale

SEBASTIAN: In our group we're already debating over what position to take

CHARLES: When I was a kid spinach was already my favorite

SEBASTIAN: To get them really smooth you know I wonder if I've used the right saucepan hers were like velvet you really need a saucepan with a thick base

CHARLES: They wouldn't name you if they didn't think you could be a crew leader

SEBASTIAN: The work I do now adjusting machines it's never monotonous and you get to move around from shop to shop keep in touch with the guys by making me crew leader they immobilize me I become responsible for a production budget makes me sort of a part of management it's a technique they often use to neutralize a guy who's a little activist

CHARLES: Absolutely no security she's living alone in that little room can just see him climb up the six floors after her give me a second helping would you Sebastian

SEBASTIAN: They want an answer tomorrow

CHARLES: What scares you is the change

SEBASTIAN: Among machine adjusters there's no lack of guys that are good at the job

CHARLES: He knows about the two of us it turns him on to do that to her in front of me

SEBASTIAN: Must be something else

CHARLES: When was it uhuh yesterday he said it just loud enough for his wife to hear she almost swallowed her false teeth there behind the cash register when am I going to put it to you eh baby? Mary and Yvonne the other two shampoo girls almost split laughing he said your place? tonight? right when a customer was coming in not just any customer imagine but Madam Charpy of the bank next door

SEBASTIAN: Want a little more?

CHARLES: She's Polish I mean she was born in Poland you wouldn't believe it a hurricane

SEBASTIAN: They're like that it comes from their history you see a lot of them Poles at the plant

CHARLES: Imagine

SEBASTIAN: They've been screwed over so many times when you've been invaded that many times you learn how to take care of yourself

CHARLES: But she

SEBASTIAN: They're tricky the Algerians we have more problems but generally I prefer the Algerians they're tricky too more or less what you see in any people that have been walked over let themselves get walked over compare them to the Chinese now the day after the earthquake the survivors set up house and shop right in the streets as if nothing had happened

CHARLES: Their government trains to follow like sheep

SEBASTIAN: Sheep aren't trained it's their nature the nature of the people

CHARLES: If you take the job nothing prevents you from going on

SEBASTIAN: With what?

CHARLES: Organizing activities

SEBASTIAN: It isn't as clear cut

CHARLES: You've got more power

SEBASTIAN: A machine when it has problems I take it in hand I live with it until it does what I want it to exactly that's what I like then on to another machine that needs adjusting I take my time talk to the boys on the shift no giving orders that way a guy is more independent

CHARLES: Like us with hair we ask the ladies what they want but in the end we it's we who make the decisions on what looks right for them

SEBASTIAN: That's the best way

CHARLES: What way?

SEBASTIAN: The way things are

CHARLES: So are you going to refuse?

SEBASTIAN: If I refuse they might stick me in some phony job exactly what they did to Chadex last month

CHARLES: Nina's coming to dinner tomorrow and then she'll move her things all right? imagine she usually eats like a bird did you see her go for seconds and thirds?

SEBASTIAN: No

CHARLES: Why sure and as for housework she'll pitch in you'll have that much more time to listen to your records

SEBASTIAN: I listen while I work

CHARLES: She'll sit you in your big chair put your slippers on customers like Madam Charpy with real bucks the ones that throw the money around give you the big tips he keeps for himself in most salons the bosses share what they get with the employees me I have seniority over the other two twenty-

one years at one place
SEBASTIAN: Is that what you wanted to talk to him about?
CHARLES: He cleared out when it comes to money no time to talk never
SEBASTIAN: What did the other two say?
CHARLES: Nothing they're happy to have the work

III. THE ARRIVAL

NINA: She died how long ago?
SEBASTIAN: Eight months
CHARLES: Well come on in put your bag down
NINA: It's fantastic everything is shining here and perfectly straightened up you
share the housework?
CHARLES: Windows that's me because Sebastian he's afraid of heights every-
thing else is him
NINA: Even the ironing?
SEBASTIAN: I have more free time than Charles I get back home at 5:30
CHARLES: You could mention that you leave the house at 5 a.m.
NINA: Me I could never
CHARLES: It's not like us ten minutes on foot to work Sebastian he does a forty-
five minute commute in the morning and an hour and a half at night
NINA: Subway?
SEBASTIAN: I've got a moped a Peugeot
NINA: Even in winter? and when it rains?
SEBASTIAN: No problem
CHARLES: He doesn't like crowds he stops off and does the shopping on the way
home
SEBASTIAN: Well miss put your things down
CHARLES: You two could drop the formalities
SEBASTIAN: We'll see
NINA: The two of you aren't at all alike thanks anyway and if I can do anything

IV. THE SHAWL

NINA: It was terrific I've really enjoyed the last three days have to be going now
CHARLES: You leaving?
NINA: No hope of getting along with Sebastian
CHARLES: Listen
NINA: I really do like him but well that's the way he is
CHARLES: It's nothing personal he's been a little nervous since he was promoted
to crew leader now he's got to enforce production schedules
NINA: It's not just him you too ever since I arrived you've been on edge (*Sebas-
tian comes in.*) I don't know which of you is more impossible

SEBASTIAN: You leave your magazines all over the place

NINA: You see Charles? my mind's made up

CHARLES: Nina's leaving

SEBASTIAN: You leaving miss?

CHARLES: Sebastian I thought you'd use her first name by now

SEBASTIAN: (*Sits in his chair.*) O.K. hit the road baby

NINA: (*Sits on Sebastian's knees.*) Won't be quite that easy

SEBASTIAN: Easy to what?

NINA: Easy for me to get used to you (*sighs*) used to all that dust

SEBASTIAN: What dust?

NINA: I know there's no dust the two of you made out of dust no it's too much

CHARLES: What Nina?

NINA: He opened the bathroom door going to pee he saw me on the throne you'd think he saw the devil himself the way he cut out of there I never lock the door

CHARLES: So it's no big deal

NINA: Sorry it's final

CHARLES: You could try a little harder

NINA: Me try a little harder me? that's all I do is try a little harder

SEBASTIAN: Don't we all no lack of effort around here

NINA: I wonder if we should

CHARLES: Should what?

NINA: Make efforts the three of us I wonder if we shouldn't each just follow our inclination like Sebastian for example suppose you said something nice to me eh? don't you like me a little bit? well then why don't you show it? (*She slowly removes all her clothes.*)

CHARLES: Why you taking your clothes off?

SEBASTIAN: I have the distinct impression she's not leaving

NINA: That's not certain

CHARLES: You're going to catch a

SEBASTIAN: All right you two here's where I get off

NINA: No Sebastian we're in this together you're wrong if you think I don't need you too come right down to it Sebastian I think you overawe me a little bit go get me your mother's shawl and wrap me in it (*Sebastian goes out.*) I'm feeling fine did your mother overawe people too?

CHARLES: She didn't own a cookbook

SEBASTIAN: Didn't even write her recipes down

CHARLES: Sebastian reconstructed everything from memory

SEBASTIAN: I used to sit there evenings

CHARLES: Watching her work

NINA: That's a way for you two to keep her alive but we three could also dream up some little things from time to time just for us

CHARLES: I doubt he'll ever let you near that oven

NINA: Well little mice can slip into all sorts of places (*Nina goes out.*)
CHARLES: I think you hurt her

V. AT THE MOVIES

NINA: Looks brand new
SEBASTIAN: It is
NINA: Nice suitcase
SEBASTIAN: Better this way
NINA: What did you pack?
SEBASTIAN: I've rented an efficiency in Clichy
NINA: They say Clichy's nice it's on the Riviera isn't it?
SEBASTIAN: Close to the plant I've been thinking along those lines for some time now
NINA: Yes all that commuting time
SEBASTIAN: By the time I get home at night it's too much
NINA: Yes especially since you have your new responsibilities
SEBASTIAN: All that time wasted I can't really do my share of the work of our group printing the brochures distributing not to mention the meetings
NINA: Oh I see how at first I figured you were taking off on vacation
SEBASTIAN: What?
NINA: You aren't putting me on Sebastian? (*Charles enters.*)
CHARLES: Where are you going?
NINA: Sebastian's moving out he just explained everything don't try and stop him
CHARLES: What are you talking about?
NINA: He's right he's convinced feels like a fifth wheel around here we'd be happier without him all he does is pick up after me not to mention that you and I have no privacy you know how Sebastian is everything on schedule and in order just last night I got home late for dinner never hear the end of it oh Sebastian there's only one thing that doesn't fit into your system which is that me I couldn't really get along without you and if you take off I'm going too
CHARLES: You leaving with him? just great great
NINA: I'll commute between the two of you come on open that suitcase let's see there they are everything in order folded shirts handkerchiefs sweaters pajamas and look at this toiletries case a bit worn you'll have to get a new one let's put this all back Sebastian and go out to a show tonight on me this time you must never play such tricks on us again just wait a while I'm going to put on my face (*Nina goes out.*)
CHARLES: So in the end the Algerian
SEBASTIAN: No not yet
CHARLES: But you will have to fire him?

SEBASTIAN: The matter isn't quite resolved yet

CHARLES: Me three days now three days my boss hasn't spoken to me not even to yell at me

SEBASTIAN: The only certain fact is that supplies are missing from stock but that's not the real issue the foreman couldn't care less about the Algerian it's me he's after he wants me down on my knees

CHARLES: After he chewed me out we used to end up laughing

SEBASTIAN: But no proof at all

CHARLES: Nina doesn't take it serious but under the surface there's something cooking (*Nina enters.*)

NINA: Zip me?

CHARLES: Right Nina? I used to be entitled to getting chewed out three times a day

NINA: Holy fucking Christ Charlie get off your ass the next customer my boy move it

CHARLES: Holy fucking Christ Charlie customers waiting and you sleeping that's the way to keep your clientele holy shit

SEBASTIAN: He talks that way in front of the customers?

NINA: Holy fucking Christ he whispers it but you can hear it all over

CHARLES: Holy fucking Christ the final touches one last little brush stroke god-damn painter he thinks he is no wonder we lose customers with you

NINA: You could get in two more customers a day easy am I right or not? well you lazy shit?

CHARLES: But you know those last few strokes of the brush it's all in that just that

NINA: It's what people come back to you for

CHARLES: Down deep he isn't a total creep

NINA: Likes to kid around

CHARLES: Kid around with shampoo girls' asses

SEBASTIAN: In our plant we tell the new female employees not to put up with that sort of thing

NINA: Easy to say but when it's your boss

SEBASTIAN: We tell them to report that to the representative now it's true that a lot of them don't dare to no matter no boss has the right to

NINA: But us in the beauty salon no representative to report it to what are we supposed to say?

CHARLES: It's a normal part of the job like getting chewed out three times a day

NINA: He's not really a total creep

CHARLES: No but under the surface it's cooking Nina she doesn't really believe it but he hasn't given me one holy fucking Christ or a single lazy bastard for three days now

SEBASTIAN: There's some lower management they take liberties we're against that

NINA: But what can we do? you two ready?

VI. THE DRAPES

CHARLES: You tell her
SEBASTIAN: Better if it's you
CHARLES: She's more afraid of you
SEBASTIAN: Still she's yours
CHARLES: I don't know anymore
SEBASTIAN: You brought her in Charles it's you that should do it
CHARLES: She's really ours now let's do it together we could talk to her both of
   us
SEBASTIAN: There has to be somebody to start though
CHARLES: Listen Nina you're a lot younger than we are
SEBASTIAN: Right
CHARLES: You've got your whole life ahead of you and we've already lived half
   of ours that does it
SEBASTIAN: What do you mean that does it?
CHARLES: I mean Sebastian and I we can't just let you break it all up like that
   we you could say something too you know
SEBASTIAN: Sure tear it to pieces like that the way we've lived our habits our
   personalities
CHARLES: If you weren't so selfish
SEBASTIAN: If you just respected our way of living just a tiny bit
CHARLES: If she didn't get so interested in you might have done better Nina and
   me upstairs you down here just like before except naturally meals together
SEBASTIAN: The lord and lady of the house and the jack-of-all-trades?
CHARLES: You know what I mean
SEBASTIAN: I warned you
CHARLES: If you hadn't starting hanging on her right from the beginning
SEBASTIAN: You crazy?
CHARLES: Just telling you what I think
SEBASTIAN: I tried to stay out of it best I could
CHARLES: Best you could
SEBASTIAN: She wouldn't let me alone and you encouraged her
CHARLES: We weren't going to live back to back (*Nina enters.*)
NINA: What's that I smell cooking wonderful really smacks you in the nose
CHARLES: Sebastian's cooking up a little corned beef and cabbage for us
NINA: Gimme a kiss Sebastian and sorry I'm late want to know where I've been?
   shh it's a surprise for the three of us you know what this house is missing? a
   bathtub I found one
CHARLES: What?
NINA: They were tearing this house down it's old-fashioned with paws for the
   feet but what's the matter Sebastian?
CHARLES: Mental anguish he's got
NINA: It's deep some of the enamel is chipped off

CHARLES: He had to fire the Algerian

NINA: Work is always a little complicated

CHARLES: Sebastian we could eat now no?

SEBASTIAN: No talk to her first

CHARLES: O.k.

SEBASTIAN: Nina

NINA: Hey you two I can take a hint

SEBASTIAN: Charles isn't the same ever since you moved in he's anxious he and I we've been thinking it over

CHARLES: Sebastian ever since you it's more his way of life turned upside down the dinner schedule the bathroom door

SEBASTIAN: I couldn't care less if it was just for me but Charles is another matter can't get used to

CHARLES: No problem for me

NINA: You both have problems and I'm going to help you with them (*Nina gets a stepladder, steps up, unhooks the drapes and lets them fall; she opens the window and throws them out.*)

SEBASTIAN: The chair coverings too

CHARLES: And the chandelier (*The covers are removed from the chairs, the chandelier is taken down.*)

SEBASTIAN: There's mother's room the bed is bigger you can take down the old pictures

NINA: No we shouldn't change anything there

SEBASTIAN: There you'll be more comfortable

NINA: Or we could make it into the living room it gets the most light by far instead of leaving it sealed up empty we take out all the furniture and I'll sew cushions hundreds of cushions

CHARLES: Aren't you hungry?

NINA: Dying

CHARLES: Let's eat

VII. FREE REIN

CHARLES: And you're staying on?

NINA: I know Charles but we can't both of us be out of work

SEBASTIAN: You walked right into his trap

CHARLES: Sure now he's got free rein

NINA: I'll keep my guard up don't worry

CHARLES: Your guard where's it been up to now and with me there?

NINA: With you there it encouraged him

CHARLES: This time it was more than the wandering hands the last customer he had left he unzipped

NINA: He took my hand and put it I struggled

CHARLES: You called me
NINA: It was a mistake
SEBASTIAN: For that you could take him to claims court you could even take
  him to criminal court
CHARLES: Sure prove it
SEBASTIAN: The other two shampoo girls were there
CHARLES: You think they'd testify
NINA: Charles hit him he fell he screamed
SEBASTIAN: Mistake you shouldn't have hit him
CHARLES: Oh well and you don't have time to think he can hire someone
  younger at a little over half of what he pays me
NINA: We didn't figure I should have just let him go on
CHARLES: And then?
NINA: Feel him up a little and that's all
SEBASTIAN: Oh sure
NINA: Whereas now
SEBASTIAN: He fire you?
CHARLES: Without severance pay even serious infraction
SEBASTIAN: After twenty-one years
CHARLES: Assault on the person of one's employer
SEBASTIAN: Take him to court counter-claim
CHARLES: Sure and meanwhile
SEBASTIAN: Maybe it's for the better Charles you're good at your work you'll
  find a more decent place better conditions
CHARLES: You know I'd swear ma was talking

VIII. THE TUB

NINA: It's beautiful
SEBASTIAN: An antique
CHARLES: How we going to fill it?
NINA: With pitchers
SEBASTIAN: In ma's room under the washstand there's a jug
CHARLES: How we going to empty it?
NINA: Didn't think of that wait Sebastian the master mechanic he'll fix us up a
  pump
SEBASTIAN: Where shall we put it?
NINA: Leave it right here
CHARLES: In the middle of the room?
NINA: Tub like this one you need room all around to walk
CHARLES: A tub usually gets put against a wall
NINA: Our tub's going to be just like it is (*Bucket brigade to fill the tub, with
  pitcher, jug, bucket.*)
CHARLES: What does he say to my customers?

NINA: I don't know

CHARLES: What do you mean you don't know don't they ask?

NINA: He tells them that after a while things didn't work out

CHARLES: What didn't work out?

NINA: His wife made up the official story but let's not talk about it tomorrow Charles I'll tell you but not today I'd like to

CHARLES: Like to what?

NINA: I'd like us to be happy

CHARLES: Tell me how does the story go?

NINA: Well you see Madam Charles took to drinking a little too much and a hairdresser you understand bad breath is out in this profession

CHARLES: He tells them that?

NINA: She tells them that

CHARLES: And the other employees say nothing?

NINA: Buttoned up tight they're good at it the shampoo girls too you can be sure the atmosphere hasn't gotten any better but there are some customers that just do an about face when they see you're not there they don't want their hair done by anyone but you

CHARLES: I'll get even

SEBASTIAN: He'll be brought to justice

CHARLES: I don't believe in justice he's going to get a knife in his belly

SEBASTIAN: You've already done one stupid thing forget it

NINA: There we are our tub's ready

CHARLES: Everybody gets a turn

SEBASTIAN: Not me

NINA: Not you?

SEBASTIAN: No never

NINA: We're going to take it all three of us together your replacement started this morning a little Italian guy

SEBASTIAN: Not me

NINA: Yes you

SEBASTIAN: I'm off

NINA: I'll undress you

CHARLES: A foreigner to boot

NINA: Talkative like you wouldn't believe puny guy skinny right out of Punch and Judy

SEBASTIAN: (*Letting himself be undressed.*) Italy land of haute coiffure

NINA: I'm a name Gino Gino fromma Napoli he gives you the cut in five minutes old lady Brooche really gets off on him man there's turnover first was Madam Brossard's daughter the tall blonde chick with the bangs remember? the one that always wants thinning shears he really took the shears to her half an inch too much off the sides but she well aren't you getting undressed?

CHARLES: I'm not in the mood for it

NINA: Well take my clothes off (*He takes her clothes off.*) you can get in Sebastian Charles is going to watch us do it maybe get him interested a bath I can't imagine a greater pleasure if you do it right

SEBASTIAN: I don't see the sense

NINA: No sense just pleasure you haven't the vaguest

SEBASTIAN: Don't feel like

NINA: Look you have to learn I don't say that it'll work the first time (*She gets into the tub.*) next he got Madam Barbereau one of your oldest customers

CHARLES: One of my very first

NINA: Yes

CHARLES: I remember when I started out she always talked to me about her divorce she insisted I give my opinion should she or shouldn't she

NINA: And you know the rule you never tell a customer oh I really couldn't say it's strictly your personal

CHARLES: No you have to give advice she wasn't that young then and me I was green her husband beat her but you see she used to tell me (*Nina washes Sebastian.*)

NINA: You see?

CHARLES: Well you see I can't get him out of my system she had magnificent hair

NINA: Even now that her hair's white it's still magnificent

CHARLES: She required a very tight perm you see he suffered such a great deal when he was a boy he never managed to free himself from the clutches of a possessive mother

SEBASTIAN: Did she get the divorce?

CHARLES: No she seemed relieved enough just talking about it about ten years later he died of cancer of the larynx smoked all the time without stopping she hated smoke (*He removes his clothes; standing next to the bathtub he washes Nina.*) didn't she ask about me?

NINA: Naturally

CHARLES: Hurts

NINA: Scrub my back that's it a little harder

CHARLES: This morning I went to the agency for work

SEBASTIAN: At the plant there's a number of them Italians those guys pass out of apprenticeship fast

NINA: Next he got Madam Colin

SEBASTIAN: Italians are enterprising sharp

NINA: You have lots of Portuguese?

CHARLES: At the agency I had to deal with this little frizzy there were two women that questioned me a heavy mama that limped too

NINA: When did you go?

CHARLES: I said this morning (*Nina gets out of the tub, Charles goes in; she washes him.*) they didn't like it when I told them the line of work I was in

NINA: How come?

CHARLES: It's very tight nowadays they had me fill out applications wanted to know if I was interested in retooling as a boiler maker look you can be sent to a training program three months paid room and board at Poitiers

IX. THE CARD GAME

(*Sebastian, head bloodied, lets Nina wash and bandage his wound.*)

SEBASTIAN: You've got the knack

NINA: Nurse it was my dream I went to school for a year was he waiting for you?

SEBASTIAN: At the plant exit yes

NINA: Crummy line of work a shampoo girl makes more when you consider the tips

SEBASTIAN: You haven't lost your skill

NINA: So he jumped you?

SEBASTIAN: No he wanted to talk

NINA: Shh don't you talk too much

SEBASTIAN: We walked together for a while I was pushing my moped

NINA: Easy you'll faint again

SEBASTIAN: He walked alongside me we were going over things calmly Tahar listen I says to him not really any choice and besides I knew you wanted to go back to Algeria in two months so two months more or less I understand he says to me he's got his wife and kids back there listen I said this matter of missing material from the stocks I dunno if it's you or it isn't personally I'm inclined to think it wasn't you I understand he says he repeated it two times I understand then it hit me I was pinned under the moped when I finally got back up nobody around Tahar was a gentle sort of fellow kept his mouth shut crack mechanic to tell the truth put him on a machine no worries you could forget about it

NINA: I wish Charles would come back

SEBASTIAN: Every night he gets home later and more loaded

NINA: And you came all the way from the plant on your moped?

SEBASTIAN: Tahar you should be the first to understand you have your union card decisions like that the boys don't make without mixed feelings

NINA: You could have passed out and got run over

SEBASTIAN: Wouldn't have been a smart idea

NINA: No but

SEBASTIAN: I had made up my mind to get back home

NINA: Situations like that you go right straight to the first pharmacy

SEBASTIAN: Situations like that that's exactly what you don't do

NINA: You're not easy to figure out Sebastian

SEBASTIAN: The pharmacist he calls medical emergency at police headquarters they take you to the hospital then questioning verbal disposition they try to get you to press charges it's already mixed up enough

NINA: In your head?

SEBASTIAN: In fact (*Sebastian, stretched out, and Nina, seated, clean beans; Charles enters.*)

CHARLES: Ten bucks quick ten bucks I need ten

NINA: Little kiss for

CHARLES: Ten bucks

NINA: What no kiss?

CHARLES: Drunks don't kiss ladies drunks got bad breath ten bucks or five

NINA: Kiss me and come join us with the beans

CHARLES: What's the matter with him?

NINA: It was really sort of funny Sebastian opened the door and fainted at my feet you see I'm making progress with Sebastian he lets me clean beans with him

CHARLES: A fiver

NINA: You going out again?

CHARLES: Middle of a card game

NINA: Stay we need you

SEBASTIAN: Let him go

NINA: Not just for the beans

CHARLES: Don't count on me for the beans (*Nina takes hold of Charles, takes off his coat, shoes.*)

NINA: He got beat up by the Algerian the one he let go

CHARLES: What are they waiting for to send those bastards back where they came from?

SEBASTIAN: Just so he stays out of my sight just so he gets the hell go back to your bar

CHARLES: What am I stranger here?

SEBASTIAN: Give him the fiver

CHARLES: Good for nothing vermin I say on the backs of real Frenchmen

SEBASTIAN: Give

CHARLES: Strangers we are in our own house the real French don't have work anymore (*Nina has gotten a pail of water which she empties on Charles's head.*) for a hairdresser's job the agency it's zero for work the bar you get leads there might be an opening on rue Saigon corner by the avenue I'm going to drag myself over that direction tomorrow morning

X. THE AWAKENING

(*A double bed and a single bed pushed together. In the double bed, Charles and Nina; in the single, Sebastian.*)

SEBASTIAN: You sleep all right?

CHARLES: Yes you?

NINA: Yes you Sebastian?

SEBASTIAN: Fine today's my last day of work stoppage

CHARLES: Me too today at noon maybe I'll know what they've decided

SEBASTIAN: Tomorrow I re-up

NINA: My two little doves fly away look at me

CHARLES: At any rate there's a chance

SEBASTIAN: It'll go all right Charles

NINA: Look at me oh it's going to make me feel really funny

CHARLES: Nina it's time

NINA: Get up Nina get up you two going to stay bundled warm under the covers?

SEBASTIAN: Tomorrow morning seven o'clock Leduc with his fat little hands behind his back the conversation takes up where it left off Pelissier I must ask you to be more firm with your crew lack of discipline in that gang Pelissier (*Nina gets out of bed, dressed, makes her face*) beg your pardon but I've upped production twelve percent over budget am I right or wrong? if you took your men in hand Pelissier you'd have done better than twelve the kind of authority over a crew we want around here you don't exercise Pelissier I beg your pardon but tell me how you measure authority I says to him only have to take a stroll through the shop he says to see it's your men stop to talk the most authority as far as I know is measured by the quantity and the quality of production I says to him my crew has the best output in the plant sure says he you've got the best machines if I got the best machines I says to him it's maybe because they're maintained the best I says

NINA: Charles my pants

CHARLES: You left under the covers bottom of the bed

NINA: I'm beautiful

CHARLES: Who's this Leduc?

NINA: His foreman

SEBASTIAN: Former union officer he's the one created the first party cell went up through the ranks and made me fire Tahar he didn't think I'd do it he wasn't happy when he heard I'd done it thought he had me

CHARLES: Now they'll have you fire one or two more you'll get named shop foreman a nice future ahead of you all laid out right Nina?

NINA: Suppose I tell you you both bore the hell outa me?

CHARLES: Me it's the other way round they're looking for somebody young one or two years on the job still maybe they'll take me I'll have to take what they offer for money that means start all over twenty years behind (*Nina goes out.*)

SEBASTIAN: She went out without saying goodbye

CHARLES: She was going to be late

SEBASTIAN: Something's not going right

CHARLES: I haven't had a drop in two weeks and I assure you it's all over with

SEBASTIAN: I know I know but it has nothing to do with you it's us
CHARLES: What should we have done?
SEBASTIAN: We didn't take the trouble to find out
CHARLES: What?
SEBASTIAN: I don't know

XI. THE DEPARTURE

CHARLES: But it's your suitcase it's the new one
SEBASTIAN: She wanted to borrow it and I said she could keep it
NINA: Charles my blouses in the top drawer Sebastian my sweater sets
CHARLES: I don't believe you
NINA: You don't believe me? I'm going to introduce him to both of you he's five
    years younger than me a child really really pretty funny face doesn't speak
    French my pullovers Charles
CHARLES: What do you see in him?
NINA: Who could say?
SEBASTIAN: Where's he from?
NINA: Czechoslovakia a refugee
SEBASTIAN: So he doesn't have a job?
CHARLES: She's making the whole thing up
NINA: I'm not he was standing on a streetcorner looking lost
CHARLES: You angry with us?
NINA: Oh no I love both of you tenderly
SEBASTIAN: You won't be coming back
NINA: I don't think so all my shoes my four pairs of shoes my boots but I'll drop
    in for visits my slippers
CHARLES: I can't bear it
NINA: Can't bear what? (*Charles takes the suitcase by the handle, throws it, the con-*
    tents spill all over the room; Nina drops into the large chair, closes her eyes. Pause.
    She gets up, smiles.) you know I didn't go about it the right way first the shoes
    then the woolens then the underwear (*Picks up, refolds her scattered things,*
    begins packing again.) so as long as he's without his work visa anyway it's not
    serious the boss gave me a whacking big raise
CHARLES: You jump in the sack with him?
NINA: No on the contrary he keeps his fat paws to himself twenty-five percent
    raise wouldn't believe the trouble I had keeping from breaking up he calls me
    solemnly to his office to tell me I've been named head shampoo girl I say to
    him but Monsieur you really shouldn't why the way business has been going
    downhill lately Nina he says I want you to help me get the shop back on its
    feet we're going to redecorate you've got taste
CHARLES: Too late it's fucked
NINA: My bottle of lavender water Sebastian I almost forgot

CHARLES: He's fifty years behind
NINA: In the medicine cabinet and my nail polishes I'm forgetting everything
CHARLES: Old hat like him
NINA: It's true the reason why he needs me is I'm full of ideas
CHARLES: You don't give a damn Sebastian she walks out on the two of us and you sit there after two months I'm making as much as I made in the old place after twenty-one years because we share tips and the clientele is different
NINA: Not to mention your old customers who left us and went looking for you Charles that's exactly what I explained to the old boy and I think that's what finally made him understand you see well best of everything to you two
SEBASTIAN: Good luck
NINA: Good luck Charles
CHARLES: Yes good luck

XII. THE VISIT

(*Sebastian, on a stepladder, is repainting a wall; new furniture from Roche-Bobois. Charles, apron on, prepares dinner. Nina enters, shakes off her umbrella.*)

NINA: You make the potatoes?
CHARLES: Sausage and whipped potatoes it's a snap nowadays with those packages of instant
NINA: Kiss for me Sebastian
SEBASTIAN: Everything going all right?
CHARLES: He doesn't have time anymore comes home late at night
NINA: And you're redoing the house revolutionary
CHARLES: Every night or almost he's got meetings but Sundays he cooks you should come on a Sunday
NINA: We go on train rides on Sunday
CHARLES: You and your refugee?
NINA: He paints landscapes with scary little people in them he paints houses that explode things like that
SEBASTIAN: He's an artist?
NINA: And the insides of trains he's a dissident he escaped from a camp
SEBASTIAN: And he paints pictures in trains?
NINA: He paints the insides of trains he paints trains that look like women and animals that look like trains I bought a camera while he paints I take pictures pictures of everything he taught me to look at things
SEBASTIAN: Like you taught us to see differently
NINA: Yes but you Sebastian you've never wanted to teach me the simplest little recipe
SEBASTIAN: Well if we could start all over and then there was the conflict
CHARLES: The management was waiting to see what Sebastian would do he

had to make a clear choice he chose the side of the strikers in fact he became one of the leaders of the movement the bosses tried to transfer him he refused there was a show of worker solidarity it led to another strike management backed off Leduc lets him alone now

NINA: Until the next incident

SEBASTIAN: No something has changed now

NINA: Good mashed potatoes

CHARLES: I added a spoonful of cream

NINA: You know I can't get over it you Charles

SEBASTIAN: Fact is Charles for the very first time he's recognized for what he's really worth

CHARLES: In this beauty salon you can go all out in your work it's called The New Coiffure no gadgets you can stay with something innovate the turnover isn't the most important thing you can stay with a customer half a day if there's a good reason

SEBASTIAN: And for dessert there's dates

CHARLES: Package arrived

SEBASTIAN: Czechoslovakia now those people there are sharp very intelligent they've let themselves get walked over too

CHARLES: Right on time from Tunisia

SEBASTIAN: The Tunisians too

NINA: That where that comes from?

CHARLES: Every year

NINA: Oh yes I remember Sebastian

CHARLES: Spent one night

NINA: Yes

CHARLES: You tell it

SEBASTIAN: I've already told it a hundred

CHARLES: Oh yes and I haven't told you he's got a lady friend now

NINA: Well go ahead tell

SEBASTIAN: She had little bells on her bracelets on her necklace

NINA: They melt in your mouth

CHARLES: Sebastian and I don't particularly care for them

SEBASTIAN: Why don't you take them along if you and your friend like them

END

THE GAS STATION
La Salamandre (France)
Directed by Gildas Bourdet

The Gas Station

a comedy

Gildas Bourdet

The set depicts a gas station which includes both the owners' flat and a repair shop. Only the shop still seems in working order; the gas pumps, of a vintage variety, have obviously been out of commission for a number of years. Wildly luxuriant vegetation has begun to invade the service area and the station itself is located on the edge of dense woods not far from an airport. We should get the feeling that there are no homes, no housing developments nearby. The set includes, in addition, a glassed-in telephone booth with a coin-operated telephone. The booth cannot be seen from the flat. At irregular intervals, with the exceptions of Act III and most of IV, we hear the overhead rumblings of cargo planes. The action takes place between the months of May and June. Act I unfolds towards the end of the afternoon; Act II the next morning. Act III begins at sundown, about two weeks later, and Act IV commences the next day in the late morning. Except for the disappearance of the Peugeot station wagon before Act IV, the set need not be changed from the beginning to the end of the play.

CHARACTERS:

Madeleine: 58 years old, still beautiful

Thérèse: 38 years old, the oldest daughter of Madeleine and Humbert, the mother of Tut-Tut, single and a high school teacher of the "humanities"

Maud: 28 years old, single, a some-time professional poll-taker, the second daughter of Madeleine and Humbert

Doris: 18 years old, in her last year of high school, the youngest of the three daughters of Madeleine and Humbert

Humbert: 58 years old, a fine-looking man, obviously an "artist"

M. Samson (Monsieur Samson): 45 years old, a car mechanic, well-built, quite tall

Tut-Tut: 18 years old, Thérèse's son, mentally retarded

Richard: about 30 years old, Maud's lover

Thomas: 27 years old, a medical student, Maud's fiancé

Winnock: 23 years old, looks like a member of a motorcycle gang, short

Nothing in the appearance or the clothing of the characters should suggest poverty or any kind of material hardship. Only Humbert's clothes in Acts I and II might appear mussed and rumpled without, however, bespeaking penury.

ACT I

SCENE 1

TUT-TUT: (*Alone, downstage. Staring attentively in the direction of the audience. Behind him, from under the raised body of a station wagon, come the sounds of hammering, of metal striking metal, of a wrench clanging on the concrete. Suddenly we hear the rumblings of a jumbo jet taking off. Tut-Tut looks up.*) Vroom Varoooom! . . . Ta ta ta ta ta! Ta ta ta ta ta! Attack! T'attack! Matchine guns wid bayernettes n'cannons. Pow! Pow! Pow! Attenshun! Yessir generalsir! . . . Bossman sir! No cry, no bad, no bad, Jezuz Christ! Meza hero Chief! (*He sings to the tune of a military march.*) Brrr! Brraa! Vroom vroom varooom!

M. SAMSON: (*From under the station wagon*) Shi . . . it! Goddammit all ta hell!

TUT-TUT: Shi . . . it! Shi . . . it! Goddam Goddam damn damn damn!!! (*Turning to the audience.*) Ladies n'gennemens, here we goes, goes. Dem clowns geh . . . geh . . . geh . . . goes. Motorodeo . . . olé . . . torero! Shh! Shh! . . . pee pee . . . pee pee! (*He runs over to the display window of the gas station and pees for a long time all over it. The urine flows in rivulets, wending its way under the car.*) Pshh . . . Pshh . . .

M. SAMSON: (*Feeling the dampness of his clothes.*) What the hell? Oh, great, great fuckin' A . . . (*He emerges from under the car.*) That little shit! Yer gonna see, jest wait till I . . .

TUT-TUT: (*Turns around and pees straight ahead, triumphant*) Pee pee! Pshh! Pshh!

M. SAMSON: Cut it out, ya . . . ya . . . Oh hell, yer gonna see . . .

TUT-TUT: (*While still urinating, he attacks.*) Kung-Fu! Kung-Fu! Keeaheetykhoo!

M. SAMSON: Okay. Okay. That's enough. Man, that one's a disaster all right. Throw 'im in with the loonies, they should. (*He tries to wipe himself off with a dirty rag, then throws it in disgust on the hood of the car.*) Can't be done. She's nuts; make it like new! (*Snaps his fingers.*) She's nuts okay and me, too, sayin' "sure" jest like it was nothin'. Not even yer simple gasket change or even a complete o-ver-haul, but she wants a motor like brand fuckin' new. An' I ain't even looked at the brakes an' the transmission yet. Bet they'll be another gorgeous sight. Man oh man . . .

TUT-TUT: Man oh man! . . . (*He pushes M. Samson downstage.*) Da beginning! Pa pa pa pa pa pa! Boom boom! Ladiesgennemens!

M. SAMSON: Hmm . . . All right, okay. An' me full o' pee; howdaya like that! (*He cuffs Tut-Tut.*) Ya asked fer that one.

TUT-TUT: No do dat! Dopeydope! (*He blows his nose.*) Rafinhotdog!

M. SAMSON: That's right! Ratfink hotdog! Man oh man! . . . (*Embarrassed, to the audience.*) Yeah, well, to make the story short, we was livin' in a period that was, well, let's say without exaggeratin' it, sort o' reasonable, I mean, a little bit o' crisis like everywheres . . . anyhow here it wasn't so much that. But the highway bein' cut off . . . well that was a year an' a half ago, an' the decision to lay a direct access road, that was a lot earlier, before the crisis anyways. Since they gone an' enlarged the main highway, that's how the old frontage road got clipped. Anyhow the crisis, it don't have no effect on them airplanes, cuz the airport has gone international, with its expansions an' all the hullabaloo an' so, us, in the meantime, click, the old road is cut right off! Otherwise, up till then, it went okay 'round here, cuz au-to-mo-biles, till we get another arrangement, ya gotta keep puttin' in the gas or the oil, an' since they keep runnin', crisis or no, there's always clutches ta replace or batteries ta change, that's ta say there's a gig for the grease monkey. But ya ain't got no idea o' how bad it can be for a gas station havin' a highway cut off. Naw, the real problem, that's cuz they wasn't enough on the fuckin' ball ta sell the place when they shoulda. An' that's the long an' short ta it. But what can ya expect! A woman runnin' a garage is like a priest operatin' a whorehouse. Let's say it jest don't go together!

TUT-TUT: Whooey, holes n' whorehouse, homes n' handbags, piggy-piggy.

M. SAMSON: (*Laughing.*) Hey, you, over there, piggy-piggy, nobody's tellin' ya to repeat everythin' that . . . (*He spots the battered camshaft with which Tut-Tut is playing.*) Where'd ya pick up that now, huh? Whadda joker, he finds the damnedest things sometimes . . . No, gimme that now, you're gonna get all crapped up. (*Tut-Tut gives him the camshaft.*) Thanks! That's a good guy. Well, look at this, can ya still call this thing a camshaft? Jest try an' do a long-distance taxi haul with that one, even fixed up! The valves would never work! Not even new! At fifty plus ya don't mess 'round with a piece o' junk like that! Here ya go, ya can have it back, it'll work in yer motorbike. (*He gives the camshaft back to Tut-Tut.*)

TUT-TUT: Crankshaft?

M. SAMSON: Jesus no wiggly piggly, it's a camshaft.

TUT-TUT: Okay!

M. SAMSON: That's all it means ta ya? (*To the audience.*) Anyhow, as I was sayin', an' ta be brief about it, it wasn't goin' so hot but at least it was calm. Ya can't have everythin'. (*To Tut-Tut*) Hey, Tut-Tut, close yer fly, yer bird'll escape.

TUT-TUT: Tut-Tut no putway pee pee matchine gun.

M. SAMSON: (*Laughing and Tut-Tut laughing with him.*) Sure, that's right, man oh man, I get a kick out o' ya. Okay pal, sheathe yer rod. Always gotta poke 'round down there, he does. Hey come to think o' it, yer eighteen years old, ain't ya? Guess it must be ticklin' ya from time ta time. (*He grabs at Tut-Tut's penis.*) Ain't it? Huh? Say, can't ya feel nothin' there, ever?

TUT-TUT: (*Pulling away.*) Boom! Boom boom boom!

M. SAMSON: Yer jest a real honest to God retard, an' that's the truth ta it. Yer real lucky I ain't female, cuz believe me ya woulda known what's cookin' by now an' maybe that woulda put yer marbles back where they belong n' you'd be usin' yer wanger fer other things than pissin! Whaddya think 'bout that!

TUT-TUT: I . . . I . . . I . . . Tut-Tut go war . . . jeds n' matchine guns.

M. SAMSON: An' ta think there ain't a chance in the world they'd draft a dude like you!

TUT-TUT: (*Suddenly very angry.*) No dude! Me Tut-Tut . . . shoulder caption Tut-Tut Chief! (*He runs off into the woods.*)

SCENE 2

M. SAMSON: At yer orders, Chief! Uh . . . what the fuck did I do with my wrench . . . Hey Tut-Tut! . . . I'll be damned, did he clear out? At least ya can say that he don't mope 'round. Blessed be the poor in spirit! Anyways, that's what they say, but I dunno . . . (*To the audience.*) An' me, ya might ask, what the hell was I doin' here? That's what I ask myself, I tell ya, with that clunker ta fix that was too fuckin' wore out ta make anythin' worth somethin' out o'. Anyhow, there wasn't no boss buggin' me an' the customers weren't exactly on my back. At one point I coulda quit ta go work in town for Magnard. He's the dude who's got the BMW dealership. It can't be no drag workin' on them beautiful big engines with all the tools ya need ta have. But that wasn't my real big dream. I was gonna be in racin'. Not the driver. Shit, I don't even have wheels . . . A hoofer as they say. Naw, I woulda been the pit mechanic, there fer the tune ups an' emergencies, all that stuff, fer Mac Laren or Porsche. Makin' all the big stops on the circuit by plane: Imola, Zandvoorte, Kyalami. Why not? I ain't no racist! I woulda even learned ta get by in English! Yeah, a life like that, it coulda been great. (*The telephone rings mercilessly in the repair shop.*) Anyhow, that's how everythin' got started. (*Indicating the telephone.*) Yeah, jest like that. Ya ask, a customer? Hell, that, my friends, would be an event. Maybe one o' the girls, or maybe some fool screwin' up his number? (*He picks up the receiver.*) Airport Garage . . . Yeah, ya got it, this is the Airport Garage . . . the repair shop . . . No, she ain't here. No, I'm here by myself . . . half an hour, an hour, I dunno fer sure . . . Whadda'll I tell her? . . . Okay, if that's what you . . . (*He hangs up.*) An' good-bye ta you, too. Don't cost no fortune ta be polite! (*He rolls himself on the creeper back under the car.*)

SCENE 3

MADELEINE: (*Just returned home and without looking at M. Samson, leans against the door of the station wagon.*) I think, M. Samson, that I've finally located a decent rear axle at Lakiani's. Only, you'll have to figure out how to bring it back here.

M. SAMSON: I'll hijack a bus, how 'bout that . . . I already told ya that the one we got can still do the trick. It's a waste o' time fer me ta . . .

MADELEINE: I don't care, I prefer the othe: one . . . Anything new?

M. SAMSON: Now what kind o' new wouldya like . . customers?

MADELEINE: I'm beat.

M. SAMSON: Well, I suppose there could be.

MADELEINE:(*Seeing the puddle of urine.*) My God, you don't have to relieve yourself all over the store. The toilets still work, as far as I know.

M. SAMSON: (*Emerging from under the car.*) Excuse me, I couldn't hold it. I'm real sorry. I'll hose it off.

MADELEINE: Oh forget it. What difference does it make . . . What *are* you doing? Are you staring at my legs? That's not like you at all.

M. SAMSON: Well then I guess I'm sorry for the second time.

MADELEINE: Don't bother, it doesn't matter . . . it's just not like you, that's all. I was surprised.

M. SAMSON: There's nothin' insultin' about admirin' what's beautiful.

MADELEINE: (*Moving away.*) Legs, in theory, you know, are the last thing to go on a woman. (*Silence, then to herself.*) I remember adoring having men look at my legs when I was a kid. (*She enters the flat.*)

M. SAMSON: (*Yelling out to her.*) I'll see what I can do 'bout the rear axle. (*To himself.*) God, I'm a fuckin' soft touch! . . .

SCENE 4

M. SAMSON: (*To the audience.*) Why didn't I say nothin' 'bout the phone call? Yet another mystery o' life. In any case, it wouldn't'a changed much. I'd had a nice quiet day, but all o' a sudden, things were startin' ta pick up. The swallows were comin' home ta nest an' I was pluggin' away on this spring on a valve stuck on the cylinder head. (*He disappears under the car. Doris, followed by Winnock, enters.*)

WINNOCK: Okay, so ya gonna ask?

DORIS: O' course not. We'll split without openin' our mouths, that's what. Can you imagine, if I said somethin' now, fifteen days before the exam, she'd blow her top. An' with you, wow!

WINNOCK: Whaddya mean, with me?

DORIS: Oh come on, I don't have to draw a picture! M. Samson, my mother home?

M. SAMSON: A couple seconds ago.

WINNOCK: Listen, I'm cancellin' if she don't give consent. Try an' get the scene; if she goes batshit at the cops', we don't even get across the border.

DORIS: Oh Christ, I mean I won't be a minor any more in a month an' a half.

WINNOCK: Whaddya think I'm sayin'? Fer now, ya still are. She's gotta sign a thing fer ya.

DORIS: Doesn't take much ta turn ya off, does it? Okay wait here an' make like ya weren't. It'd be better if she didn't see ya.

WINNOCK: Ya know, sometimes yer a real pain . . . What the fuck are ya doin'?

DORIS: (*Rapidly changing her fake leather miniskirt and high-heeled pumps for jeans and flat-heeled shoes.*) M. Samson, don't look!

M. SAMSON: I got enough troubles with this valve; ya think I wanna add to 'em by watchin' ya undress?

DORIS: (*To Winnock.*) You neither. I told ya ta disappear.

WINNOCK: Geez, listen ta me a minute!

DORIS: I'm on my way.

WINNOCK: Ain't ya gonna say nothin' ta me? Didn't ya like it this afternoon?

DORIS: Sure, yeah, but not in front o' . . . Come on, I gotta go. (*She runs off disappearing into the living quarters of the gas station.*)

SCENE 5

WINNOCK: (*Shouting at her after the door has been slammed shut.*) Anyhow, it was great for me, real great. Okay . . . okay . . . okay . . . sure, sure, sure. Yeah, an' I still haven't showed ya everythin' I know. (*He violently kicks a gas can which goes flying under the station wagon.*)

M. SAMSON: Easy now, easy, the personnel's still under here. An' the blocks ain't so solid.

WINNOCK: Okay, since yer stuck there, okay.

M. SAMSON: Sometimes, ya can't do nothin' else ta put in a gasket.

WINNOCK: Are ya a Einstein with cycles too?

M. SAMSON: Depends on the make.

WINNOCK: A "Kaw."

M. SAMSON: 500?

WINNOCK: 250 S 1.

M. SAMSOM: Yeah, that's a lot better.

WINNOCK: Better than the 500?

M. SAMSON: Nope, I mean, I was thinkin' 'bout the driver's weight.

WINNOCK: The problem's the clutch.

M. SAMSON: Ya mean their clutch with the plastic worm gear; the one where they were able ta eliminate the ballbearins' an' the rods?

WINNOCK: Uh . . . Well, I dunno 'bout that . . .

M. SAMSON: Usually pretty solid, them clutches.

WINNOCK: Yeah, but mine . . .

M. SAMSON: Anyways, don't have no time. Gotta finish this one first.

WINNOCK: So what's it got?

M. SAMSON: Everythin'.

WINNOCK: When'll ya finish?

M. SAMSON: Three or four years.

WINNOCK: Yeah, I guess that *is* a while, a real long while.

M. SAMSON: If yer gonna be a biker, ya gotta know how ta stick yer fingers in the grease from time ta time.

WINNOCK: (*Menacing.*) I don't need nobody preachin' ta me, buddy. Understand? Or da ya need me ta explain better?

M. SAMSON: Not me, I gotcha, man. Everybody does what he wants with his hide; an' me I ain't had ta fight since Algeria, twenty-eight months o' parachutin'. Ya lose the habit an' anyhow I don't like ta fight. I never liked it, even back then.

WINNOCK: Shouldn't o' gone.

M. SAMSON: That's easy ta say.

WINNOCK: Fuck it, I don't have nothin' ta do with yer problems.

M. SAMSON: Me neither, I don't have nothin' ta do with 'em myself, that's the pity o' it. So, anyhow, yer cycle, I ain't ready ta get involved, 'specially since, considerin' yer situation in this family, it'll probably be a freebie. Now you'll have ta 'scuse me, I still got problems with this valve. (*He disappears under the car. Sounds of the engine revving up and the car door shutting.*)

SCENE 6

HUMBERT: (*Entering.*) Can I use . . .

M. SAMSON: Hello there!

HUMBERT: Sorry, hello to you, too . . . Can I use your phone?

M. SAMSON: It only eats large silver an' it don't give ya back the change.

HUMBERT: That's okay.

WINNOCK: Say, sorry to interrupt, but yer taxi is gettin' ready ta peel the fuck out o' here.

HUMBERT: I know.

M. SAMSON: Ya mean ya took a cab just ta telephone from here?

HUMBERT: Yes.

M. SAMSON: Then do whatever the hell ya want.

WINNOCK: Great, I'm leavin'.

M. SAMSON: Whatever turns ya on. (*To the audience.*) As a matter o' fact, that musta been when things started happenin'.

(*Humbert dials the number. Doris comes out of the flat, followed by Madeleine.*)

SCENE 7

MADELEINE: Dory, shouldn't you be studying?

DORIS: I'm goin' for a walk. I have ta think. I can't think here.

MADELEINE: Think about what?

DORIS: Things.

MADELEINE: Don't you think you'd do better to think about your exam? It's only a month away. You know what a state I'm in. What'll you do if you fail?

DORIS: If I flunk, well, we'll see, it'll be tough luck for Dory, I guess.

(*The telephone rings inside the flat.*)

MADELEINE: Will you answer? (*Doris goes in to answer the call.*) M. Samson, do you think you'll manage. . . ?

M. SAMSON: Well, she ran before so it can't get any worse. That is, 'less I put 'er back together upside down; anyhow, not long now before I'm gonna see that the brakes an' the suspension are as bunged up as the rest. With all that, we'll 'a changed just about everythin' 'sceptin' the back seat. Might's well invest in a new . . .

MADELEINE: With what?

M. SAMSON: That—I can't answser. Anyways, if I get it fixed, I ain't guaranteein' yer participation in the Paris-Dakar run.

MADELEINE: That's not what I'm asking.

M. SAMSON: What *are* ya askin'? That's just what I was wonderin' myself, it's *your* dream but I ain't no goddam fairy godmother. I can't grant wishes. Poof poof; rise an' roll.

MADELEINE: I didn't know you had such a sense of humor.

M. SAMSON: Well, we don't talk much either.

MADELEINE: You think I'm a prude.

M. SAMSON: Didn't say that.

HUMBERT: (*Only the audience hears his voice, as if offstage.*) Hello, hello, I . . . I . . . who is this? . . . Is that you . . . my baby . . . Doris? Maybe this is going to surprise you . . . but it's me, me, your father. You *are* Doris, aren't you? . . . Yeah! You see! It's terrific, huh, to be able to guess like that, I mean we . . . well, we don't really know each other. That's right, yeah, I wanted to speak to Mommy . . . to your mother, that is. Sure, I know she's there . . . I can even tell you she's wearing a grey blouse . . . So, well, meanwhile, ask her to come . . . And, you know, you can call me Pop . . . Hello? . . . Hello? . . .

M. SAMSON: Ya know, I ain't exactly the chatty type myself. Always caught between replacin' a starter an' repairin' a radiator. Anyhow, ya could say . . . since we got no more customers . . . we mighta found the time.

MADELEINE: Yes, surely, but it's not the way we do things. You know . . .

DORIS: (*Appearing from the station, visibly very upset.*) It's for you, Mom . . . It's a guy . . . Well, you'll see . . .

MADELEINE: A customer?

M. SAMSON: Hallelujah!

DORIS: No, it's a guy I'm tellin' ya . . . Oh, shit on yer problems. Shit an' fuck an' shit! (*She runs towards the woods.*)

MADELEINE: But Dory, wait, what's going on?

DORIS: Go get the phone, I'm tellin' ya. He knows yer here, even knows what yer wearin'. (*She disappears.*)

MADELEINE: I'll take it. (*She disappears into the flat.*)

M. SAMSON: Mystery—an' all the suspense o' a bowlin' match. (*He disappears under the car.*)

SCENE 8

HUMBERT: (*As before.*) Hello, hello, is that you? It's me . . . Don't you recognize my voice? Hello, are you there? Sure, it's strange for me, too, when you think about it: 18 years . . . Hell, no, I'm not calling you out of the blue. No, I'm calling you . . . No, please, I want you to listen to me. My God, you haven't changed . . . No, of course I'm not insulting you. Listen, we have to talk. Well, it's just that, you don't know it yet but I wanted you to know . . . and for us to talk about it . . . What? Listen to me, goddammit! I just had a terrible blow, real awful bad luck . . . So, can I go on? . . . Well, it's like this: I had a warning last year, my lungs, but then I acted like a jerk, as usual, and I didn't take care of myself. Yeah, you know, you know me . . . So, anyway, now I've really got it, only I looked into it a year too late. Had so much pain I finally got myself examined. Well, I just got out, just got the results. And the results: they give me a year, and guess what else? There's nothing to be done. It's too late for an operation, not even worth a try. So there you have it! . . . In a year, you'll be a widow. It's only natural that I wanted to warn you. You know, it gives you a weird feeling when you hear it. I still don't realize it. Ah well! At least I'll know. Life after death—God—all those kinds of questions . . . And only 58 years old, Christ, not even retirement age. Still, right now, I'm not suffering too much . . . So what do you think about that for a bomb being dropped? And them, they just announce it to you like that: "You know, life's no picnic, old man . . ." Pow . . . So right away I felt that I had to see you again, you and the kids . . . Oh no, no I tell you, it was official, one year, no longer . . . You can take a look at the X-rays. It's for sure, they told me, not a shadow of a doubt . . . What are you afraid of? It isn't catching, you know. In any case, I insist that we see each other to clear up all the inheritance business.

(*We stop hearing Humbert who, nevertheless, is visibly continuing the conversation. Maud and Thomas enter. They are carrying groceries.*)

THOMAS: And then I saw Dehours, and then Dehours says to me . . . You see who he is, right? . . . the head of neurosurgery. I already told you about him, and I knew that he liked me, I mean, he knows my father pretty well. There was this problem once and my father was part of the legal commission, anyway, to make a long story short . . . He feels, I guess, indebted to my Dad, so, it carried over to me. Anyway, he's taking me into his service. Well, I kind of planned on heart surgery, but to be Dehours's assistant . . . it's . . . You see what I mean . . . Dehours, he's sort of a star after all. Oh yeah, another thing, I forgot to tell you: my father completely agrees to lend us the apartment in Cap d'Antibes for our honeymoon.

MAUD: We'll stay in France, then?

THOMAS: Sure, it's better that way. You'll see. The apartment is dynamite. You don't know Cap d'Antibes. I used to go every year. Some memories! . . . Besides, we'll go in September—late September, early October. It's better because it's still warm and nobody's left on the Riviera.

MAUD: So the Mauritius Islands are out?

THOMAS: We can always go another time, can't we? Say, do you think I bought enough?

MAUD: Don't worry about it.

THOMAS: So you think I can stay for dinner? If not, I'll just drink the champagne with you. Hey, we better put it in the fridge, huh? It's great, don't you think, what Dehours said to me. You know, that'll advance me at least a year, easy.

MAUD: Go bring the champagne to Momma.

THOMAS: Aren't you coming?

MAUD: Of course, I'll be there in a minute, but go on. She'll be so happy to see you. And tell her about the conversation you had with your boss. She'll be thrilled.

THOMAS: Sure, okay. I guess you're right. It's important for our future. It's really going to launch us with the big-wig physicians in the clinic. We're going to have to give cocktail parties, you know. Oh yes we are, sweetheart. What about it, kitten?

MAUD: Purr. Go along now.

THOMAS: Aren't you coming?

MAUD: Yes of course, I mean no, I mean I have to talk to M. Samson about something.

THOMAS: I'll wait for you then.

MAUD: No, no, go on, please.

THOMAS: Well! . . . Hello down there, M. Samson!

M. SAMSON: Hi, how are ya? . . . uh . . . (*To himself as Thomas enters the flat.*) Has ta talk ta me about somethin'! Another mystery an' *bullshit*!

(*Maud walks over to the telephone booth.*)

HUMBERT: . . . No, but I think that you don't really understand the situation. To begin with, I think that the first thing to do, in your own interest, is to put everything that belongs to us in the name of the survivor. Otherwise when I die you might have to sell the whole works if one of the girls claims her part . . . Uh uh, I'm living alone now. I mean when I found out what was in the cards for me I preferred to break it off, wipe the slate clean. It was better for her not to have to deal with me in that state. Can you imagine a girl twenty years younger than me having to play nurse? And then, you can attest to it, I'm no easy patient. So, you see, I've changed my mind about the will I made for her. That's why this business about the last survivor. (*Maud opens the door to the booth and doesn't budge, very obviously indicating her impatience to Humbert.*) And then there's the matter of my paintings! . . . Most of all I want them to come back to the family. And above all, to you. Of course, it doesn't mean money in the bank right away, but it *can* mean it. You know, all it takes is for me to have disappeared for them to discover me . . . Just the same it's a pretty sizable bunch of canvases, about a hundred. And I'm only talking about the big ones. For the moment everything is at her parents', in their garage. But, you can imagine, I don't want to leave them there! Huh? Hey if you've got guests, I'll let you go. You wouldn't want me to stop by tonight, would you? I only want a couple . . . Okay, but anyway, I'll be calling you again because this is serious, this business about the inheritance. (*We understand that Madeleine has hung up in a huff.*) Gotta take care of it, right? . . . Oh shit!

MAUD: (*To Humbert who is looking for another coin to call back; she has overheard the last part of the conversation.*) I'm sorry, but I just want to make a real quick call, and I'm in a super hurry.

HUMBERT: (*Who recognizes her without being entirely sure about it.*) Huh? Yeah, sure, I mean, it only works with five franc coins.

MAUD: I know.

HUMBERT: Yeah, of course.

MAUD: What?

HUMBERT: Nothing, I . . .

MAUD: (*Into the phone.*) It's me, listen, I can't talk long. No, he brought me home. He's staying for supper . . . It's just not possible, no, he bought champagne, pâté, caviar, vodka, blintzes, I can't tell him to leave . . . Maybe this evening, late . . . You boob! Me, too, I feel like it . . . Of course I'm thinking about it. No, definitely not, *I'll* call you . . . In a little bit . . . Don't know . . . You'll be . . . Okay. Yeah, yeah, me too, oh boy. No, tell me, then I'll hang up. Oh wow, yeah, me too. (*She hangs up. To Humbert.*) So, that wasn't too long?

HUMBERT: Right, sure . . . Do you . . . do you live here?

MAUD: Uh huh, I live with my parents. I mean . . .

HUMBERT: Right.

MAUD: You can go ahead now, the line's free.

HUMBERT: Yeah, yeah, I . . . it's not important, I'm gonna call a cab and go home.

MAUD: Okay if that's what you want! You are odd, you know.

SCENE 9

DORIS: (*Leaving the flat.*) Maud, where are ya? Come on in, that's enough, okay? Hey, yer Superman is suckin' up ta Mom. He just gave her God knows what – probably some thousand franc perfume an' she is completely out o' her tree. She just got a call from her ex.

MAUD: Your father?

DORIS: An' yers, too, ya might recall, that is if it's really him. Don't know what bull he was handin' her, somethin' 'bout inheritance, paintin's or somethin'. She hung up on him. Seems to have really bugged her, meanwhile yer honey is lookin' all over the pad for a champagne bucket.

MAUD: What's this? Hold on. Wait a sec! (*Pulling Doris with her, Maud slowly approaches the phone booth.*)

M. SAMSON: Disconnect the accelerator cables an' the starter cables. Replace the heater hose an' the belt ta the fan. Flush out the heater, remove the cover ta the air filter an' wash it out. Boil out the carburetor an' grind the intake valve. (*To the audience.*) It's undeniable that from that moment on, we was goin' towards bigger 'n bigger surprises, which weren't gonna be pleasant fer everybody.

HUMBERT: (*Thrusting the chewed-up remains of an old phone book at M. Samson.*) Pardon me, but you wouldn't happen to have a phone book that's in better shape?

M. SAMSON: Well sure, but we ain't the post office here.

MAUD: (*To Humbert.*) You know . . . I'm Maud and this is Doris, my sister, the baby of the family. Doris, this is my father, your father, and the father of Thérèse even though she isn't here.

DORIS: (*To Humbert.*) Is that true?

HUMBERT: Yes.

DORIS: Well! Wow! Gee! Pleased ta meet ya, anyhow. Aren't you Maud? Well, I guess you already know him. You're the guy who called Mom a while ago, huh? What did ya say ta her?

HUMBERT: The truth.

DORIS: And just what's that? Can we know?

HUMBERT: It's that I'm dying. (*Silence.*)

DORIS: Wowey . . . that's a scoop!

HUMBERT: At the most a year from now. Doesn't it do anything to you to hear you're going to lose your father?

DORIS: Hey, you're the one who lost me! An' that was already a long time ago.

MAUD: Take it easy, Dory.

DORIS: Shit, ya aren't gonna start playin' poppa's little girl at yer age.

MAUD: I don't know what to do. I just don't know.

DORIS: Whaddya think ya *can* do? Anyway, Mom doesn't want ta see him; I'm sure o' it. She doesn't want ta see him again an' that's the story. Given that, what else can ya do? Nothin'. Ya do: nothin'!

MAUD: I don't know, I just don't know. What does it mean, him coming back here like this, unexpected? . . . You should've come down the chimney while you were at it! What do you want, huh? Why did you come back? Why?

HUMBERT: I already told you, I told both of you: because I'm going to die.

MAUD: And . . . and . . . and so you decided we should all benefit from it.

HUMBERT: Obviously, I couldn't stand the idea that the three of you and your mother, you'd be wanting for anything because of my death, I mean because of technicalities about wills or inheritance. You do understand?

MAUD: You're the one who doesn't understand, that's not what I was talking about. I mean, you expect us to profit for a year by knowing, by accepting the even worse kick in the face that our father, who we haven't seen for eighteen years, who we have carefully avoided speaking about, is going to die. Am I lying, Doris? It's just something understood between us. Doris, am I lying?

DORIS: No, no it's true.

MAUD: So you've come to unload this on us, on purpose.

DORIS: (*To Maud.*) Wait, wait just a minute! How do we know it's even true? Besides, what does it mean, within a year? Maybe it'll be in two or ten or fifty years? And why not tomorrow mornin'?

MAUD: Yeah, besides in a year maybe I'll be the one who's dead, or Momma, or M. Samson, could be just about anybody.

M. SAMSON: Hang on there . . . (*He shrugs his shoulders and raises his eyes to heaven.*)

HUMBERT: You want proof? Don't worry (*he shows the X-rays*), I brought them. Take a look at these X-rays. A good look. Not like that, for Chrissake, naturally if you look at them upside down . . .

MAUD: That's a cancer? . . . Is that it?

HUMBERT: Right on.

DORIS: (*Laughs.*)

MAUD: Stop it, Dory, please, cut it out.

DORIS: But didn't ya hear what he just said . . . I'm sorry, but . . . shit . . . ya don't need to get on my case, too. Nobody needs ta give me lessons. I never saw the guy before. What the fuck do I care about his cancer cells.

MAUD: Oh shit, shit, shit. I've gotta go in, I can't leave Momma . . . (*To Humbert.*) Listen, you can't stay here. God, and Thomas who's having supper with us, and after that . . . and then I have I don't know how many surveys to compute before tomorrow. Oh Christ! I can't think about it all . . . Why, just why did you come back, and why did it have to be tonight to top it off?

HUMBERT: Because I wanted to see you again before I left for good. Because I'm dying, sweet Maud.

MAUD: And me, I'm getting married without a dowry or a trousseau. If you think it's a piece of cake . . .

DORIS: Ya only got ta pull out.

MAUD: Go tell Thomas and Momma that I'm coming.

DORIS: Why don't ya just say ya want ta talk ta him alone? Geez, go right ahead.

MAUD: Listen Doris, you don't understand, I . . .

DORIS: Sure I do, you bet, it's private, just between the two o' ya. So long, have fun. I'll be 'round ta hold the john door, big sister. (*She enters the gas station.*)

HUMBERT: Good God, so that's how she raised her, that mother of yours!

MAUD: Wait just a minute now! Objectively, you're really going too far.

HUMBERT: (*Starting to head towards the house.*) Anyway, I'm going in, after all, it's my home here, and I want to see her.

MAUD: (*Stopping him.*) No! My God, you have no idea.

HUMBERT: Indeed I do, I know that I still have the right to speak to my wife and my daughters. Not only the right, I have the duty.

MAUD: Besides I don't want you to run into Thomas.

HUMBERT: This Thomas, he's my future son-in-law?

MAUD: It isn't that, I need to talk with you. Uh uh, I forbid you to enter the house. Momma could never take it. Later, okay, just give us the time to get her used to the idea.

HUMBERT: Because you think *I'm* the one who's gonna frighten her? That'd be a new one. I can't wait, besides I don't have the time. Hey, give me a cigarette, would you?

MAUD: Are you smoking? With what . . .

HUMBERT: Uh huh, oh, you know . . .

SCENE 10

THOMAS: (*Coming out of the station.*) What're you doing, Maud?

MAUD: Hide, hide quickly. I don't want him to see you.

M. SAMSON: (*Indicating the back seat of the station wagon to Humbert.*) In here, come on! (*To Maud.*) Okay, sure, see what I can do. Tell 'im ta bring it ta me next week. (*To Thomas.*) Okay, M. Thomas, fer yer Peugeot 104, I'll take care o' it. See 'bout it with Maud here. Okay?

THOMAS: Are you coming? That's terrific, M. Samson. Come on Maud.

MAUD: Okay, darling, I'll be right there. Go help Momma.

THOMAS: But we're waiting for you for the bubbly . . . (*Thérèse enters.*) Hey, here's Thérèse. How are you? Hey, dynamite, great! We'll all be here for the champagne. M. Samson, you'll drink with us, right? It's the least we can do.

Don't you think so, Maud?

M. SAMSON: As soon as I finish adjustin' this valve, I'll wash off my grubby hands an' I'm all yers.

MAUD: . . . Sure, I think so! Well, I'll wait for you. I'll wait for M. Samson.

THOMAS: But Maud, he's only got two steps to go before . . .

M. SAMSON: Hey now, ya'll have her ta yerself all the time, soon enough.

THOMAS: Okay okay. But you're becoming quite the mystery lady, my love. (*He re-enters the flat.*)

SCENE 11

THÉRÈSE: Something wrong, Maud?

MAUD: Oh no, oh no, no, everything's perfect, just fine, perfect, great, sure, great!

THÉRÈSE: Well if nobody needs me here I'll just . . .

MAUD: Oh no you don't, I mean sure, why not, sure, great!

THÉRÈSE: What is wrong with you?

MAUD: What's wrong with me? What's wrong? I'm, I'm, oh, nothing, sure, just the opposite, oh . . . great!

M. SAMSON: (*To Humbert who is still hidden in the car.*) Ya better show yer face again. She'll never get it under control.

MAUD: Wrong? Oh hell, shit goddammit. Wrong is that Poppa's hiding here.

THÉRÈSE: Poppa?

MAUD: And I'm afraid he and Thomas will run into each other. And he looks like he just stepped out of a novel by Tolstoy. And Momma doesn't know he's here. And he'll spend hours in the phone booth. And she'll hang up because she doesn't want to see him of all people. And as an added vacation bonus, he'll be dead in six months of lung cancer.

THÉRÈSE: But where is he?

HUMBERT: (*Climbing out of the car.*) I'm here. (*To Maud.*) And it's not six months, it's a year.

THÉRÈSE: What's this story about cancer?

HUMBERT: That's what the sawbones say . . . I don't know.

THÉRÈSE: What do you mean? You don't know.

HUMBERT: I'm telling you, it's the docs. I've got the X-rays. I came to let you know and to put our affairs in order. It's not difficult to understand.

THÉRÈSE: Where is Tut? Maud, do you know? Is he inside?

M. SAMSON: In the woods, in strict formation, out there huntin' lions 'n deer with bazooka chops.

THÉRÈSE: Poppa, I'm sorry but it's better if you don't stay.

HUMBERT: So, you're really going to stand together on this!

MAUD: That's at least one thing we'll have got from you.

THÉRÈSE: *Gotten* from you.

MAUD: Okay, if you insist, "gotten." Nobody'd mistake you for anything but a teacher, geez . . .

HUMBERT: You're not going to start quarrelling, the day of my homecoming, especially when we've so little time.

THÉRÈSE: Of your homecoming? You intend to move in here?

HUMBERT: I didn't say that. I just said it . . . offhand, you know, but nobody wants to listen to me around here, anyway.

THÉRÈSE: Oh listen, Poppa. I know your problems; I've heard them before. I'm tired; we had teachers' meetings all day; the kids are already in a vacation mood; we could hardly keep them in their seats. Please, not tonight . . .

HUMBERT: But what do the three of you have against me?

THÉRÈSE: He saw Doris?

HUMBERT: I'm not the bogieman, for Chrissake.

MAUD: For us you are, at least a little bit.

HUMBERT: But Maud, you knew me, you were ten years old when I left. Don't you remember? We adored each other! Thérèse was even jealous. Remember, Terry? Thérèse was tough, but you, you were all hugs and squeezes, big kisses for Poppa, just the opposite of your older sister. And then Doris came along . . . And Doris, well I didn't want us to keep her. Except Madeleine! . . . God, Madeleine! . . . "Maybe it'll finally be a boy" . . . And what-do-you-know, another repeat, I mean, a repeat little girl. Well, at that point, I felt really trapped. Three kids, all girls, and a gas station weighing on me, going all right, but me working all alone, those fifteen-hour days. And suddenly I knew that I'd never be able to paint again, because that was, after all, my real calling. I'd accepted the idea of the gas station because it was true that we weren't making it when I was drafting for architectural firms, not to mention that, because of you, your mother had to stop singing. But then, that was kind of her choice. Because it was either you or her career, even if it *was* only light opera. What I mean is, I didn't leave to have fun, it was to dedicate myself to my painting. That's what you have to understand. And now that I have all this work backing me up, it's up to you to profit from it, because I'm finished, it's over for me. That's why I want to make a gift of it to you.

MAUD: How come? Are you well-known?

THÉRÈSE: You've got to be joking, Maud, or dreaming.

MAUD: What do you know about it?

THÉRÈSE: I'm telling you that Poppa is finished without being known. If he wants to give us his paintings, it's because he's still got them. How many do you have?

HUMBERT: About a hundred.

THÉRÈSE: And if he's still got them, it's because he hasn't sold them. And if he hasn't sold them, it's because nobody wanted to buy them. And if nobody wanted to buy them, it's because they aren't worth anything, *et tutti quanti*.

HUMBERT: Well of course, if you're talking about worth in terms of money! I was talking about my work, not about money. Nobody can know the value of my work ahead of time. But there are precedents. Just wait till I'm dead, then you'll see. You told me yourself that you thought what I did was quite interesting.

MAUD: You mean you know his work? You've been seeing him?

HUMBERT: Tell her the truth.

MAUD: It doesn't matter. I'm not an idiot.

THÉRÈSE: Well I don't know why I shouldn't have.

MAUD: In any case, with the airs you put on, whatever they mean, you're ending up smelling like a dirty hypocrite. So—you were seeing him . . . You knew where he parked himself . . . And you never said a word to me about it. Okay. So what? I could care less! Meanwhile, don't forget that I was his favorite, he said so, and you were the bitch. And even so, he still plays the long lost father to you! That's great, that's absolutely great; because losing your father when you're ten, that really forms your character, and you, sister dear, you didn't have that kind of luck. Well, Thomas is waiting for me and he, at least, is not the type to abandon his children. Now I've said it, and that's what I mean and that's all I have to say. (*She returns, crying, to the flat.*)

SCENE 12

HUMBERT: (*After an embarrassed silence.*) So, she's going to get married?

THÉRÈSE: Three weeks from now, supposedly . . . What's gotten into you?

HUMBERT: Everything that I was saying. When you feel the end approaching, it makes you ask a lot of questions about your life.

THÉRÈSE: Sure, that's just like you. You've always acted like a kid who was incapable of accepting his responsibilities. Listen, it's better that you go away. Give us some time to think about this. Momma isn't in good shape. We're going to have to leave this place, sell it if we can, if *she* can. She's got enough problems as it is.

HUMBERT: She can't sell unless I agree to it.

THÉRÈSE: Unless you're dead.

HUMBERT: Naturally. But it'd be better to take care of all that while I'm still alive, even if it only straightens out the inheritance rights.

THÉRÈSE: Poppa, listen to me, I know very well that you don't have a centime, so I would really like to know what your game is.

HUMBERT: My game? Honestly, I don't have one.

THÉRÈSE: I'm afraid, Poppa. I don't know, all this makes me nervous. It'd be better for me to leave you now. I don't like being outside when the sun goes down. I want to be near Momma. You know, it didn't help me, seeing you again last year.

HUMBERT: It helped me.

THÉRÈSE: Not me, really . . .

HUMBERT: It must be because I wasn't doing too well then. Of course you might say . . . Okay! Okay. So we won't cry about it, huh? Stiff upper lip!

THÉRÈSE: Stop playing the clown. You know how much I hate it.

SCENE 13

TUT-TUT: Nommee, Nommee, yippee, all dead baddies, dead, dead, boom, boom, blockhouse boomed, boom, boom, boom. Tut-Tut no 'fraid, no 'fraid baddies, yippee Nommee!

M. SAMSON: (*Catching him.*) Tut-Tut, scram, get the hell outa here!

THÉRÈSE: Never mind, M. Samson, don't bother . . . Look at him, Poppa, you're a grandfather. Grandfather to that.

M. SAMSON: Hey, now! He's a nice kid.

THÉRÈSE: Sure and in six months, he'll be able to vote.

HUMBERT: That Terrenoire boy, the one that was the student, is he the father?

THÉRÈSE: Yeah, he gave me this present and then (*snaps her fingers*), good-bye and thanks very much. You set the example, you know. End of school for me . . . and all the rest! You wanted to know why, last time. Well, here's the real reason. Maybe you can understand now why men and me—my own father and all the others included . . . Anyway, I'm ugly, so that really takes care of the problem.

HUMBERT: Terry, don't . . .

THÉRÈSE: Oh, you know, being ugly . . . it's as if I were already dead. And then if that weren't enough, there's him. Before, I was really angry with you and Momma for having made me, for being so ugly, but since he was born . . .

TUT-TUT: (*To Thérèse.*) Nommee, stoppee, no, khhh . . .

HUMBERT: It's funny, you'd almost think he knows you're talking about him.

THÉRÈSE: Sure, it's funny, isn't it?

M. SAMSON: Thérèse, don'tcha think they're waitin' fer ya?

THÉRÈSE: Yes, of course, and for you, too.

M. SAMSON: Oh, me . . .

THÉRÈSE: Of course they are. Poppa, let me be the one to call you, please.

HUMBERT: I don't have a phone anymore.

THÉRÈSE: I'll find a way.

HUMBERT: Sure, sure you will, we'll just see!

THÉRÈSE: Don't make that face. (*She hugs him briefly.*) It's hard enough as it is. (*She enters the flat.*)

SCENE 14

HUMBERT: Hard enough, I guess.

M. SAMSON: Stiff upper lip!

HUMBERT: Is it far on foot?

M. SAMSON: Ten minutes till the bus stop. It's none o' my business but maybe they're right. I mean, maybe ya shouldn't 'a come, even if ya save some money on death notices. But I ain't said nothin', okay? Anyways, I'm sort o' glad ta get ta meet ya.

HUMBERT: That's the first kind thing I've heard since I got here.

M. SAMSON: Well, all the same, I dunno what I woulda done in yer place. Guess it's normal ta wanna see the family 'fore ya kick off fer good. An' it ain't yer fault if ya was called ta art. Look at me, in my family, the dream was I'd have a army career. Commandin' maybe, that wouldn't'a bothered me too much, but obeyin'! . . . O' course, ya might wonder . . . if I'd 'a known! Cuz it's pretty clear this ain't gonna last a coon's age. Anyhow! Guess we'll see. There's a bus at 9. You just got time. (*Looking at Tut-Tut who seems to be fascinated by Humbert.*) It's sure strange, the kid seems ta be completely hypnotized. He ain't tellin' no more stories, an' he's only got eyes fer you. Should see how he's lookin' at ya. Ya oughta be a lion tamer, ya should, cuz, man oh man . . . Hey, nine o' clock, huh? Don't hang 'round here cuz I dunno how they do it, but they come right on time . . .

TUT-TUT: (*To Humbert.*) Poppa!

HUMBERT: And somehow through all this mess I've gained a grandson.

M. SAMSON: Ya see, ya ain't completely wasted yer time. Well, so long. (*M. Samson walks into the flat.*)

SCENE 15

HUMBERT: So long to you, too.

TUT-TUT: Poppa pop . . . pop . . . poppa!

HUMBERT: No, not Poppa! Gotta name, huh? What's your name?

TUT-TUT: BOOM!

HUMBERT: I'm just Grampa, and that's pretty damn good.

TUT-TUT: Poppa.

HUMBERT: No, you knucklehead, Grampa, Grampa, your Mommy's poppa. Can't you understand? But we're buddies, right, buddies? Yieeee! WOAH!

TUT-TUT: Yieeeee! Yieeee!

HUMBERT: Ugh! How now Injun Chief! Me old cowboy, me no know where sleep tonight, no have teepee. Squaws no want me. No open fort. Can't go to Geneviève's. Anyway, she wouldn't have me. Huh? No you don't. Let go!

TUT-TUT: Come woods, come sleepy-bye, Tut-Tut, poppa.

HUMBERT: Go away now, leave Grampa alone.

TUT-TUT: Ka ka come Tut-Tut blockhouse.

HUMBERT: Say, that's right, I remember . . . that blockhouse. So it's your house? Can I see it? (*They exit into the woods.*)

SCENE 16

THÉRÈSE: (*Running out of the flat followed by Madeleine.*) Tut? Tuuut?! My God, suppose he left with . . .

MADELEINE: Who exactly could he have left with? M. Samson is still here. No, don't worry, he's still in the woods, in his blockhouse. He's sleeping there more and more often. And besides, if he's hungry, he'll come empty what's left to empty out of the fridge in the middle of the night.

THÉRÈSE: Momma . . . I take awful care of him.

MADELEINE: Nonsense. He's happier here than he would be anywhere else.

THÉRÈSE: But Momma, what about when we have to leave?

MADELEINE: We still have lots of time to think about it . . . You know, I know he'll be a doctor soon, but he doesn't seem very much on the ball to me, Thomas, I mean.

THÉRÈSE: Momma, she's old enough to know what she's doing.

MADELEINE: Of course, Come on, let's go back in, I don't like the sundown.

THÉRÈSE: No kidding? You neither!

ACT II

SCENE 1

(*The next morning.*)

RICHARD: (*Getting out of the station wagon.*) HO-LY FUCK, we fell asleep! Hey! Wake up Maud! Move it! Shit, I was supposed ta meet some pals. (*He glances at his watch.*) That coffee machine–it still workin'? What do I need? Hand me some dough, wouldya? Man, I tell ya, we sure crashed. Ya really took me for a ride this time, babe. I'm sore everywhere.

MAUD: Be quiet, you nerd! You'll wake up everybody.

RICHARD: Give me some francs. Hold on, I got 'em . . . (*He puts some coins in the vending machine, but it doesn't deliver any coffee.*) Shit, out o' order. Everythin's broke. Won't ya make me a cup o' coffee, pretty lady? Without my coffee in the mornin', I'm . . .

MAUD: (*Emerging from the wagon and straightening her clothes.*) Oh my God, I can't believe it. Six thirty? Don't look at me. I must look like a witch. Do you think they heard?

RICHARD: Heard what?

MAUD: (*Sarcastically.*) The gas pumps.

RICHARD: So what?

MAUD: Richard, you have no idea . . .

RICHARD: What?

MAUD: Come here.

RICHARD: Again?

MAUD: Yeah, c'mere.

RICHARD: Babe, I need some coffee.

MAUD: I must really be crazy about you.

RICHARD: Ta get married ta that quack?

MAUD: No silly, to bend to your slightest whim.

RICHARD: Not every little one! But after all, that's your business–

MAUD: Shithead!

RICHARD: Wouldya rather hear what I really think about the whole thing?

Course not. So, in that case . . . Coffeeee.

MAUD: But after that . . .

RICHARD: When do ya see 'im again?

MAUD: He's picking me up this morning.

RICHARD: Wow! Doesn't it get ta ya?

MAUD: *I'll* deal with it.

RICHARD: An' zap, zap, shot down again! What's buggin' ya? Hey? An' besides, look who's cryin'.

MAUD: Leave me alone, it was so good, why do you want to spoil it? If you think it's easy . . .

RICHARD: Body an' soul? Or a piece o' ass an' a lot o' dough?

MAUD: Richard!

RICHARD: Don't yell! You'll wake up your tribe.

MAUD: I don't care.

RICHARD: Liar. Go on, get goin' . . . Coffeeee!

MAUD: Can't you see that I don't want to live here the way I've been living?

RICHARD: An' Richard ain't rich . . . Sure, I see. Coffeee.

MAUD: You make me want to puke with your coffee.

RICHARD: I want some all the same.

MAUD: Why don't we make non-stop love, you and me, to hell with the world.

RICHARD: Because it's too damn exhaustin' . . . Cof . . .

MAUD: Okay. Instant all right?

RICHARD: I don't care, just make it strong. (*Maud disappears into the flat.*)

SCENE 2

M. SAMSON: (*Arriving and discovering Richard.*) Never figured I'd meet a soul at this hour o' the mornin'. That G.T.V. parked at the fork, it's yers, huh?

RICHARD: That's right.

M. SAMSON: Yer radio's still on. That's an Alfa fer ya, mechanically brilliant, a real star, but fragile. What's the year?

RICHARD: 79, but I had everythin' replaced.

M. SAMSON: So what's wrong with it, any idea?

RICHARD: Nothin's wrong, I'm waitin' for some coffee.

M. SAMSON: Well, don't count on that machine.

RICHARD: So I found out.

M. SAMSON: (*To the audience.*) The plot thickens. (*To Richard.*) 'Scuse me but I'd prefer it if ya'd wait away from the Peugeot, cuz I gotta work underneath it. (*Plunging into the back seat of the car.*) These panties 'n stockin's yers?

RICHARD: No.

M. SAMSON: Didn't seem yer style. All the same, they weren't there last night. (*He hangs them on the car's antenna.*) Anyhow, this way, if the owner passes by, she ain't likely ta miss 'em.

SCENE 3

MAUD: (*Leaving the flat, a cup of coffee in her hand.*) I made you a big one. (*Seeing M. Samson.*) Oh, hi, M. Samson. Working already?

M. SAMSON: Woke up in the middle o' the night an' after that, no way . . . So, 'stead o' tossin' an' turnin' in bed, I figured I'd take the mornin' by the scruff. O' course, I take the afternoon that way too—always better ta work than ta drink away yer paychecks. I mean, when ya live alone . . .

RICHARD: (*Ironically.*) Ahhmen!

M. SAMSON: Sorry, just felt like gabbin'. Guess I'll get goin'. By the way, the clean-up crew found this stuff on one o' the seats. The kid probably stole 'em to play with.

MAUD: Ah, yeah, I guess, sure that must be it.

M. SAMSON: That said, we all gotta find things ta play with from time ta time, nothin' wrong with a little fun.

MAUD: Would you like some coffee!

M. SAMSON: How'd ya guess? Huh? (*He takes down the underclothes.*)

MAUD: Don't bother, it'll just clutter up the shop. I'll take care of them. (*She re-enters the flat with the panties and stockings.*)

M. SAMSON: Two lumps o' sugar, please, Maud.

RICHARD: She's a sweetheart, huh?

M. SAMSON: What's he sayin', that fella with the G.T.V.? I don't get it.

RICHARD: I was sayin' that she . . .

M. SAMSON: That's what I was sayin', I don't get it.

RICHARD: My name is Richard.

M. SAMSON: Good fer *you!*

RICHARD: So who are you, Uncle Angelbear?

M. SAMSON: If that's what ya want.

RICHARD: Jealous.

M. SAMSON: I'm just an employee here.

RICHARD: One month out o' three.

M. SAMSON: That's my business . . . Ya shouldn't'a set down there.

RICHARD: (*Realizing that he has, unfortunately, sat down on an old oil can which has left oil spots all over his pants.*) Oh shit! Thanks a lot for tellin' me before it was too late.

M. SAMSON: Don't mention it.

MAUD: (*Coming out of the flat with a second cup of coffee.*) Here you go, M. Samson.

M. SAMSON: Thanks.

SCENE 4

THÉRÈSE: (*Emerging from the flat in her robe.*) Maud, what's going on? What's happening? M. Samson, are you here too? What is it? It's Tut, isn't it? Something's happened to him!! Tell me! Oh God!

MAUD: Calm down Terry, nothing's happened. These gentlemen are just having a cup of coffee.

THÉRÈSE: And Tut, have you seen him? He didn't sleep in his bed again. One of these days I'm going to set fire to that blockhouse. Besides, I can't understand why they don't blow up those things.

M. SAMSON: But whaddaya think's gonna happen ta 'im, Thérèse?

THÉRÈSE: Oh I'm just fed up! Maud, you know, I've been thinking, I hardly slept. I'm going to put that kid in a home. Besides, I should have done it years ago. At least they'll take care of him. You know, here, I can't really count on Momma anymore. What do you think?

MAUD: Listen, I really don't know.

THÉRÈSE: Naturally. It isn't even worth asking you what you think. Except for your wedding, nobody can talk to you about anything.

MAUD: Don't start up again, Thérèse.

RICHARD: (Making gestures of leaving.) Well, thanks for the coffee.

THÉRÈSE: (Taking the cup from him; he's at a loss about what to do with it.) My pleasure, that'll be two francs. (She laughs.)

RICHARD: Your francs are in the machine.

THÉRÈSE: (To Maud.) Who's this?

MAUD: A friend of M. Samson's, apparently. I made them some coffee.

THÉRÈSE: I know, I can see that. Besides, you already told me. Twice.

MAUD: Listen if I can't even open my mouth around you . . . (To Richard.) Good-bye. (She walks over towards him to shake hands goodbye.)

RICHARD: (Going over to shake hands with Thérèse.) Well, good-bye.

THÉRÈSE: Now that you know the way . . .

MAUD: My God, you don't need to . . .

THÉRÈSE: Jesus, Maud, we never see anybody here. If he's a friend of M. Samson's. (To Richard.) You'll have to excuse me, I just fell out of bed. I didn't even have time to get dressed. It's a bit early for a visit, you know.

RICHARD: Well, in that case, the next time I'll bring some croissants.

THÉRÈSE: Oh my, then you might just make some people very happy. in the morning, I'm as hungry as a tigress.

MAUD: Thérèse! That's enough. My God.

THÉRÈSE: You wouldn't have a cigarette, would you? I like lights.

RICHARD: Gitanes.

THÉRÈSE: Well, beggars can't be choosers.

MAUD: I have what you want upstairs.

THÉRÈSE: Don't put yourself out, his'll be fine.

RICHARD: Gotta run, gotta see some pals o' mine.

THÉRÈSE: Some pals!

MAUD: Yes, some pals. He has to see some pals. So please don't keep him any longer.

THÉRÈSE: Why? I'm not stopping him from doing anything he wants. (*Richard smiles at both of them.*) Good-bye, Richard!

SCENE 5

MAUD: You're out of your mind.

THÉRÈSE: He's not bad, not bad at all. Is there any more coffee?

MAUD: Instant, you can make it yourself.

THÉRÈSE: You're unbearable this morning.

MAUD: Listen, just go to hell. I didn't blab on you and Poppa last night to Momma, so consider yourself lucky. Anyway, he obviously wasn't interested in you.

THÉRÈSE: Whom are you talking about?

MAUD: That guy.

THÉRÈSE: Can't we call a truce?

MAUD: You're the one who started it.

THÉRÈSE: You're unbelievable.

MAUD: I'm going to change.

THÉRÈSE: You've hardly been up and dressed and you're going to change already?

MAUD: I have the right, don't I?

THÉRÈSE: Of course.

MAUD: You'd better get dressed, too. Thomas is picking me up any time now. If you want to go into town with us, you'd better get a move on.

THÉRÈSE: I'm not teaching this morning . . . I mean, we're on strike.

MAUD: You're striking again?

THÉRÈSE: Well you know I'm a member of the union. And besides my principal is with the Federation, so I don't want to mess up.

MAUD: You used to get more excited about moral issues.

THÉRÈSE: Now, all that, you know . . .

MAUD: You gonna use this chance to talk to Momma?

THÉRÈSE: I don't know; you mean, about Poppa? I don't know what I could say to her about him.

MAUD: You know, in fifteen days, I won't be able to help her out any more . . . I don't know what made me say that.

THÉRÈSE: (*Seeing Thomas who is entering from the outside.*) Here comes your dream man. Say, does he drive like a farmer, or is it the car?

MAUD: Uh uh, he's an awful driver.

SCENE 6

THOMAS: (*Entering with an enormous bag of croissants in his hand.*) Up already?

And I thought I was going to wake you. Hi, honey, hello, Thérèse. I hope you haven't eaten, 'cause I brought some croissants.

THÉRÈSE: So many?

THOMAS: Sure, why not? (*To Maud.*) Boy did I have a scare when I got here, you know, there was this guy parked at the fork in a pretty banged-up sports car and the jerk took off just when I arrived. He forced me off the road. I tell you, just like it was on purpose, you know. I had to make a helluva swerve. My legs still feel like cotton. You think he stopped? Not for a minute. And I'm sure he saw me. You know, there really are some maniacs out there. And you know what else? I didn't really see his face, but I got the impression that he was laughing at me when he took off. Really! Can you believe it, Thérèse? Isn't it incredible, honey? It's incredible today how aggressive people are. A little bit faster and you would've been a widow before you were even married.

THÉRÈSE: If it's going to happen, it'd be better right after . . . for the pension, I mean.

THOMAS: (*Laughing.*) Yeah!

MAUD: You can laugh about it? Oh you drive me nuts.

THOMAS: But hon, what's wrong, are you upset?

MAUD: What? Yes, I'm upset.

THOMAS: I'm sorry.

THÉRÈSE: You're a peach, Thomas. It's fantastic, you say you're sorry . . .

MAUD: Terry, will you please . . .

THÉRÈSE: Not poke my nose into your business. Okay, dear little sister.

MAUD: I'm going to change.

THOMAS: But you look great. I love you in that dress. It's the one you had on yesterday, isn't it?

MAUD: Well, yes, that's the problem.

THÉRÈSE: You know, Thomas, a woman is mysterious and capricious, a totally unpredictable being.

MAUD: (*To Thérèse.*) To each her mysteries and her secrets, okay, Thérèse?

THOMAS: (*To both of them.*) I'm sorry but I think I've lost you on that one.

MAUD: Stop apologizing all the time.

THOMAS: I'm really sorry.

MAUD: My God!

THOMAS: Hey M. Samson, do you want some croissants? I guess I bought too many.

M. SAMSON: (*From under the car.*) Well, ain't that nice. Put 'em in the front seat. I'll find a way ta gobble up one or two before noon.

THOMAS: How's it going, M. Samson?

M. SAMSON: Why, you bet, just fine. Why wouldn't it be goin' just fine? We're baskin', baskin' everywheres, as they say. (*During M. Samson's aside, Maud and Thomas walk away, towards the highway, while Thérèse walks towards the woods. All three return when Tut-Tut enters. To the audience.*) Sometimes, it's better to seem even more of a asshole than ya really are. That said, it didn't necessarily change the way I intended ta act towards the girls. I was 'specially thinkin' 'bout Thérèse. I'm not one o' them erotic types, but all the same, almost naked under her robe, them magnificent breasts, o' course, they didn't hire me fer that, great legs too, even in bedroom slippers. An' I remember once seein' her in high-heeled satin shoes. Same legs as her mother! Just cuz o' them, she wouldn't'a had ta ask me twice. Maud, well Maud woulda turned me off, I think. An' as fer the kid sister, didn't even think about her. I knew 'er as a baby, so gotta block against it, I guess.

SCENE 7

TUT-TUT: (*Surging out of the woods.*) Brrrrr! Eeeek! Brrrrr! Eeeeeek!

THÉRÈSE: Tut, come here. You know your mother doesn't like you sleeping in there.

TUT-TUT: Tut saved hurted general. Ssh! Sleepie, no sick, Chief. (*Seeing the bag of croissants that Thomas is holding.*) Nommee, kassant, kassant?

THÉRÈSE: Okay, calm down. This kid is dying of hunger. Is it all right, Thomas? Are they for him too?

THOMAS: Of course. I'll go in with you, Maud.

MAUD: While I change my clothes? (*She enters the flat and calls back a warning to her sister.*) Terry!

SCENE 8

THOMAS: I suppose I'll stay here then. Say, guess I'll make some coffee. Who wants some? M. Samson?

M. SAMSON: Not again. I tell ya, everybody's tryin' ta make me drink coffee. An' comin' from you, a doc . . . I bet ya ain't no heart man.

THOMAS: I'm sure your heart is in perfect shape.

M. SAMSON: D'ya see that in the whites o' the eyes?

THOMAS: I'm positive, in fact, that's not what'll give you trouble. Coffee, Thérèse?

THÉRÈSE: Yes please.

THOMAS: For the kid, too?

THÉRÈSE: What? Do you think he's too calm?

TUT-TUT: Offee offee Tut pissonner.

THOMAS: We'll give you a thermos for your prisoner.

THÉRÈSE: You can't be serious. He'll drink it all.

THOMAS: All right, I'm sorry, I was just playing.

THÉRÈSE: Thomas, he isn't a child, he's a mentally retarded a-dult!

TUT-TUT: (*At the same time as Thérèse.*) A-nult!

THOMAS: Obviously. I'm sorry. Well, I'm going in now. You can drink it inside, okay? I'll call you. (*Tut-Tut, unable to control himself, grabs the bag of croissants from Thomas's hands.*) Hey, he's taking all the croissants. Give them back! Come on! . . . (*He struggles with Tut-Tut, trying to retrieve the croissants. From this confusing melee, Thomas emerges defeated while Tut-Tut runs off into the woods, brandishing triumphantly the bag of croissants.*)

THÉRÈSE: Let him go. You can make toast instead.

THOMAS: If that's what you want, but all the same I went all the way to Roblot's to buy them.

THÉRÈSE: It doesn't matter. Anyway, we usually eat toast in the morning. (*Thomas enters the flat.*)

SCENE 9

THÉRÈSE: (*Yelling in the direction of the woods.*) Tut! Come back here, Mommy has to give you a bath this morning. (*To herself.*) At least the strike will guarantee that Tut gets cleaned up.

M. SAMSON: So the workin' class struggle is good fer somethin'.

THÉRÈSE: (*Laughing.*) You know, you're pretty funny this morning, M. Samson.

M. SAMSON: Well me, I think yer a bit too half-dressed ta think about what I am.

THÉRÈSE: Oh, sorry. (*She tightens her robe.*)

M. SAMSON: No problem. (*He starts working again on the car's engine.*)

THÉRÈSE: (*Following him.*) Anyhow, my sister is about to make a major mistake . . . You're not saying anything, but I'm sure you think exactly like I do. She's always lived *here*, she'll never get used to it. And then, you don't need . . . with men . . . I mean you don't need to get married to have men. I don't understand how somebody her age can only see things through marriage. Of course you're a man, so you don't necessarily have the same point of view. But, just the same, take the example of my parents! Do you know what's happening, about my father coming here yesterday, I mean? Are you in on all this?

M. SAMSON: I sort o' understood, yeah.

THÉRÈSE: Well, I'm not eager to get married. That's one thing you can be sure of.

M. SAMSON: Say, I believe ya; I really do.

THÉRÈSE: It's interesting how I've always enjoyed talking with you. Even 'tho, and it's true, isn't it, we don't have the same educational background. Still, I guess I didn't go as far as all that after all.

M. SAMSON: Ya know when people get on together, it ain't necessarily a question o' schoolin'. Fer example, did ya know that I listen pretty regular ta classical music: the *Egmont Overture*, Tchaikovsky's *Nutcracker* . . .

THÉRÈSE: *Egmont?* Who's the composer?

M. SAMSON: Beethoven!

THÉRÈSE: Oh, sure, of course. In other words, for certain things you know as much as I do, maybe even more, despite the fact that I'm a . . . teacher.

M. SAMSON: I'm sure that when it comes ta compression-ratios, I know more 'n just a glimmer more 'n you do.

THÉRÈSE: He doesn't get in your way too much, Tut, I mean? You seem to have things worked out with him.

M. SAMSON: Yeah, sure I do. But I gotta 'scuse myself here, cuz if ya keep talkin' ta me, I'll never finish this job on time.

THÉRÈSE: Oh, of course. Besides I have to take my shower and get dressed. Momma must have taken something in order to sleep. She should have gotten up by now. She sleeps so lightly normally, you know.

SCENE 10

DORIS: (*Emerging from the flat, only half awake.*) Holy cow, everybody's up in this pad. What is it—the Revolution or somethin'?

THÉRÈSE: Well, I'm *very* surprised to see you on your feet so early with everything you managed to put away last night.

DORIS: I guess I really tied one on, didn't I? I think I'm a little hung over. Anyhow, no way ta sleep with you guys around! It's that M. La-Dee-Da's champagne. I can't stand the stuff.

THÉRÈSE: You'd rather drink beer, I suppose?

DORIS: Never less than a liter an' a stiff shot o' cognac ta wash it all down. That shock ya?

THÉRÈSE: You do what you want. It's not my life.

DORIS: Ya sound just like my head "teach": "Doris, dear, I don't want to intrude in your business but blah blah blah blah." Don't worry. I won't force ya ta watch the tragic spectacle o' yer little sister wreckin' havoc with her life.

THÉRÈSE: *Wreaking* havoc . . .

DORIS: Okay, Jesus, wreakin', wreckin', who the hell cares . . . Not too far down the pike, I won't be a minor no more an' I'm splittin' fast. Hello world an' good-bye this dump! Besides, maybe I won't even wait till then.

THÉRÈSE: And do you mind telling me just what you plan to do, what you think will become of you?

DORIS: Nothin' worse than Maud, or even you, or even Mom. Hey, is it true that ya saw what Pop is doin', I mean my father?

THÉRÈSE: Did Maud say something to you about it? Yes, in fact, last year I had this urge to see him again . . .

DORIS: That's not what I'm askin' ya. I don't give a shit that you saw 'im without tellin' us. What I wanna know is whaddaya think o' his paintin's?

THÉRÈSE: You know, I don't know. I, I saw a few things, these big sort of abstract things. I can't explain it to you. I'm not sure I like them; still, there's something . . .

DORIS: So ya think it wasn't worth it, his splittin' an' everything?

THÉRÈSE: It's unbelievable how badly you speak.

DORIS: So answer me.

THÉRÈSE: Why are you asking me this?

DORIS: I dunno . . . just because . . . sometimes I wonder if I might 'a had a genius for a father. It'd be funny, ya know.

THÉRÈSE: In my opinion, it would already be known.

DORIS: Tough luck.

THÉRÈSE: For him.

DORIS: Especially for us, cuz him . . . BAM!

THÉRÈSE: Please, let's not talk about it.

DORIS: Hey, the burial'll give us a reason to see each other again, all four o' us, an', ya know, I never set foot in a cemetery before. D'ya see me followin' the hearse with a stiff in it that I never even knew till he got inta the coffin, in the middle o' the three o' ya, moanin' an' groanin' like the Holy Virgin an' Mary Magdalene? Weird, huh, Marie Madeleine bein' Mom's name an' all? They said a year from now, huh? Hey, what're ya doin'? Ya goin' in? I'm not comin' with ya. I think my future brother-in-law is makin' eyes at me. Know what I mean? Last night, he was starin' at me all the time, an' if I have ta put up with it at breakfast too, well, I won't be able ta keep my mouth shut. Anyway, guess if we get sick, we get free prescriptions. Hey, ain't ya goin' ta work?

THÉRÈSE: We're striking.

DORIS: No shit! Yer loco; ya still believe in all that crap?

THÉRÈSE: One day, when you're older, you'll understand.

DORIS: Don't worry. I'll X myself before that happens—

THÉRÈSE: You really have to be your age to say such a thing.

DORIS: Cuz after, ya ain't got the guts! It's funny, I was thinkin' 'bout it, yesterday. Ya really could be my mother, ya know, instead o' Mom. Ya should'a had another kid.

THÉRÈSE: (*Slaps her violently.*) You little bitch!

DORIS: Oh shit, are you a jerk or what? You must be sick. you really hurt me. (*She throws herself into her sister's arms.*) I'm sorry, I'm sorry, really. I didn't mean anythin'.

THÉRÈSE: It's my fault. I'm sorry, too. I couldn't control it. I don't know what happened, why I . . .

DORIS: No, it's my fault. I'm a creep to have said that. But I wasn't thinkin' . . .

THÉRÈSE: Have you eaten?

DORIS: No.

THÉRÈSE: Are you going to your review session?

DORIS: Dunno.

THÉRÈSE: You don't know if you're cutting or not?

DORIS: No, that's not it, it's just . . . we might go fer a ride.

THÉRÈSE: Without a helmet?

DORIS: Relax, don't be stupid, I stashed one in the stadium.

THÉRÈSE: So you're in love with your biker. (*She starts to sing the Piaf lament* "L'Homme à la moto.")

DORIS: Are ya nuts? Besides, I'm gonna drop 'im. There's this super dude in the gang. I'm crazy about 'im. Silver Wing an' everythin'. But I ain't gotta prayer. He's married, the fool. O' course, his old lady, she's pretty super too . . .

THÉRÈSE: Come on, let's go, we'll breakfast away in my bedroom, just the two of us.

DORIS: Okay! Great! Super! You bet! Sometimes I really love ya, ya know.

THÉRÈSE: How come, then, you act like the same little piss?

DORIS: Hey, will ya tell me a bit about Pop, just, just some things, ya know, just ta know.

THÉRÈSE: If you want.

SCENE 11

MAUD: (*Coming out of the flat, followed by Thomas.*) Guess what! Momma's not in the bedroom. Her bed's all messed up but it's cold. You haven't seen her, have you?

THÉRÈSE: What about her things?

MAUD: I don't know; I didn't look.

DORIS: D'ya think she could'a flew the coop?

THÉRÈSE: You're the only one who's trying to get away from here.

THOMAS: But why are you making yourself all upset like this? It's idiotic, you know. Besides, here she comes now.

MAUD: Momma? . . .

MADELEINE: (*Entering, a carton of cigarettes and a newspaper in her arms.*) I went all the way to the airport.

THÉRÈSE: On foot?

MADELEINE: Tsk, tsk, tsk. Of course on foot. It's no big deal. I didn't have any more cigarettes. I had to wait till they opened the shops. So I figured I might as well buy a carton.

MAUD: You could have had one of mine.

MADELEINE: I did go to your room.

MAUD: Uh. . . ?

MADELEINE: But you were sleeping like an angel, so I didn't want to wake you up.

MAUD: Gee . . . well, gee! . . .

MADELEINE: Hello, Thomas; are you feeling all right?

THOMAS: Fine, just fine.

MADELEINE: Well that's fine. (*To Thérèse.*) Thérèse might be the eldest, but she's always the last one to get dressed.

THÉRÈSE: Okay. I'm going.

MAUD: Us, too, we're taking off. Come on Thomas, let's get going.

THOMAS: Sure. So long Thérèse, bye Doris, bye Madeleine . . . bye to you too, M. Samson.

M. SAMSON: I'm not kissin' ya, got grease all over me.

THOMAS: Please, don't trouble yourself.

M. SAMSON: That's what I say.

DORIS: (*Laughing and pointing to Samson, to Thérèse.*) God he's weird.

MAUD: Are you coming? Otherwise we won't have any time to play. (*Maud and Thomas leave.*)

THÉRÈSE: (*Laughing.*) What's gotten into him? (*Thérèse enters the flat.*)

SCENE 12

DORIS: Mom, I . . . I wanted ta tell ya yesterday, that phone call from my father . . .

MADELEINE: Don't you have school this morning?

DORIS: Mom! I'm sick ta death o' yer never listenin' ta me. I'm not ten years old anymore. Seems like ya take any chance ya get ta treat me like a baby.

MADELEINE: I'm sorry, maybe you're partly right.

DORIS: It's okay.

MADELEINE: So, tell me.

DORIS: No, it's nothin' . . . I mean, if ya feel like seein' 'im, as far as we're concerned, I mean, it's yer right. That's all. D'ya think he's still in love with you?

MADELEINE: What does that mean, "in love," according to you?

DORIS: I dunno. See what I mean, yer makin' fun o' me. But people yer age, yer generation, people who've been married an' everythin', it means somethin', doesn't it?

MADELEINE: Maybe, I guess so . . .

DORIS: (*Pointing at the newspaper her mother's holding.*) What's that, that rag in yer hand?

MADELEINE: Nothing. (*Doris takes it from her.*) It's the real estate guide.

DORIS: Ya wanna ditch this dump?

MADELEINE: I don't know, maybe, take over a little business . . .

DORIS: What kind? A sex shop?

MADELEINE: Now that's an idea! . . . No, I don't know.

DORIS: Great, wow, yeah! You get a sex shop, an' I'll be the sexy salesgirl who brings in the customers. We'll make a ton o' dough an' after that it's fat city. We'll travel . . .

MADELEINE: A sexy salesgirl with her baccalaureate!

DORIS: Sure . . . I mean, I'll try, ya know.

MADELEINE: It'd make me very happy if you got it.

DORIS: Me, too, as a matter o' fact, I'd really prefer ta. (*Silence.*)

MADELEINE: Your father slept in the blockhouse last night . . .

DORIS: Are you kiddin' me?

MADELEINE: He's most likely still there. Otherwise he would have shown up here.

DORIS: Did ya see 'im?

MADELEINE: I took a blanket and something to eat out to Tut-Tut during the night. He was sleeping next to him. For a second I thought it was sóme sadist or I don't know what, and then, it's odd, but when I got closer, I recognized his snoring. After eighteen years, I recognized your father by the way he snores. (*She laughs.*) Maybe that's the love you were talking about.

DORIS: Did ya talk to 'im?

MADELEINE: He didn't even hear me. You would've almost thought they were two animals. For a minute I thought they were dead. I remember at the end of the war, I found a dead German soldier, in a woods too. I even cried over him.

DORIS: (*Touching her mother's eyelids.*) An' last night, ya bawled too.

MADELEINE: Not for the reasons you think. (*Pause.*)

DORIS: Mom, I haven't said anythin' ta ya yet, but if everythin' goes all right, I'm splittin'.

MADELEINE: When is that? You know I don't approve.

DORIS: I know. But I don't feel like bein' here for Maud's weddin'.

MADELEINE: Do you think she's really going to go through with it?

DORIS: She better, after what she's put us through.

MADELEINE: Like you say, she better!

DORIS: So, yer kind o' for it?

MADELEINE: She's twenty-eight years old.

DORIS: An' I'm eighteen an' I don't wanna end up a jerk.

MADELEINE: She isn't one either.

DORIS: She's doin' everythin' possible ta become one, ya gotta admit it.

MADELEINE: She sees Thérèse. She's looking for a way out.

DORIS: Well fer a way out, thank you no! I'd rather choose a dead end, like our road. 'Cept for tennis, o' course. We really didn't have the opportunity.

MADELEINE: Are you really sorry?

DORIS: Oh hell no! Anyway, she plays like a piece o' wood. "Mme snob, V.I.P." It gives her dude a hard-on ta see her runnin' 'round in that little skirt, that's all. Besides, I'm positive he's a pervert. He has this way o' lookin' at me sometimes; even *you*, right?

MADELEINE: Dory!

DORIS: Okay, all right, I'll shut my trap. But just wait an' see the life she'll lead once he's hooked 'er fer good.

MADELEINE: If only I'd have been more clever at making money, the three of you would have had an easier time getting out of here . . .

DORIS: Don't make me cry with yer super guilt trip.

MADELEINE: You know what my super guilt trip is going to do to you? Go on, scram, leave me alone.

DORIS: Okay, okay, exit the baby. But I still gotta talk ta ya . . . D'ya think he'll be back here?

MADELEINE: If he slept in there, then that must be what he's planning.

DORIS: Well, anyways, don't let 'im wrap ya 'round his finger, if ya don't want him to.

MADELEINE: I don't want to see him. But I know what I'm doing!

DORIS: Ma, I'm gonna ring up this guy so he'll come an' get me.

MADELEINE: The motorcycle freak?

DORIS: How d'ya know?

MADELEINE: I know . . . he's ugly . . .

DORIS: Well . . . yeah, he is . . . (*She disappears into the flat.*)

SCENE 13

MADELEINE: Samson!

M. SAMSON: (*From under the car.*) Yes sir.

MADELEINE: Forget about the station wagon.

M. SAMSON: (*Climbing out from under the car.*) What?

MADELEINE: We're going to stop spending money on that car. It's not worth it.

M. SAMSON: No more money, ya mean *me*? Yer cannin' me? Well I say no. I'm strikin' an' occupyin' as of now. I ain't forgettin' nothin' no way. Jesus, ain't it just like a woman! My own wasn't no better. Whayddaya think . . . I'm gonna spend a month breakin' my ass on this pile o' shit. No way. I'm finishin'! You'll have yer donkey cart, ya can go 'round the world in it or ya can go right through the roof the first time ya hit a hole, that's yer problem. But I'm deliverin' the goods for the weddin', just like we agreed. God Almighty, fuck, I can't believe it.

MADELEINE: And what if I sell the place first?

M. SAMSON: I'm not gonna hold my breath fer that one. Who ya gonna pawn it off on—some group wantin' a home fer the deaf an' dumb? Cuz, at the end o' the runway, the "Quiet Haven Home" seems a bit dicey ta me, unless ya find a oil well in the basement, but I doubt it. You got a taker? Sell it? Je-sus!

MADELEINE: And what exactly else do you think I can do? Even you're starting to get on my nerves. Always sitting on your high horse, playing the good Samaritan. I have to pay you, don't I? Maybe the Chamber of Commerce . . . when they enlarge the airport . . . I'm not going to stay here alone when my daughters have left . . . I don't see any other solution.

M. SAMSON: That's yer problem! I ain't paid ta find solutions. Still, maybe there's somethin' . . . course I'm not sayin' nothin', but . . . obviously it'd take special equipment that I don't have here, but, after all, what are banks made for . . .

MADELEINE: I don't understand a word you're saying.

M. SAMSON: Naw, I just thought, gettin' engines ready fer stock car racin' . . . I always dreamed 'bout doin' it an' as far as investments are concerned . . .

MADELEINE: I'm too old, M. Samson, even to think about starting something else. I'm sorry about a few minutes ago, but, you know, sometimes these cannonballs hit you . . .

M. SAMSON: Ya mean like a husband.

MADELEINE: So you know about it, too?

M. SAMSON: Ya can't imagine what ya learn when ya spend yer life spread out on the floor. Naturally, nobody even thinks about ya. Like when I was a kid, I'd go hang out in a air vent an' I'd jest get ta see people's legs. Sometimes it's real pretty: nice stockin's, even lace, sometimes ya can't look at it, varicose veins an' all the rest. Ya can see everythin' from below, ya know.

MADELEINE: You're a strange duck, Samson.

M. SAMSON: No I ain't. It's just, well it worries me ta see ya all worked up an' hassled like this.

MADELEINE: It's not worth your being worried.

M. SAMSON: How can ya say . . .

MADELEINE: S . . . Samson . . . (*She leans against his shoulder.*)

SCENE 14

HUMBERT: (*Entering from the woods.*) Maddy, I . . .

MADELEINE: Maddy! . . .

M. SAMSON: 'Scuse me, it's time fer my union break.

MADELEINE: M. Samson!

M. SAMSON: Think I'll take a walk. Ain't it the truth? At our age, ya get all stiff. (*He walks away.*)

HUMBERT: So, have I changed a lot?

MADELEINE: In eighteen years? No, of course not, not at all! And me, why I look splendid, top form, more beautiful than ever, isn't that it? Thanks but no thanks, you can keep that line of patter to yourself.

HUMBERT: I didn't open my mouth. I only asked you . . .

MADELEINE: I answered. So beat it, will you!

HUMBERT: Can't we even talk.

MADELEINE: To say what, old friend, to finally decide whose fault it was and why you left for good. But we've already been through that, haven't we? Your painting, your art, your mid-life crisis, and what else was there?

HUMBERT: That's what I said, sure. But the real reason, it wasn't . . . The real reason, well, I . . . I was jealous! Really, it was jealousy that kept me from working, from painting, from doing anything.

MADELEINE: You're lying. I have never, never seen you jealous.

HUMBERT: Is that right? And these letters, huh? (*He shows her a packet of letters.*) There's nothing in them to make me jealous?

MADELEINE: *You* have them? But . . . how? Since when?

HUMBERT: You never wondered about it? Since the day I found them stashed behind the motor of the refrigerator.

MADELEINE: (*Closing her eyes, on the verge of hilarity.*) My God!

HUMBERT: Nearly twenty years. It was the day they brought back Jean Moulin's ashes.

MADELEINE: I'd completely forgotten; I didn't even notice they were missing.

HUMBERT: Hot stuff they are, real hot. (*Reading.*) "My sweet love, my darling

Madeleine," that's you all right. "Since yesterday afternoon, I haven't stopped thinking about you, about your stomach, your thighs, your ass, the gift
of your body, about the words you pronounced as I penetrated you, about
your frenzy, about my overwelming desire for you" . . . he forgot the "h."

MADELEINE: Stop it, stop it, what use is it . . .

HUMBERT: You asked me to explain, I'm explaining.

MADELEINE: I didn't ask you anything at all. You'd practically stopped making
love to me. It was a stupid thing, it wasn't important. Besides it had been
over a long while when you left.

HUMBERT: But I was going crazy every time you got near a customer. I saw you
humping half the world. Who was it?

MADELEINE: Is that why you got me pregnant again?

HUMBERT: If Doris even is my daughter.

MADELEINE: She is.

HUMBERT: Hmm! Who was it?

MADELEINE: It's not important. So you left without saying a word, without
daring to talk to me about it. Do you want to know what I really think? I
think you did it because you're gutless.

HUMBERT: In any case, I've got enough guts to come back.

MADELEINE: Just like you had enough to run away. That ridiculous motto you
used to repeat all the time to make you seem so profound: "In love the heroic
action is flight." Is that what you mean?

HUMBERT: That's right, it's from . . .

MADELEINE: Napoleon.

HUMBERT: So you remember! After I left, were there many others?

MADELEINE: Enough to know for sure that I didn't want any one of them every
night in my bed.

HUMBERT: Did the girls know?

MADELEINE: No more than they did about the letters . . . (Pause.) It's true,
though, isn't it, it really worked for us, sex, I mean. And then, and I never
understood why, as far as you were concerned, you got less and less interested. I couldn't seem to excite you at all, but, still, it was almost
miraculous to have known what we had together. I still think so. Anyway, I
never experienced it again like that, I mean, to that extreme.

HUMBERT: Well, to tell you the truth, I didn't either.

MADELEINE: Do you think I give a damn? I'm telling you about me, only about
me. You don't exist and haven't for a long time. Whether you disappear
from here in a year the way you say or if I'd read about your death ten years
ago in the newspapers, for me, it would amount to the same thing.

HUMBERT: You can't say that, Madeleine.

MADELEINE: If I said it, it's because I can say it.

HUMBERT: I want to come back here for the time I have left.

MADELEINE: You can't do that!

HUMBERT: It's only for a year.

MADELEINE: If it were just for a day, it would still be too long.

HUMBERT: So, for you, it's really over, the two of us?

MADELEINE: My God, how dare you, after . . .

HUMBERT: Okay, I understand. You don't even want to listen to me, at least you haven't changed about that. I'll set myself up in the blockhouse next door. That's easy enough. But I insist, do you hear, I insist on being able to store my canvasses in the old wash house where it's dry. I've just got enough to rent a pick-up, I'll go get them. Be prepared for a surprise, though, but I won't say anything about them yet. You'll see that you'll come around to understanding me. Do you still have a minute? Because I want to tell you a few things about me that you never understood, about us . . . (*Madeleine moves imperceptibly away from him and slips into the repair shop. He continues speaking, thinking she is next to him. However it is M. Samson who appears onstage and begins to listen without Humbert knowing it.*) . . . it's not easy, but nothing's easy. No, but now that I think about it, I'm not joking about the blockhouse. Since I'm going to die anyway, drop dead like a stinking dog, at least it'll be only 200 meters from here, from you. Anyhow, what was I saying? . . . You're right, I mean, you're right to think I should have talked to you, tried to see if we could give it a second chance, especially after Dory was born. But I must have told myself then that it was all over, no matter what. And then, I was nearly forty and nothing that I'd dreamed about as a young man had happened. You were acting like the Holy Virgin, the perfect mother. I know I'm being hard, but it was true. And then you were obsessed with making money and, at the same time, I had proof that you were cuckolding me. There's no other word for it; that's what it was! You know, I'd tried to stop painting so it wouldn't be a barrier between us, but it was always stronger than me. I still had the ambition, even if I wasn't sure I had the talent. In any event, I realized I wasn't being either a real artist or a businessman, even though I did more than my share around here. Maybe you'd say, not as much as you did. I guess that's possible. Only you had given up on your singing of your own free will; I mean given up the life of the artist. Today I'm at the end of my rope. Maybe I didn't really succeed but you can't blame me for having tried. I know you're going to say: what about your responsibilities! (*M. Samson walks slowly into the shop and begins working again, unseen by Humbert.*) That's exactly what I want to talk to you about. Because it's all a part of my work, you might say, in the sense that you can consider my paintings as a kind of life insurance for the four of you. Do you see, Madeleine? Maddy? . . . Where is. . . ? But I was just talking to her . . .

M. SAMSON: Uh . . . when I saw Mad . . . I mean yer wife walkin' away, well, I said to myself, they're finished, I guess. I'll go back ta work. But ya kept on talkin' all by yerself. I didn't wanna disturb ya.

HUMBERT: I guess I am a little disturbed.

M. SAMSON: Then that explains it 'bout the kid. Yer the antecedent, so ta speak, in the family. It's true, ya know, it can easily skip a generation. An' then, if I understood right, ya got some health problems.

HUMBERT: Yeah and not just anything, either. Well, she asked for it. I'm gonna set up right here.

M. SAMSON: Where's that? In the wagon? Listen, I've had enough.

HUMBERT: In the blockhouse, over there in the woods. That'll do me fine for the time I have left.

M. SAMSON: Sure, why not? You don't risk ruinin' yerself in gas an' electricity bills, anyways.

HUMBERT: Did you two have a little something, by any chance?

M. SAMSON: Ya mean yer wife an' me, by any chance? . . . Not that I know o'. That said, ya weren't exactly policin' her. O' course, I ain't sayin' nothin' by that. Hey, what're ya doin'? (*Humbert is opening a metal cabinet in the garage.*) That's my locker.

HUMBERT: Oh! . . . Well I'm just seeing how I can fix myself up, if there're some things I can take out there.

M. SAMSON: No way. I ain't givin' ya my locker, 'less it's the boss who asks me to.

HUMBERT: She gets what she wants from you, huh?

M. SAMSON: Let's not exaggerate; but all the same, I'd like ta keep my locker.

HUMBERT: I'll take care of things all by myself, as usual . . . All right?

M. SAMSON: Hey, you got an insane situation here, okay? But everybody's got his problems. I got my own bunch just like everybody else. So I mind my own business.

SCENE 15

WINNOCK: (*From offstage, then entering.*) What the fuck she doin'? She was supposed ta wait for me at the fork cuz o' her old lady.

M. SAMSON: Would ya like me ta tell 'er yer here? Oh, (*indicating Winnock*) this here is Doris' chauffeur an' this (*indicating Humbert*) is her father, a guest o' the woods, so ta speak. (*He enters the flat.*)

WINNOCK: Didn't think she had a father.

HUMBERT: You always have a father.

WINNOCK: Mine died o' cancer last year.

HUMBERT: I'm very sorry.

WINNOCK: Don't be. He was a asshole. Hey, why don't I ask you?

HUMBERT: Why not?

WINNOCK: Ta sign an authorization so Doris can blow this joint. (*He takes a piece of paper out of his wallet.*) Sign right here. Otherwise, she can't cross the border. We're goin' ta San Sebastien, the biggest rock festival in Europe. It's even more stupid when ya think that in a month an' a half she won't even need it. She's fabulous, Dory, a super chick, ain't she? It's funny, ya know, she talks about her mother, but you . . . not a word. Hey, don't bother readin' it, those things are just bureaucratic junk. Anyway you can count on her not ta act like a stooge. Say, listen, if . . . I mean if ya could give 'er a little dough, cuz down there . . . They say it should be cheaper, but all the same . . .

HUMBERT: Nyet! Dear boy, I simply can't.

WINNOCK: Afraid o' the dope, huh? Whaddaya want, it's here too, ya know . . . Anyway, down there at least it's legal. The Socialists are less backwards than here. For the dough, I dunno how she's gonna manage. I got some, but, seein' as she has nothin', it unbalances the relationship, if ya know what I mean.

HUMBERT: I understand. (*He signs.*)

WINNOCK: (*Gathering up the document.*) Fab! Thanks a lot fer her sake.

M. SAMSON: (*Coming back out of the flat.*) Her mother would like ta see ya.

WINNOCK: Won't make no difference now; he signed it, her father I mean.

M. SAMSON: I dunno. (*Humbert disappears into the woods.*)

WINNOCK: He's a pretty good guy, her old man.

M. SAMSON: I dunno. (*Doris comes out of the flat.*)

SCENE 16

WINNOCK: He's a good guy, yer old man, he signed it.

DORIS: What? He signed what?

WINNOCK: The authorization so ya can leave France.

DORIS: My father?

WINNOCK: Yeah, yer father, the batty guy with the beard. So, let's get goin', we'll take a detour ta the sea. They're not waitin' fer us. Anyway, we go a lot slower. We'll meet up with 'em down there.

DORIS: Stash that paper somewheres. I don't want my mother ta see it. An' wait a sec; I wanna say good-bye ta her.

MADELEINE: (*Coming out of the flat, to Winnock.*) Just a minute there. I want a word with you. It is out of the question that Doris leave before her baccalaureate exam.

WINNOCK: Don't worry 'bout it, Lady, it's okay with your husband. He signed the authorization.

DORIS: Shut up, you moron.

WINNOCK: She can shout an' scream all she wants. All they got ta do is get together on this. (*To Doris.*) So let's split before she starts goin' weird on us.

M. SAMSON: Unless maybe I go weird on yer face first!

WINNOCK: Why's he always askin' fer it, yer proletarian hero here?

M. SAMSON: Cuz ya get on my nerves.

WINNOCK: (*Cautiously withdrawing, to Doris.*) It's yer scene; take care o' it!

DORIS: Mom! . . .

MADELEINE: I don't give a damn about you and the sooner you leave, the better.

SCENE 17

THÉRÈSE: (*Emerging from the flat, dressed.*) What's this all about? Doris? Mother? What is it?

DORIS: (*On the verge of tears.*) Nothin', it's Mom who's makin' a big deal out o' nothin'.

M. SAMSON: Doris, tell that helmeted tadpole o' yers that if he wants ta park his tricycle 'round here, he better learn ta speak politely ta people cuz helmet or not . . .

MADELEINE: It's okay Samson, it's between her and me. After all, it's my fault if she doesn't understand.

M. SAMSON: Well, it's her charmin' Hell's Angel that's givin' me a pain in the butt.

DORIS: (*To Winnock.*) Take me ta school.

WINNOCK: But we're goin' . . .

DORIS: I'm tellin' ya, take me ta school. (*They leave.*)

THÉRÈSE: (*To Madeleine.*) Momma, will you explain?

MADELEINE: There's nothing to explain. I'm an hysterical old fool, that's all, incapable of any authority. The worst is that it seems completely natural to me that she wants to leave.

THÉRÈSE: Come on, I'm going to do your hair. I've got time today. We'll do your roots, too, okay? I want my mother to look pretty.

MADELEINE: If you'll enjoy it, but you'd be better off doing something for yourself on your free day. (*They enter the flat.*)

SCENE 18

M. SAMSON: (*To the audience.*) Gaskets an' hairdos. Drama or no, ya always have ta contend with them kind o' things. O' course it's thanks ta them that life goes on. What I remember the best 'bout Algeria, fer example, is poker an' soccer pools; when, in point o' fact, we spent three-quarters o' our time in the mountains in useless maneuvers gettin' ourselves knocked off by the Arabs. But that's what I can hardly remember. Guess that shows ya don't live things the way ya think ya do when yer in 'em. (*Humbert emerges from the woods and heads towards an old car seat pushed into a corner of the garage. Samson indicates what he's doing to the audience.*) An' that one, durin' all this time, was goin' 'round takin' care o' settin' up his hideaway. Enough ta make ya wonder if the whole thing was gonna blow sky high. O' course I'm not sayin' nothin' by that. Besides, I wasn't there ta think. (*Richard enters.*) Hey, I was startin' ta get lonely fer ya.

RICHARD: I must 'a dropped my bread in the car.

M. SAMSON: Ain't seen it, why don't ya go ta the lost an' found.

RICHARD: That's not funny.

M. SAMSON: Okay okay. I'll take a look. (*Bending over the back seat of the station wagon, he finds a switchblade.*) Jeez, look at what I found instead.

RICHARD: Relax, I'll look myself. An' the blade, it's mine, a remembrance of my mother.

M. SAMSON: Oh yeah? Prove it.

RICHARD: There weren't two hundred dudes who fucked in that car last night.

M. SAMSON: Sure, but that don't make it any less dangerous.

RICHARD: It's a remembrance, I'm tellin' ya. (*Finding his wallet in the car.*) Here it is! (*He pulls out a wad of bills.*) Nine thousand, ten, ten thousand five hundred.

M. SAMSON: It all there?

RICHARD: Uh huh.

M. SAMSON: Woulda been a cryin' shame ta lose all that.

RICHARD: (*Holding out his hand.*) The blade.

M. SAMSON: Here ya go. (*He gives it back.*)

THÉRÈSE: (*Coming out from the flat.*) M. Samson . . . (*Seeing Richard.*) Why, you've come back already!

M. SAMSON: Yes, Thérèse?

THÉRÈSE: Never mind, it was about Tut-Tut and my father, but it's not important. (*To Richard.*) It's really nice of you to come back to see us so soon.

M. SAMSON: Yeah, I think so too.

RICHARD: Uh huh, only, well, I gotta leave now.

THÉRÈSE: Already?

RICHARD: I got a lot o' things ta do.

THÉRÈSE: That's a pity, you could have stayed to lunch with us and given me a lift into town afterwards. I have a meeting at three.

RICHARD: Sure, if I could 'a, but right now, I can't. Another time, though. Me, too—gotta meetin'—ya know what it's like.

THÉRÈSE: Well, gosh, maybe I could . . . Wait just a second. I'll be right with you. M. Samson, if you see my little boy, tell him he's got to take his bath. It's been over a week. Have to tell my mother something, then I'll be back in a jiffy. (*She returns to the flat.*)

M. SAMSON: That's the big problem here, when ya ain't got a car.

RICHARD: How old is she . . . Thérèse? Right?

M. SAMSON: She ain't a kid no more, Thérèse ain't. Her younger sister, her name's Maud, but I guess ya know that already.

RICHARD: What intuition!

M. SAMSON: Observation.

SCENE 19

MADELEINE: (*Leaving the flat behind Thérèse.*) So you're leaving me alone. I thought you were going to spend the day with me and do my hair. (*Seeing Richard.*) Who's that?

THÉRÈSE: A friend of M. Samson's. Listen, Momma, I really have to find a present for Maud and Thomas.

MADELEINE: Why don't you give them one of your father's paintings?

THÉRÈSE: Stop thinking about it, Momma!

MADELEINE: You're a fine one, you are. There he is, creeping around in the woods, spying on the house, and your son is with him. What do you think about that?

THÉRÈSE: And what do you think'll he'll do? Come off it, Momma! I have to go, the gentleman is waiting for me.

RICHARD: How d'ya do?

MADELEINE: At least try to get back before M. Samson goes home.

THÉRÈSE: Momma, dear, I promise I'll try. Shall we go?

RICHARD: (*Looking at his watch.*) If it's all right with you.

THÉRÈSE: You can drop me off wherever it suits you best. (*They exit.*)

SCENE 20

MADELEINE: I hate to be here alone. Lucky for me that you're around.

M. SAMSON: If I was you, I'd buy a dog.

MADELEINE: (*Laughing.*) Oh sure, that's right, a dog, I guess I'm at that stage.

M. SAMSON: Naw, I don't mean that . . . a big one ta guard the house! Listen, I didn't say it fer that.

MADELEINE: But you said it just the same.

M. SAMSON: Oh shit, Madeleine.

MADELEINE: (*Throwing herself in his arms and crying a bit.*) Do you think he's gone?

M. SAMSON: I'm 'fraid he's movin' in. Hey, c'mon now, c'mon.

TUT-TUT: (*Charging out of the woods.*) Nadline! Nadline! Brrrrm! Eeeerk! Brrrr! Eeeeeek! Took duck bath Nommie. No tub Tut-Tut. (*Separating Samson and Madeleine,*) Top! Top! Go pad boat! Fff–Fff . . . Pshuu pshuu . . . Fff–Fff . . . (*He pummels M. Samson.*)

MADELEINE: (*Pulling him away from M. Samson.*) Okay. Come on now. (*She re-enters the flat with Tut-Tut who shoots at M. Samson with his imaginary gun.*)

M. SAMSON: I dig. He means Samson equals the King o' the assholes.

(*Humbert reappears to grab an old blanket. Then he disappears again into the woods while M. Samson watches him. Black out.*)

ACT III

SCENE 1

(Same set, early evening, about two weeks later.)

M. SAMSON: (*To the audience.*) From time to time, I could hear the old guy slinkin' 'round not too far from here, like a fox stalkin' a chicken coop. Madeleine an' the girls pretended not to notice. More than once I felt like goin' ta find 'im an' chattin' a bit, but as soon as he figured somebody had seen 'im, he made a beeline fer the blockhouse an' hunkered down. You could say it didn't exactly make fer a crazy happy atmosphere 'round here. The kid was spendin' the better part o' his time with 'im, an' robbin' everythin' that, accordin' to his thick skull, he thought might be useful ta 'im: old newspapers, oil cans, a comforter, my lunches . . . The wagon was practically finished an' I wasn't dissatisfied with the job, but what was makin' me so fuckin' nervous was that I didn't know what the fuck I was gonna do after. A couple o' times, a real estate agent came by ta take a look, apparently it never amounted to nothin'. But, o' course, I'd already predicted that, an' I'd decided ta mind my own business. After all, if I'd gone an' got myself single again, it wasn't so as I could get mixed up in family problems that had nothin' ta do with me. (*Seeing Tut-Tut who has slipped into the garage in order to steal a sandwich wrapped in aluminum foil.*) Not that one, Tut-Tut, it's yesterday's. (*He takes another sandwich wrapped in foil out of his pocket and offers it to Tut-Tut.*) Here, take this one. (*Tut-Tut runs away.*) Obviously, what interests him is stealin', otherwise, it ain't no fun. It's like offerin's to his God.

TUT-TUT: (*Showing up again.*) Gimme, gimme Tut-Tut, nit good?

M. SAMSON: So now yer makin' a liar out o' me? So much fer theories! Yer retarded but ya got a practical side all the same. Here ya go, it's got mayonnaise, don't know if he'll like it. (*He gives the sandwich to Tut-Tut.*)

TUT-TUT: Nyes!

M. SAMSON: (*To the audience.*) So, all's a sudden, I'm fixin' two sandwiches instead o' one . . . naturally! . . . In short, I was doin' like the girls, actin' like

I wasn't payin' no attention but I couldn't ignore the situation. (*To Tut-Tut, near him and getting all worked up.*) Whaddaya want? The naked ladies in the cupboard?

TUT-TUT: Dyes!

M. SAMSON: (*He gives the key to Tut-Tut.*) Here, don't put yer fingers on 'em. (*Tut-Tut opens the metal locker and contemplates the girlie photos taped to the inside of the doors. M. Samson looks at him. To the audience.*) The weddin', theoretically, was fer the next day. Shoulda seen the circus with the kid: Thérèse gettin' 'im ta try on a new jacket an' tie an' all. I kept goin' back an' forth 'bout whether ta show or not. 'Fraid o' bein' uncomfortable, but it was the son-in-law, I mean, the future son-in-law, who kept insistin'. I think if I'd let him, he woulda stuck me with best man. All cuz I unplugged the carburetor o' his 104 by blowin' in it. 'Cept for 'im, who was always enthused about everythin', considerin' the climate 'round here, it was lookin' like it was gonna be pretty bizarre. Meanwhile, I could see I had my work cut out fer me fer part o' the evenin', if I wanted the Peugeot ta be 100 percent fer the weddin'. An' I'd promised.

SCENE 2

THOMAS: (*Coming out of the flat.*) So, M. Samson, you've finished it, almost.

M. SAMSON: Almost.

THOMAS: (*Noticing Tut-Tut who is finishing masturbating in front of the photos.*) What's wrong with that kid? My God, look, he's . . .

M. SAMSON: Nothin's wrong, he's doin' what you an' I do; he ain't sick.

THOMAS: You . . . you let him do it?

M. SAMSON: I'm kinda liberal when it comes ta raisin' kids, 'specially when they ain't my own.

THOMAS: You have to admit that it's strange, I mean, seeing that he's not normal.

M. SAMSON: Fer that he sure is! Course yer the doc, not me.

THOMAS: Well, anyway, the station wagon is dynamite . . . it's dynamite that you finished it.

M. SAMSON: Two or three little things ta fix an' tomorrow mornin' it's ready ta take off fer the big day, guaranteed.

THOMAS: Oh, the big day, it's really just a formality, except for my parents.

M. SAMSON: My weddin' day, man, I remember we sure laughed. (*Tut-Tut laughs.*) Three days later, I was leavin' on a troop ship from Marseilles, an' I was laughin' a lot less! When I got home in '59, my wife was long gone. So ya see, already back then marriage wasn't sacred . . . That said, everybody got ta have his own experience.

THOMAS: Maud and me, it's different.

M. SAMSON: If ya say so.

THOMAS: Besides you know her.

M. SAMSON: Uh huh! . . .

THOMAS: Come on . . . sure you do.

M. SAMSON: Well let's not make a big deal out o' it.

THOMAS: I know there were guys before me, but I think that's even better. Because I can tell that with me, she's truly involved. And just the fact that my mother likes her a lot and trusts her completely . . .

M. SAMSON: Well, now, if yer mother. . . !

THOMAS: I really believe in feminine intuition for these things, especially when it comes to my mother . . . By the way, her father . . . have you heard anything much about him?

M. SAMSON: Not much.

THOMAS: The other day I heard her talking about him to Thérèse and her mother, but I didn't get her to . . .

M. SAMSON: (*To Tut-Tut, who has climbed into the car and eaten the sandwich.*) Okay buddy, all chowed down?

TUT-TUT: Tut-Tut nungry. Tommandant too.

M. SAMSON: (*Taking a second sandwich from his pocket.*) Take this one too, but behave yerself now, ya hear? (*Tut-Tut runs into the woods.*)

SCENE 3

THOMAS: Don't they feed that kid?

M. SAMSON: Sure they do, I mean it's not . . . it's a game. He pretends he eats a lot.

THOMAS: Better watch out for that. Bulimia can bring on all kinds of neurogastric complications.

M. SAMSON: Jesus yes!

THOMAS: So, her father . . .

M. SAMSON: 'Scuse me, but if I really wanna finish . . .

THOMAS: I'm keeping you from your tasks! I just left her alone long enough for her to try on her dress. I haven't seen it on her yet. She thought it was a little too . . . sexy, but I'm all for it! There's no reason to be ashamed of . . . Sexuality, all the same, is fundamental to the health of the couple. And as far as that's concerned, between her and me . . . Gee, I keep on talking and I know I'm bothering you!

M. SAMSON: Naw, naw, o' course not.

THOMAS: So you agree with me?

M. SAMSON: Since we're confidin' in each other here . . . me, ya know, I go ta whores. It's easier. And if ya do some calculatin', it's not necessarily pricier.

THOMAS: Gee, well, of course, that's one solution.

SCENE 4

MAUD: (*Leaving the flat in her wedding gown.*) Thomas, sweetheart, take a look.

THOMAS: You're . . . let's see, turn around. You're . . . gorgeous. I mean, your shoulders . . . no, I guess it doesn't matter. No, you're magnificent. You see, didn't I tell you?

MAUD: It's cut too low in back, that's what you mean, isn't it?

THOMAS: No, not really, and besides Mother was there with us when we picked it out, right!

MAUD: Okay, you don't like it. I understand.

THOMAS: Well, you couldn't, maybe, wear a bra with it?

MAUD: Are you crazy or something?

THOMAS: You think it'd show? No, listen, it's not important. You'll be very pretty. You'll be just right.

MAUD: If it bothers you so much, I can wear a tee shirt underneath.

THOMAS: Well, that'd certainly be unique.

MAUD: Will you please stop it!!

THOMAS: Honey, you'll be the prettiest bride of the whole year. Won't she, M. Samson? Isn't she gorgeous?

M. SAMSON: 'Cept fer gaskets an' pistons, I . . .

MAUD: (*To Thomas who's trying to kiss her.*) Be careful, you're going to wrinkle it.

THOMAS: I'll get you sooner or later.

MAUD: (*Unenergetically fighting him off.*) Love, please, let me go now.

THOMAS: Too late. You shouldn't have let yourself get caught on my tenterhooks. Too bad for you, even the law's on my side, kitten. Right, M. Samson?

M. SAMSON: In theory, anyways.

THOMAS: (*Very amorous.*) Honey, think about how great it's been all week. I'm going to spend the night.

MAUD: Please, don't I'm too nerved up. Besides, we have to get some sleep for the long day tomorrow.

THOMAS: Maybe you're right. We'll have all the time in the world, later. (*He hugs her.*) Wow, you don't have anything on underneath. (*He laughs.*)

MAUD: Be careful! My dress!

THOMAS: Tomorrow, 11 o'clock sharp! For once be on time, okay? Don't work too late tonight, M. Samson. Tomorrow you'll have to partner . . .

M. SAMSON: All the single ladies o' the family. Rock 'n roll, waltzes, tangos. Don't worry, I won't ley ya down.

THOMAS: Good night, love, think a little of your doctor-husband before you fall asleep.

MAUD: A lot, honey. I love you.

THOMAS: Say goodbye to . . .

MAUD: Don't worry, I will. (*Thomas exits.*)

SCENE 5

MAUD: I'm twenty-eight years old.

M. SAMSON: I understand.

MAUD: I'm going to make a phone call.

M. SAMSON: It's only natural.

MAUD: (*Goes into the phone booth and dials the number. It's obvious that she's speaking to an answering machine.*) Richard, it's me again. This is the fiftieth time I've called you. If you got my message, call back soon, whenever you want, before tomorrow. Kisses, I'm thinking about . . . Shit. (*She dials the number again.*)

M. SAMSON: (*Seeing Richard coming out of the woods, a bottle of anisette in his hand.*) Well how 'bout that? Our forests are definitely bein' repopulated.

MAUD: (*Into the phone.*) It's me again . . . I want you, us . . . I need you, I have to see you . . .

SCENE 6

RICHARD: (*Behind her.*) That part's easy.

MAUD: Richard! But how? . . . Where have you been these last few days? You . . . you just disappeared. I looked everywhere for you. I was so afraid, I even almost . . .

RICHARD: I was with some pals.

MAUD: No! No, you don't have to explain anything to me. You've come back. That's enough . . . That's the important thing. Oh baby! Am I glad to see you. If you only knew how glad!

RICHARD: That's what this's about, I've come ta tell ya that I'm gettin' outa here . . . He was right, you look great in that dress. No foolin', you'd make any guy get his knocker up. Yeah, well, I've got this buddy who's openin' this video business in Tahiti. I'm leavin' with him.

MAUD: You're leaving?

RICHARD: In the middle o' the week. Don't look at me like that. Direct from Paris to L.A. One night at a hotel, four or five hours, an' then L.A. —Papeete. Twenty hours o' flight time all together an' then coconut palms, blue lagoons, an' native girls . . .

MAUD: Are you really going? Is that the truth?

RICHARD: If I was him, I'd ask ya ta save that dress for the weddin' night. An' I got one thing more ta tell ya, ya shouldn't wear anythin' underneath.

MAUD: I already figured that out. (*She takes the bottle from him.*) Give me that!

RICHARD: Don't be stupid. It's pure alcohol.

MAUD: Is this how you drink it. (*She drinks.*) Je-sus!

RICHARD: I warned ya.

MAUD: I don't believe your story about Haiti, so there.

RICHARD: Ta-hi-ti. French Polynesia, it's even farther away. (*He takes an air-*

plane ticket out of his wallet.) So what's this, a subway ticket? You read: Papeete FAA one-way! Now whaddaya think? (*She takes the ticket from his hands.*)

MAUD: I'm going to tear it up! Anyway, that's the kind of country where you catch typhus and malaria.

RICHARD: (*Grabbing her around the waist.*) Stop it! (*He takes the ticket from her.*) You want everythin', don't ya?

MAUD: Why are you doing it?

RICHARD: To make the maximum amount o' dough I can in five ta six years without killin' myself.

MAUD: And what about me all that time?

RICHARD: *You* make Doctor's babies.

MAUD: Do you realize this means we won't make love any more, you and me?

RICHARD: Sex is only an accessory ta life.

MAUD: That sounds terrific coming from you. And what if I love you?

RICHARD: What would that change?

MAUD: You have no right to do this.

RICHARD: See, ya won't even answer.

MAUD: And you? What would it change for you?

RICHARD: I dunno, two tickets instead o' one . . . Naw, I haven't even thought about it.

MAUD: And what would I do there? I don't even have the right bathing suit. (*She laughs.*) I'm laughing, but it's not funny.

RICHARD: So I see! . . .

MAUD: I suppose you'd like it better if I were crying. Give me that! (*She takes back the bottle and drinks.*)

RICHARD: Hey, easy now . . .

MAUD: Oh shit, get off my case!

RICHARD: Lower your voice, for God's sake.

MAUD: You make me sick.

RICHARD: Am I crazy or what? Aren't you the one getting married tomorrow?

MAUD: Yes, tomorrow I get married. So what? I'm getting married, period. You're not going to keep on telling me for seven hundred years? And you, you're leaving. So, everything's working out just fine. We don't have anything more to say to each other. And that's that.

RICHARD: You bet. I'm gettin' out. I got a chance ta bask in the sun for a couple o' years, thanks ta this buddy, an' I'm not gonna let it slip away.

MAUD: Then I'm delighted for you.

RICHARD: Hey, don't think that . . .

MAUD: Think what? I'm delighted. I said so. What do you think I think, huh?

RICHARD: Well . . . nothing!!

MAUD: So we agree.

RICHARD: I only want ya ta recognize that this decision, I mean leavin' or not, you decided it for me. You made the choice, right?

MAUD: It was never, never a matter of choice between us. You've known about this marriage from the beginning, and it never bothered you before. So what's this story about choice that you're handing me now? You don't seem to know what you're saying, my sweet.

RICHARD: Get off it! I came by ta tell ya that I was leavin', period, that's it. You're the one who's turnin' this into a screamin' match. Get it into your head that nothin' forced me ta stop over.

MAUD: You shouldn't have put yourself out for so little, Richard dear. I'm a big girl, I would have understood. But all that aside, I'm glad you came here to tell me. Now I can call Thomas and tell him the truth.

RICHARD: You're really askin' for the weddin' eve blow-up, aren't ya?

MAUD: He's not necessarily an idiot, you know.

RICHARD: No, I don't know.

MAUD: Well, I'm telling you.

RICHARD: Then why aren't ya fuckin' him tonight?

MAUD: What's it to you? It's not your problem anymore. If you really want to know, it's you I wanted. But, relax, I got your message.

RICHARD: As far as "message" is concerned—me, too, I want you.

MAUD: Well I don't any more.

RICHARD: Come here.

MAUD: No.

RICHARD: C'mon, don't be like that.

MAUD: It doesn't make sense now.

RICHARD: Ya mean it made sense before?

MAUD: Maybe not for you, but for me, yeah, it did.

RICHARD: Sure, the sense was ta get fucked once by your lover, then again by your husband an' vice versa.

MAUD: You poor ass.

RICHARD: That's right! But meantime, the ass is splittin'. You can go ahead now an' call 'im, spill all the beans an' tell 'im that from now on he gets a double portion. (*Maud slaps him.*) I feel real sorry for you. Here, take the bottle. (*He walks away.*)

MAUD: Richard!

RICHARD: What? Richard!

MAUD: (*Throwing herself into his arms.*) Forgive me.

RICHARD: Forget it, kiss me.

MAUD: No, *you* kiss me. (*He kisses her.*)

RICHARD: So, d'ya wanna?

MAUD: Yes.

SCENE 7

WINNOCK: (*Entering from the outside.*) Hi!

RICHARD: Oh shit!

WINNOCK: Ya wouldn't know if Doris was ready?

MAUD: Doris, ready for what?

WINNOCK: Ta hit the road. Everybody else took off 'bout two hours ago, but I got a problem with my throttle.

RICHARD: Jesus, shit!

WINNOCK: Yeah, think how shitty 1000 kilometers'd be with a bad throttle!

RICHARD: I bet.

MAUD: (*To Richard.*) Cut it out! (*To Winnock.*) 1000 kilometers to go where?

WINNOCK: Ta the festival in San Sebastian.

MAUD: Tonight?

WINNOCK: Yeah, but if I'm too wore out, I'm stoppin', tough shit.

MAUD: But tomorrow . . . is my wedding.

WINNOCK: Well, yeah, I can see . . . I mean, I know.

RICHARD: (*Growing impatient.*) Maud!

MAUD: I said wait a minute!

WINNOCK: (*To Richard.*) Well good luck, ta each his own, old buddy.

MAUD: (*To Winnock.*) He's not the one.

WINNOCK: Oh, well, uh, good luck ta the other dude, then, huh?

RICHARD: He can't be real.

WINNOCK: Sure I am, old buddy! Well, shit, she's runnin' late again!

MAUD: (*To Winnock.*) You know there's no chance she'll go with you. Besides, she's got her exam in less than a week.

RICHARD: Maud, forget it! C'mon.

WINNOCK: She's gotta come. I don't wanna look like I'm gettin' jacked around. They're already mad at me in the gang. Anyway, what'd she mean "I don't want no part in my sister's weddin', eccectera." . . . Ya see? Hey, 'scuse me, but yer her sister, ain't ya? We already met once, right? (*Yelling.*) Dooris! Dooris!

RICHARD: You sick or somethin', yellin' like that?

WINNOCK: Hey, you keep an eye on the bride's garter, okay old buddy, an' shut up.

M. SAMSON: (*Appearing from the rear of the garage, to Winnock.*) Cool it, shrimp, 'less ya wanna eat yer handlebars.

WINNOCK: Shit. Is he still here?

M. SAMSON: I'm the night watchman; that bug ya?

WINNOCK: Oh fuck. What the fuck do you care? This is private. Ain't none o' yer business.

SCENE 8

DORIS: (*Coming out of the flat, to Winnock.*) That you screamin' my name like that?

MAUD: (*To Doris.*) Is it true that you've decided to leave tonight?

DORIS: Stop yellin', you'll end up gettin' Mom out here. (*To Maud.*) No, I mean, not really. (*Seeing Richard.*) What's he doin' here . . . Thérèse's friend?

WINNOCK: (*To Doris.*) Ain't ya ready yet? This is worse'n hell.

MAUD: (*To Doris.*) Are you talking about Richard?

RICHARD: Maud, can I tell you something?

DORIS: (*To Maud.*) Ya mean you know 'im too? I nearly fell over 'em in town.

WINNOCK: (*To Doris.*) So what's this scene yer playin', huh?

MAUD: (*To Richard.*) You saw my sister again?

WINNOCK: (*To Doris.*) Ya don't wanna split tonight?

RICHARD: (*To Maud.*) I ran into her by accident.

DORIS: (*To Winnock.*) I dunno anymore . . . You're gonna drive me nuts about it. (*To Maud.*) I just screwed up, right?

MAUD: And how do you think you screwed up?

WINNOCK: (*To Doris.*) I'm makin' *you* nuts? Yer the one who's freakin' me out. Jesus Christ!

MAUD: (*To Doris.*) Huh?

DORIS: Yer with 'im, too?

MAUD: Are you crazy? I wouldn't touch him with a ten foot pole.

DORIS: Anyhow, it doesn't have nothin' ta do with me.

WINNOCK: Fuck it, Doris, ya coulda told me if ya weren't sure. Cuz I woulda planned ta take Sabine with me.

DORIS: Ya mean yer ex, the fat slob? Don't wait a minute longer! Ya still got time ta pick her up—great picture, yer tramp on yer wreck.

MAUD: Richard, can I have a word with you?

RICHARD: If ya want, but I think we said everythin' we had ta say.

WINNOCK: (*To Doris.*) I must be dreamin'. I really must be dreamin'. This can't be happenin'. I oughta bust yer head in.

M. SAMSON:(*To Winnock.*) Ya think so? . . .

WINNOCK: (*Disgusted.*) Nooo! Geez if ya can't even talk! . . .

M. SAMSON: Yeeah, sure! . . .

MAUD: (*To Richard.*) I'll go get Thérèse. I'm sure you'd like to see her.

RICHARD: Maud, please, wait a minute.

WINNOCK: So what's it gonna be? Doriis!! . . .

DORIS: Stop screamin', yer gonna wake up Mom.

SCENE 9

MADELEINE: (*Coming out of the flat.*) He already did! But I told you Doris, you do what you want. Your father signed the paper so it isn't even worth the trouble to try and stop you.

THÉRÈSE: (*Arriving right after her mother.*) Richard? Showing up without even a warning! Momma, you know Richard, don't you?

MADELEINE: I don't know anything.

WINNOCK: (*To Doris.*) Ya can see she don't give a fuck. So c'mon, hurry up!

MAUD: (*To Doris.*) You know that I was counting on you for tomorrow.

DORIS: I know, but that's not the problem.

THÉRÈSE: A propos, Maud, you wanted to know who my mysterious wedding guest was, well it's him.

MAUD: Rich . . .

THÉRÈSE: Yes, Richard, and since he does photography, he promised to document the festivities for us.

RICHARD: (*To Thérèse.*) Well, now, I'm not sure I can.

THÉRÈSE: Oh nooo! Richard!

DORIS: I can't pull this number on Mom, Winnock.

MAUD: Well thanks for thinking about *me*. Why don't you invite him too? You might as well. And you must come too, M. Richard.

WINNOCK: Did ya hear that "Monsieur" stuff, all of a sudden?

DORIS: (*To Winnock.*) Will ya please put a lid on it!

THÉRÈSE: (*To Maud who's drinking from the bottle Richard gave her.*) Is that straight pastis you're drinking like that?

MADELEINE: Maud, take it easy.

MAUD: I'm burying my life as a single girl. It's Richard's round.

DORIS: (*To Maud, stealing the bottle from her.*) Hey, give me a slug. This evening is colossal.

MADELEINE: Doris, please . . .

DORIS: Come off it, huh? I'm not leavin', so . . .

MAUD: Hand me my medicine, Doris. (*She takes back the bottle.*) To the health of my sister and her white knight.

DORIS: (*To Maud.*) I'm startin' ta find you pretty colossal too.

MADELEINE: You two are crazy. I don't believe it.

WINNOCK: Ya weren't just talkin'? I'm invited too?

THÉRÈSE: (*To Richard who's trying to leave discreetly.*) What are you doing, Richard? Are you leaving? . . . Tomorrow at eleven, don't forget.

RICHARD: Really, I . . .

MAUD: You have to come, Richard. It'd be cowardly not to show up.

THÉRÈSE: Why cowardly?

MAUD: Because he promised you, there're the pictures and all that; and then he hasn't seen you in the new dress you bought. She's terrific in it, you know. So come, and I promise you a door prize before you leave for Tahiti.

MADELEINE: What are you talking about?

MAUD: A little secret, Momma dear, between Richard and me.

THÉRÈSE: Are you leaving for Tahiti, Richard?

WINNOCK: Tahiti, no shit? That's fantastic.

MAUD: (*To Thérèse.*) Richard didn't tell you? He did me.

RICHARD: I didn't have the chance. I'll explain later, Thérèse.

THÉRÈSE: If you could, yes, I'd like to hear . . .

RICHARD: But now, really, I gotta go.

WINNOCK: (*To Richard.*) You got wheels? Cuz I only got my bike, otherwise . . .

RICHARD: Don't worry. I'm fine. See ya tomorrow, everybody.

THÉRÈSE: But Richard, I mean, you just stopped by like that?

M. SAMSON: He came ta say hi ta me. He knew I had ta work late. So long Richard.

RICHARD: Yeah, so long Samson. (*Richard exits.*)

MAUD: M. Samson!

M. SAMSON: Yeah!? . . .

WINNOCK: What kind o' duds do we wear tomorrow?

DORIS: Ya mean yer comin'?

WINNOCK: Why not, he's goin', ain't he!

MADELEINE: (*To Winnock.*) Weren't you supposed to go to a festival in Spain?

WINNOCK: In a way, yeah. But if I ain't there, they'll work things out. An' the bride invited me.

MAUD: Cor-rect!

MADELEINE: (*To Maud who keeps on drinking.*) You're going to hurt yourself like that.

MAUD: Hurt myself?

THÉRÈSE: Can I speak with you, Maud?

MAUD: I don't feel like it. I need to meditate about things before the ceremony. You shouldn't disturb me while I'm meditating.

SCENE 10

M. SAMSON: (*Noisily closing the hood on the station wagon.*) Well! This car is finished.

MADELEINE: (*Tender.*) Samson!

M. SAMSON: That's the way it is, that's all. She's finished. Whaddaya want me ta say? (*To Winnock.*) Say there, biker, can ya give me a lift?

WINNOCK: Me?

M. SAMSON: Yeah, sure, you. I'm not talkin' ta the gas pump.

WINNOCK: The dude's a class act.

M. SAMSON: Okay, get it together an' speak normal cuz yer smart talk is givin' me a headache.

WINNOCK: Doris!

M. SAMSON: (*To Winnock.*) Yer comin' tomorrow, it's settled. Ya only gotta put a bow tie under yer leather an' it'll be swell. So get the lead out, an' let's go.

WINNOCK: The man is colossal!

M. SAMSON: (*Giving him the once-over.*) With you, it ain't hard. (*They exit.*)

SCENE 11

MAUD: Eleven o'clock! (*Silence.*)

MADELEINE: I don't know what's the matter with the three of you, but you all seem like you're at some kind of armed vigil.

THÉRÈSE: Not me; Maud's the problem. For once I meet somebody and she's jealous. She has to try everything to break things up. Pssst!

MAUD: You're so wrong. As a matter of fact I insisted that he come.

THÉRÈSE: Sure you did. And do you think I didn't see all the little games you were playing?

MAUD: (Sings the first line of Piaf's "Mon manège à moi c'est toi.")

THÉRÈSE: Stop it Maud! I'm warning you.

DORIS: Geez, it's all my fault. I told Maud that I saw ya with him.

THÉRÈSE: So what?

DORIS: So, nothin'. Anyway, she's half smashed.

MAUD: Half?

THÉRÈSE: (To Maud.) Richard said something to you about going away?

MAUD: Shhh! It's a secret.

DORIS: C'mon Maud. Stop askin' for it.

MADELEINE: That's enough young ladies! Do you know how fed up I am with you sometimes; sometimes more than fed up. I can't even stand you. I see it all clearly now, I finally realize I would have been better off not having you, so I could finish my life in peace and quiet instead of risking cardiac arrest over your problems with . . . with . . . that I don't understand in the slightest.

THÉRÈSE: We never understood what yours were either.

MADELEINE: My problems are my business.

THÉRÈSE: I'm sorry but even if you didn't mean to, you got us all involved in them, and look at the results.

MADELEINE: Let me finish, Thérèse, okay? I'm just telling you that any way you look at it you're all going to have to clear out of here because sooner or later, whether you like it or not, the station is going to be sold.

DORIS: An' then, ya'll have enough bread ta get somethin' on with Pop again?

MADELEINE: That's idiotic. You know as well as I do that he won't be around in another year.

DORIS: I don't believe it.

MADELEINE: Do you realize just how much, because of you, your mother is aging, and aging badly? It's simple, really. I don't know where I'm going any more. Up till now, I thought I'd at least manage to be useful to you in some way, but I see that it's exactly the opposite.

MAUD: Oh boy, you aren't much fun.

MADELEINE: You neither.

MAUD: Sure I am! The bride is looped! Dear sisters, no kidding, I just had a funny idea. Let's go look for Poppa. We'll bring him back here. The fatted calf routine, how about that! And we'll have a bash like nobody's ever seen and tell everything to each other; him—everything he's been doing all these years and us—the same.

THÉRÈSE: You have no respect for Momma.

MAUD: You don't wanna? Too bad cuz I'm gonna go see 'im. I'm gonna have a few drinks with my daddy in his castle.

MADELEINE: Stop it Maud! What about your dress? You're going to make a mess of it.

MAUD: I am? Tough! What's important is findin' my daddy. Who cares about the dirt?

DORIS: Maud sure is a gas when she's loaded.

THÉRÈSE: I don't think so.

DORIS: Should I go with 'er?

MAUD: A young page to hold my train? Uh uh, I'm goin' all alone. (*She trips and laughs.*) Oh boy, somethin's tellin' me my weddin' is gonna be a complete wash-out.

THÉRÈSE: (*To Maud.*) If that's what you want, why don't you say so right now?

MAUD: Don't worry Momma. I won't bring 'im back here. Anyway he knows he's got the right. I mean—he doesn't have the right. I just need him ta talk ta me, I mean with him about me. Geez, I'm havin' some trouble articulatin'.

MADELEINE: And with me? You don't want to talk with me?

THÉRÈSE: Momma's right. If you've got a problem, talk to us. We're more able to help you than he is.

MAUD: But what're ya tryin' . . . what're ya sayin? I don't need help.

DORIS: Mom, should I get Pop?

MADELEINE: No!

THÉRÈSE: Momma has her reasons, Doris.

MAUD: (*To Doris.*) Sweet Dory Baby, yer the most orphaned o' all o' us. So no tricks, no can understand, dig?

DORIS: Maybe I'm more orphaned, but I'm sure not as much of a jackass.

MAUD: Tsk tsk tsk . . .

MADELEINE: Doris, don't talk like that to your sis . . .

THÉRÈSE: Don't bother, Momma.

MADELEINE: Maud! Stay . . .

THÉRÈSE: Let her do her thing.

DORIS: Hey Maud, ya look like a ghost in the woods. Huh? Don't ya think so, White Lady?

MAUD: (*Stumbling.*) An' here's the White Lady fallin' on 'er ass. Hey, where's the old bottle? (*She yells while laughing.*) Poppa, Poppa, it's the Anisette Fairy on her way ta see ya. Get the ice out. We're gonna have a ball! (*She disappears into the woods.*)

SCENE 12

MADELEINE: Doris, won't you go with her?

DORIS: You kiddin'? Ya saw how she squashed me.

MADELEINE: (*Sighing, then noticing Thérèse stretched out on the ground.*) What're you doing Thérèse?

THÉRÈSE: Well, I'm looking at the sky. You know, the infinite silence of the stars. I guess I really am afraid.

MADELEINE: Don't you think we'd be better off going to bed?

DORIS: Chickens to the coop!

THÉRÈSE: Shh! Be quiet, Dory.

DORIS: Why.

THÉRÈSE: I'm listening.

DORIS: Extra-terrestrials?

THÉRÈSE: Shhh! I'm staying here a little longer.

DORIS: Mom, if ya don't mind, I'd like ta watch a movie. I won't turn it on loud.

MADELEINE: Okay, if that's what you want. (*Pause.*) Would it bother you if I watched it with you? I promise I won't talk! What is it?

DORIS: *Star Wars II.*

THÉRÈSE: Again!

DORIS: (*To Thérèse.*) You look at yer stars an' I'll look at mine. (*Madeleine and Doris enter the flat.*)

THÉRÈSE: (*Getting up.*) Come to think of it, I haven't seen that one either. (*She gets up and follows Doris and Madeleine. Silence.*)

SCENE 13

TUT-TUT: (*Leaving the woods.*) Nommee! Nommee! Nadline! Tut see Sno White . . . woods. Nommee Sno White! Tut all lone. Tut killed. Arghhh! He dead . . . (*He lies down on the ground with his eyes wide open. Blackout.*)

ACT IV

SCENE 1

(*The next morning. The station wagon has disappeared from the garage. Almost everywhere, outside of the repair shop, inside it, around the pumps, huge colorful abstract paintings have been hung, exactly as if exposed in a modern art gallery. Thomas is seated behind a small table. All the characters are dressed for a wedding according to their own particular taste and style.*)

RICHARD: (*Arriving from the outside with a camera slung over his shoulder.*) What's this mess?

THOMAS: No idea, paintings apparently.

RICHARD: Odd ta have set 'em up like that.

THOMAS: Indeed.

RICHARD: Are they gettin' ready?

THOMAS: No, nobody's here. I don't understand, we said eleven o'clock. Are you a guest?

RICHARD: Yeah. You the groom?

THOMAS: Yes.

RICHARD: Mighta guessed. (*Pointing to one of the paintings.*) That smallish blue one there, it's not bad.

THOMAS: You think so? I kind of like them, myself.

RICHARD: That said, I don't know much . . .

THOMAS: What's worrying me is that I've been here half an hour and I haven't seen anybody yet.

RICHARD: The station wagon gone?

THOMAS: Yeah. Have we met?

RICHARD: Nope.

THOMAS: I sure had the feeling.

RICHARD: No, you're wrong there!

THOMAS: (*Offering his hand.*) Thomas.

RICHARD: Richard.

THOMAS: You're a friend . . .

RICHARD: Of Thérèse.

THOMAS: A teacher too?

RICHARD: Nope.

THOMAS: Oh! . . . Well, I'm finishing med school, but I'm going to specialize. So, you're a photographer?

RICHARD: Only amateur.

THOMAS: Well, I don't know anything about it!

RICHARD: Are you sure nobody's here?

THOMAS: I've been all over the house.

RICHARD: The bride?

THOMAS: Evaporated like the rest.

RICHARD: You're not losin' hope then?

THOMAS: (*Laughing.*) No, but I don't understand what's going on, and it's beginning to get on my nerves.

RICHARD: I know what ya mean.

THOMAS: I'm not going to make a scene, a day like today, but really.

RICHARD: It'd be a mistake as long as she hasn't said "yes."

THOMAS: Obviously!

RICHARD: It's funny . . .

THOMAS: You think so?

RICHARD: No, I was lookin' at ya. Ya look like a museum guard.

THOMAS: (*Politely upset.*) That doesn't make me laugh.

RICHARD: I didn't mean ta hurt your feelin's. You don't know where they came from . . . all these paintings?

THOMAS: I already told you, no idea at all.

RICHARD: I wonder if it's her father.

THOMAS: Whose father?

RICHARD: Mau . . . Thérèse's.

THOMAS: My God! What the f--- are they doing?!

RICHARD: When's the ceremony?

THOMAS: In less than an hour at the Mayor's office. The blessing is this afternoon.

RICHARD: Blessing?

THOMAS: My parents wanted a mass, but Maud and I didn't. I've never been one to like displays . . . This can't be happening, where in hell could they've gone?

RICHARD: Gatherin' bluebells in the woods for the bride's bouquet?

THOMAS: Don't try. You can't make me laugh.

RICHARD Hey, I'm a nice guy. I'm keepin' ya company. You sure they haven't left already for the Mayor's Office?

THOMAS: We said eleven o'clock here.

RICHARD: It's eleven fifteen. Not tragic yet.

THOMAS: If you think like that, nothing is ever really tragic.

RICHARD: Even a weddin' that falls apart at the last minute?

THOMAS: Why are you saying that? Do you know something?

RICHARD: Me? Hell no! I was just thinkin', a chic weddin' gettin' out o' hand.

THOMAS: Why chic?

RICHARD: Cuz you look chic to me.

THOMAS: My family, maybe, but hers . . .

RICHARD: An' there she is.

THOMAS: Maud?

RICHARD: Well, her family, anyways.

SCENE 2

(*Madeleine, Doris, and Thérèse entering from the outside.*)

MADELEINE: Oh Thomas, you're here! Is Maud with you?

THOMAS: I haven't seen her since last night. Isn't she with you?

DORIS: We haven't seen 'er all mornin'. Course, gotta say that last night . . .

THÉRÈSE: Doris!

THOMAS: Hello Thérèse!

THÉRÈSE: Hello Thomas, hello Richard. You're both looking chic.

RICHARD: (*To Thomas.*) Ya see!

THÉRÈSE: This is a real nightmare! Nobody knows where Maud is?

MADELEINE: We waited for her and then we figured it was useless. So we went to get some gas to try out the car. We were hoping that she might already be with you!

THOMAS: Excuse me, but really, I don't understand what's going on. You're really very strange, I'm sorry to say it! But you organize ex . . . exhibits of paintings the morning of your daughter's wedding and you don't even worry about trying to find out where she's disappeared to!

MADELEINE: Look, Thomas, what you're calling an exhibit, we don't have a thing to do with it. As for my daughter, she's not a minor anymore.

THÉRÈSE: What are you going to do, Thomas?

THOMAS: What am I going to do; what am I going to do? How do I know? We have to find her, that's all. You don't expect me to unearth someone else this afternoon?

RICHARD: (*In a fit of hysterical laughter.*) That's very funny. You're a very funny guy.

THOMAS: Meanwhile, I don't think it's funny. Do you realize what it means if something's happened to her? Or maybe she doesn't realize.

THÉRÈSE: Well, now that that's been said, I suppose Thomas is right. It's not normal.

SCENE 3

(*Tut-Tut enters from the outside, followed by M. Samson.*)

TUT-TUT: Brrrrrm eeeeeek brrruuum grrrr. Reverz! . . . Tut drive stachuntank! Namson make drive Tut-Tut! Varoom.

M. SAMSON: (*To Tut-Tut.*) Ya see ole buddy, it ain't so hard.

THÉRÈSE: (*To Tut-Tut.*) What is it, sweetie?

M. SAMSON: I let 'im drive a little. He figures things out pretty good!

MADELEINE: Are you insane, Samson?

M. SAMSON: I'm sure he's got it in 'im ta get his license.

THÉRÈSE: Oh come on now! He has problems with motor coordination.

TUT-TUT: Varoom! Varooom! Grrrr!

M. SAMSON: Don't matter!

THOMAS: The *really* insane thing is that nobody seems to be upset.

M. SAMSON: So the bride still ain't here, if I understand right. You ain't seen her, have ya, Richard, fer example?

THOMAS: Why would he? Really now, I was here before he was.

RICHARD: Nope, I ain't, ole buddy Samson!

M. SAMSON: That's too bad, ole buddy Richard!

SCENE 4

(*Winnock enters from the outside with a bouquet of flowers.*)

WINNOCK: Hey! Who d'I give it to? Doris, hold 'em a sec, huh, while I say hello. Hope they ain't gone an' died too much on the baggage rack . . . cuz o' the shocks, I mean. (*Noticing the paintings.*) Geez, what're these things? They're kind o' okay. This a expo or what? Who did it, huh? Hey, hi there Ma'am, how's it goin'? Hiya, hi, let's hear it! (*He shakes hands "hello" with everyone present except Tut-Tut.*)

M. SAMSON: Hello good pal.

WINNOCK: (*To Samson.*) Still kickin' after last night?

TUT-TUT: (*Offering his hand to Winnock.*) Hewoo!

WINNOCK: Uh! . . . (*He tries to grab Tut-Tut's hand who's already lost control of it.*) Uh, well, guess I ain't too late yet, huh?

MADELEINE: Does anyone want a drink while we're waiting? Pastis, whiskey or orange juice. Easy choice. Doris, you serve, all right?

DORIS: Winnock, come an' help me. (*She disappears into the flat followed by Winnock. (Pause.)*

THÉRÈSE: How about a couple of pictures now, Richard?

THOMAS: Listen, all the same, we have to do something. Are you sure the kid didn't see her?

MADELEINE: Ask him!

THOMAS: Uh, sure, okay. (*To Tut-Tut.*) You see Maud, my fiancée? This morning, you know where she is?

TUT-TUT: Naud? Put pitures wid Poppa. Poppa!! Poppa!!

THOMAS: Pitures, he mean paintings?

MADELEINE: Well, it's obvious that these are my husband's canvases. He must have hung them last night.

THOMAS: Poppa! The man he calls Poppa, is that your husband?

MADELEINE: It's too complicated to explain.

THOMAS: And Maud would have done it with him?

THÉRÈSE: How should we know? We can't trust what he's saying.

TUT-TUT: It thrue Nommee. It thrue! Tut see! Got faiwry dess, snowey, pretty pretty!!

THOMAS: What am I supposed to think! This whole thing is absurd.

M. SAMSON: It sure does seem ridiculous, a weddin' without a bride. Ya don't get married ta yerself now, do ya?

THOMAS: I'm not the one who said it.

THÉRÈSE: I have to admit that coming from her, it's pretty astonishing. She wanted this marriage. She did everything to make it happen.

THOMAS: Everything?

THÉRÈSE: I mean we didn't *expect* her to get married. But since it's you, well it's fine, on the contrary . . .

DORIS: (*Leaving the flat behind Winnock who's carrying a tray with bottles and glasses.*) Great, so we do the apértif scene, huh? Momma?

MADELEINE: Nothing, thanks.

WINNOCK: M. Samson?

M. SAMSON: Take care o' the leadin' man first. He needs a little lift.

THOMAS: No, thanks, really, nothing.

DORIS: Richard?

RICHARD: Orange juice.

THÉRÈSE: (*To Doris.*) Give one to Tut-Tut too. Tut-Tut come here. Tut-Tut, this is Richard.

TUT-TUT: Niitcha . . .

RICHARD: Ya, ta you too. Hi. So what's his real name? (*Richard offers his hand to Tut-Tut who squeezes his fingers with astonishing strength and knocks into him violently with his head.*) Hey stop! He's strong, this dope. You're hurting me.

MADELEINE: Tut, stop.

TUT-TUT: (*Who stops abruptly. Pause.*) Tut. Stop. Nommee pretty! Dancey? Nommee?

THÉRÈSE: Yes my sweetie, you're my handsome knight. (*She dances with Tut-Tut.*) la la la la la . . .

TUT-TUT: (*Falls and laughs.*) 'all! (*Thérèse turns away from him. Pause.*)

WINNOCK: So, Samson, what's yer poison?

M. SAMSON: Whiskey.

DORIS: Thérèse?

THÉRÈSE: I'll have a pastis, but very light. I love it, I mean, I love the taste of pastis. You don't mind, Richard?

RICHARD: Of course not, babe!! (*Everybody drinks.*)

MADELEINE: Sincerely Thomas, I don't know what to tell you.

THOMAS: Don't worry; it's perfectly simple. If she's not here in five minutes, I call the whole thing off. So it's up to you.

DORIS: (To Thomas.) He's colossal! It's up to us! We can't make 'er appear by wavin' a magic wand. O' course, there's still Thérèse an' me . . .

MADELEINE: Dory, be quiet, please.

WINNOCK: (To Doris.) Genius idea, but not with him, with me!

DORIS: Are you completely freaked or what?

THOMAS: (Pause.) Fine, well I'm going to wait in my car. If she shows up, you can send her to me. (He leaves.)

SCENE 5

RICHARD: In that case, maybe I won't stay either.

THÉRÈSE: You can just stay with me for the day, Richard. You're my beau, marriage or not.

M. SAMSON: (Pause.) He ain't takin' it real good, the young doc.

WINNOCK: (To Samson.) Geez, just think about it! How d'ya 'spect the dude ta stay cool? His bride ain't showin' up, it's sort o' shitty, ya know what I mean? Put yerself in his place.

DORIS: I'm startin' ta like my sister, ya know.

THÉRÈSE: Sure, that's you; my students are exactly the same. One little thing goes wrong and they're hysterically happy. I don't understand the way you think. (Pause.) God knows I didn't push her into this marriage, but she committed herself . . .

RICHARD: Maybe she changed her mind. Spent the night with her Poppa, talked to him about it . . .

MADELEINE: Monsieur . . . Richard? I'm not sure we need your comments.

THÉRÈSE: Momma, Richard is just giving his opinion.

RICHARD: Sorry.

MADELEINE: No, I'm the one who should be sorry. But this is starting to get to me too.

SCENE 6

THOMAS: (Returning from the outside.) Whose red car is that parked next to mine?

RICHARD: The G.T.V.?

THOMAS: Who knows, the sportscar that's half dented in.

RICHARD: It's mine.

THOMAS: It's yours? Do you know the other day you almost knocked me into a ditch. That's why I thought I recognized you.

RICHARD: Oh yeah? I didn't notice.

THOMAS: You're a public menace, old man. And you're nearly a killer. Thérèse, I don't know if you've been going out for a long time, but if I'd known it was him, I wouldn't have allowed you to invite him.

RICHARD: Hey, accept my apologies. I drive a little fast.

THOMAS: A little fast! You very obviously tried to run me down! Maybe you don't remember, but I sure do.

RICHARD: I offered my apologies.

THOMAS: I don't give a shit about your apologies. I ought to punch you in the mouth.

M. SAMSON: (*Stepping in.*) Hold on now; c'mon, Richard! Take it easy.

WINNOCK: (*Separating Thomas and Richard who are about to fight.*) Okay you dudes, ferget the rumble, you'll get all junked up. Yer too nice an' clean now.

DORIS: Winn, leave it alone.

THÉRÈSE: Richard, please, everybody's a little touchy. What can you expect?

MADELEINE: Don't forget you're a gentleman, Thomas.

THOMAS: A gentleman who would really enjoy bashing this jerk's head in.

DORIS: Hey, here comes Poppa an' Maud.

SCENE 7

(*Humbert enters followed by Maud. Each one is carrying an enormous canvas. Humbert is wearing the same clothes as in Acts I and II. They are considerably dirtier, however, from the two weeks spent in the blockhouse. Maud is wearing her wedding gown which is torn in several places and spotted with mud and vomit.*)

HUMBERT: You mean you started the opening without us? Come on Maud, I'll buy you a drink!

THOMAS: Maud, do you have any idea?

MAUD: Of what? I helped Poppa hang his show, but we didn't finish on time.

THOMAS: Have you seen the state you're in?

MAUD: You mean my dress? I'll go change it.

THOMAS: Change it?

MAUD: I'll wear my beige silk suit. It'll be just as good.

THOMAS: Just as good? Do you know what my parents spent for that dress? All that so you can get married looking like a bag lady?

THÉRÈSE: A bag lady! I gave her that outfit. And it's very cute. Isn't it, Momma?

MAUD: Anyhow, you think this one s indecent.

RICHARD: It is!

MAUD: Richard, dear, nobody asked you.

RICHARD: Not again!

THÉRÈSE: Yeah! What do you have against him?

MAUD: You can just shut up! You're already stealing other people's things, enough's enough . . .

THÉRÈSE: What did you say? I didn't take a thing from you.

MAUD: I said what I said. Okay, I'll go change and then we're off. Oh, by the way, I decided that Poppa should come too.

HUMBERT: No, Maud. I'm going to wait for the newspapermen and the gallery owners. I have to. They should be here by two o'clock.

MAUD: Can't you at least come to the Mayor's Office?

MADELEINE: Maud, if he comes, I'm staying here!

MAUD: Momma, Poppa is a very nice guy. Maybe he's even a genius. You'll both come and that's that.

THOMAS: Are you screwing up everything on purpose? Is this amusing you? Honey, listen.

MAUD: Don't scream!! My head feels like somebody's beating on it. When you yell, it throbs.

THÉRÈSE: Maud, you're doing anything you feel like and saying even worse. And I'm warning you . . .

MAUD: Thérèse darling, big sister, take care of your revolving mystery guest and don't be such a ballbuster. Right Richard? Balls!

HUMBERT: Madeleine, don't you have anything to say about what I'm doing?

MADELEINE: What do you want me to say? I don't understand any of this.

HUMBERT: You don't understand!

MAUD: But it's so simple . . . It's Poppa's first major show.

DORIS: Here? That's nuts!

HUMBERT: (To Thomas.) You're my son-in-law, right?

THOMAS: Shit Maud, do something!

MAUD: I tried . . . my silk suit. But you didn't like it. Tough. Guess I'll go like I am.

THOMAS: But you look like you've just been raped by an army of Cossacks!

MAUD: Hey, if you're ashamed of your wife! . . .

WINNOCK: (To everyone.) Is this marriage gonna happen or not? Cuz if not, Dory an' me're clearin' out. There's a great gig in Belgium an' if we get a move on we're there fer the blast off.

MAUD: Ask him. I'm ready. He's the one . . .

THOMAS: Stop it Maud. Stop it right now or I'll stop you. (He chases and tries to catch her.)

HUMBERT: Watch out for my paintings!

DORIS: S.O.S. Battered Women!

MAUD: Let go of me! Let go of me! Richard!

M. SAMSON: Keep yer cool, Thomas!

DORIS: Mom, I told ya he's the violent type.

THOMAS: Richard? Why Richard? Why're you calling him?

MAUD: Because . . . he's my lover! There! Are you satisfied?

HUMBERT: It's him? (To Richard.) It's you?

THOMAS: You mean everybody knows about it?

RICHARD: Hey now, she's just runnin' off at the mouth. Can't ya see that?

THÉRÈSE: (To Maud and Richard.) Tell the truth.

THOMAS: For how long?

MAUD: Six months, since the day after you announced our wedding to your parents.

THOMAS: That's why he nearly killed me the other day.

MADELEINE: (*To Maud and Thomas.*) Maybe you need to talk about this alone?

THOMAS: Uh uh. We're going to settle it now. (*To Maud.*) Why did you do it?

MAUD: Because I liked him.

THOMAS: And I suppose he's your sister's lover, and Doris's, and you mother's, too, huh?

THÉRÈSE: Richard and I, well we're together, but I didn't know. I swear. You're a miserable rotten creep Richard!!

RICHARD: Jesus, gimme a break, huh! Ya both came lookin' for it. Anyhow, I'm splittin' for the Pacific Ocean next Thursday. (*To Thomas.*) So you can have your little wifey back an' everythin's A-O.K. that way.

MAUD: Coward!

RICHARD: If it makes ya happy . . . Well, I'm gettin' out o' here.

MAUD: Richard!!

THOMAS: What do you want from him?

MAUD: It's none of your business.

THÉRÈSE: Maud, please, can't you try to fix things up instead of making it worse?

THOMAS: Richard, you're wanted.

RICHARD: They gimme a pain with all this back an' forth business. I'm leavin'.

THOMAS: Wait just a minute there, old man. We're gonna get to the bottom of this.

RICHARD: Drop it, will ya!

THOMAS: You see the frigging mess you've made? You aren't just going to walk away whistling with your hands in your pockets. (*Thomas goes for Richard, threatening him with his fists. Richard reaches into his pocket.*)

M. SAMSON: Watch out fer that pocket!

THOMAS: I oughta fix that pretty face of yours.

RICHARD: Try it.

MAUD: Richard, don't provoke him.

THOMAS: Are you afraid for him? Think I'll hurt him on you?

RICHARD: Cut it out, I'm tellin' ya. (*He pulls the switchblade out of his pocket and springs the blade.*)

WINNOCK: Holy fuck, looka that!

HUMBERT: (*To Richard.*) You can't do that. It's not fair.

MADELEINE: What *is* this foolishness?

WINNOCK: Doris, whose side am I on?

DORIS: If ya get mixed up in this, ya never see me again.

MADELEINE: (*Breaking them up.*) It's not bad enough as it is, you have to find a way to kill each other while you're at it. You're grotesque. Both of you. A couple of mangy dogs fighting over a brainless female in heat.

THOMAS: Isn't she your daughter?

MADELEINE: That's exactly why I know what I'm talking about.

HUMBERT: She's mine, too.

MADELEINE: Shut up Humbert!

RICHARD: You givin' up, quack?

MADELEINE: Drop that knife!

THOMAS: I'm waiting for you. (*Thomas grabs an old muffler or a drive shaft and brandishes it as though it were a sledgehammer.*)

MAUD: Thomas!

THOMAS: Would you rather he kill me? (*To Richard.*) Come on, now, come over here, c'mon and let me mash your pretty face into a pulp.

THÉRÈSE: My God Thomas, remember you're a doctor. (*Suddenly Tut-Tut throws himself on Richard and clutching onto him, he empties a bottle of kerosene all over his clothes.*)

RICHARD: The shithead, it's . . . it's gasoline.

M. SAMSON: Nope, it's kerosene. Think he intends ta set fire ta ya.

RICHARD: For Christ's sake, stop him!

TUT-TUT: Bic bic, psstt! (*Samson gives Tut-Tut a box of matches. He tries awkwardly to light one over Richard's head.*)

MADELEINE: (*Taking the matches from Tut-Tut's hands, she slaps him. Then she takes a flip-top lighter and lights it.*) That's enough now. Samson, grab him. (*Samson pins Richard. Humbert picks up his knife.*) I'll be the one to set you on fire if you don't stop. And we'll say it was an accident. Maud, you decide right now: marriage or no marriage. The joke has gone on long enough.

MAUD: I'm still game.

MADELEINE: First point! (*Threatening Richard with the lighter.*) Richard, you don't intend to oppose it?

RICHARD: It's not my fuckin' problem.

MAUD: That's why you tried to turn me on last night?

THOMAS: After I left?

RICHARD: As per usual. (*To Thomas.*) We always did it after ya left. (*To Samson.*) This stuff stinks! (*To Thomas.*) More excitin' for her, I guess.

MADELEINE: Don't start that again! If everybody's in agreement on this wedding, then let's get it over with. Richard, the best thing would be for you to disappear and never show up again.

THÉRÈSE: If Richard doesn't go to the wedding, it'll take place without me. Maud you can go find yourself another witness.

THOMAS: It won't be necessary, because I won't be there either. And let me tell you I consider this entirely Maud's fault. You can keep the ring! On second thought, no you can't. I want it back. I've been made a fool of enough as it is.

MAUD: But listen, I still want to.

THOMAS: You! You're going to . . .

MAUD: Hit me! Go ahead! Here. (*She holds out her hand with the ring on it. Thomas removes it from her finger with difficulty.*)

MADELEINE: Under these conditions, Thomas, you should leave right now. Afterwards, we'll let Richard go.

THOMAS: That's fine, just fine. Why don't you fix up their bed too? Maud, I have nothing to say to you except that I'm more undone by this than you could ever imagine. I . . . I loved you. It's stupid, but that's the way it is. I thought that happiness was possible, that it existed for us and that . . . You know, everyone was ready to adopt you, to adore you. Everyone was waiting for you, as if you were a queen. Oh . . . shit! . . . (*He sobs.*) You had to ruin everything. Keep it! Keep the ring. It makes me sick now. (*He throws the ring at Maud's feet. Tut-Tut picks it up and puts it on.*)

TUT-TUT: Trezure ta blockhouse!

MADELEINE: Samson, help him to his car.

THOMAS: If you knew how much this was going to hurt my parents . . .

MAUD: (*Obstinately, her eyes lowered.*) Thomas, I still want to . . .

RICHARD: After all the stuff you blabbed to me about him?

MAUD: But Richard, I mean Thomas, you can't believe . . .

THÉRÈSE: There're certain slips of the tongue you really shouldn't make.

M. SAMSON: (*To Thomas.*) It's better if ya don't hang around here. C'mon.

THOMAS: How did you ever manage to survive in such a nuthouse?

M. SAMSON: Gotta understand, ya poor kid, it ain't always so easy fer them, either.

SCENE 8

RICHARD: Can I have my blade back?

WINNOCK: It's only natural ta give it ta him.

HUMBERT: What isn't natural is pulling it out at the slightest provocation.

THÉRÈSE: Come off it! Richard isn't a killer. It was Thomas who got hostile.

HUMBERT: For civilized people, there are rules usually, when you fight.

WINNOCK: (*To Humbert.*) Hey now partner, war is war.

DORIS: Jerk!

WINNOCK: (*To Doris.*) Bug off!

RICHARD: Okay. Well, can I leave now?

SCENE 9

M. SAMSON: (*Entering from the outside.*) The way is clear.

THÉRÈSE: Richard, take me into town, that is, if my sister doesn't object.

RICHARD: I don't feel like it. Maud, I'm leavin' Thursday at the earliest. Ya can call me; I'm not movin' from my place.

M. SAMSON: I see he's found his cool, old buddy Richard.

MAUD: I don't know, Richard.

RICHARD: Do what ya want. But I could put off my trip some. I mean . . .

MAUD: Richard, I don't know.

THÉRÈSE: The boy is incredibly tactful and sensitive.

MAUD: Nobody asked you to throw yourself at him.

THÉRÈSE: He's irresistible, what do you expect? And then, in bed, he's really something else, at least with me!

DORIS: (To Thérèse and Maud.) Okay over there in the big girls' dorm, truce! I fuck, too, but I don't make a recordin' o' it. Huh, Mom?

THÉRÈSE: All I mean is, I can't believe she can find fault with me, in her situation.

MAUD: My situation is just fine, thanks!

M. SAMSON: Hey old buddy Richard an' young pal biker, let's get some air! These people need ta be left alone fer a bit. Guess I'm really doin' the mop up squad today, ain't I?

WINNOCK: Okay, sure, Doris?

DORIS: I'm stayin' here.

WINNOCK: Oh shit!

DORIS: Maybe tomorrow, later, I dunno . . .

M. SAMSON: Closin' time!

WINNOCK: Good-bye everybody, see ya! Okay fer tomorrow, Dory?

RICHARD: Maud, did ya hear what I said?

THÉRÈSE: Of course.

RICHARD: (To Humbert who gives him back his knife.) I don't understand anything about your paintin's, but they aren't bad. (He exits.)

HUMBERT: (To himself.) They aren't meant to be understood.

MADELEINE: Samson, don't come tomorrow. I'm closing. Keep the Peugeot. It's barely enough to cover what I owe you.

M. SAMSON: I'll think about it. You keep it for now. (To the audience.) Well, looks like I don't get the last word. Hard on a big mouth like me. I spent the rest o' the day bent over a pinball machine, dressed ta the fuckin' nines. I must 'a looked like a class A fool! But that's another story! . . . (He exits.)

MADELEINE: Don't feel obliged to stay, Humbert.

HUMBERT: Of course I do! I sent out 400 invitations to my opening!

DORIS: Lousy timin'!

HUMBERT: How was I supposed to know . . .

MADELEINE: You girls agree with this?

THÉRÈSE: He'll finally understand when nobody shows up.

MAUD: You know, Momma, he told me about the letters last night.

MADELEINE: Why are you telling me now?

MAUD: Maybe I seem to be out of control.

MADELEINE: You're not the only one.

THÉRÈSE: What letters?

MADELEINE: Just some letters . . .

MAUD: From her lover; Poppa found them. He says that's why he left.

DORIS: Is that true, Pop?

HUMBERT: No, I made it up.

THÉRÈSE: Momma?

MADELEINE: You heard what he said.

HUMBERT: I even had somebody else write some of them so it'd seem more true. (*We hear a plane take off.*)

MAUD: Gee, guess the controller's strike really is over. (*Pause.*)

MADELEINE: I think I've found a buyer for this place. It'd be best to split the profits between the five of us and then everyone can go their own way and take care of themselves.

HUMBERT: But what if the show's a success?

THÉRÈSE: Poppa, you never even had one customer. You're not going to see hoards today. (*Pause.*)

HUMBERT: What about that bum who's leaving for Tahiti? Huh? . . . I almost ran off to Reunion Island myself. If I had, I would've stayed and I'd have died there without seeing you again. Yep, that could've happened . . . (*Pause.*)

DORIS: (*To Humbert.*) Is yer cancer fer real?

MAUD: I'm going to bed. I'm pooped. Momma, wake me up.

MADELEINE: Sorry, I'm going to town. I won't be back till late. I'm going to the movies and after that I'm having dinner at Trottier's. I haven't done anything like that in ten years.

DORIS: Will ya take me with ya?

MADELEINE: I'll give you a lift into the city; but after that I want to be left alone. (*She exits followed by Doris.*)

THÉRÈSE: Maud, don't you want to talk?

MAUD: I'm too sleepy. (*She walks off into the flat.*)

THÉRÈSE: Well, I'm going to take a week off before the final student evaluations! I'll go to the union's chalet in the Pyrenees. Can't look at another kid!

HUMBERT: What about yours?

THÉRÈSE: He manages just fine with you. (*She takes her shoes off and approaches the edge of the woods.*) I really never do go in there, in the woods, I mean.

HUMBERT: Wait up! I'll go with you.

THÉRÈSE: If you want to. But what about your show?

HUMBERT: I'll pick up everything tonight. (*He disappears into the woods behind Thérèse.*)

TUT-TUT: (*Alone onstage, stretched out on the ground staring at his ring, then standing up and looking at the audience.*) The 'nd. . . !

END

Exiles

Enzo Cormann

EXILES
Théâtre Bastille (France)

First you will be in darkness.
Your hands will snap a woman's fragile neck.
Your ears will strain to hear the cartilage popping.
Your legs will try to absorb the final convulsions
of her young body struggling in its last great effort.
Then the light will come slowly in.
Suddenly you'll release her and let her slide to the floor.
You will be gasping for breath and sweating, your whole body
will be trembling.
You will remain motionless a long time, staring at her, and then
as if coming to a sudden decision, you will relax and stretch
the way you do after making love, enjoying the air that your mouth
will draw in hungrily and the light touch of your right hand
through your hair.
You'll be unable to say how much time has passed
when you turn to her once again and speak:

I won't wait any longer.

Sitting here like a lump.

I heard the screech of car tires, you must have, too; just as you must have imagined that a dog barely escaped being hit, or a cat.

A long time ago, several months at the most, I don't really know how long it was, one minute or one life, like these landscapes in the distance that tremble in the hot air. . . . What was I saying?

There is always a man, lost, in the city, who talks and talks and gets himself worked up, an empty bottle. I've often been that man, like now. Stop that. Oh yes, I'd wanted to get to know you for some time. I had said, Why not invite that girl from the publisher's to dinner? Go dancing, too, perhaps?

I contemplated it a long time, stuck here on the edge of Paris, really the EDGE, so foreign to the Paris we imagined those opium evenings, dancing at a little bar on the Kantstrasse, whispers in the hollow of a tiny ear, everything coated with the smell of woman. . . .

Did that car stop after all? I think I heard a woman scream. Perhaps the police got involved.

You came to our rendezvous.

You said, Strange for a writer, you don't have any books.

I said, This is where I sleep, here inside these four bare walls. Books would die of boredom in this rat hole. I can survive without them. Here I only wait.

—Wait for what? you asked.

—For tomorrow, I said. Or for you to come. Or for some money from a book. For illness or triumph. For the rope to break and I plunge into the ravine. You looked at me without understanding, and yet, with some tenderness, it seemed to me. You asked me to tell you about it.

They burned the Reichstag, Goebbels was named, we were all deprived of our German citizenship: Toller, Feuchtwanger, Heinrich Mann, Tucholsky and so many others. And little Carl Sturm, too, with his habit of stammering out vague reminiscences for your benefit, here inside these four bare walls, furnished with all these tottering things. The Man who BECAME Carl Sturm. Who is not Carl Sturm except when he writes his prose poems of fabulously antediluvian inspiration that have instantly made him famous throughout Europe. As you can see, I said, I am a conceited bastard.

The woman has stopped screaming outside. No one wants to listen to her anyway. Strange, the way these pimples seem to fester as if the air were corroding them. The atmosphere is so acidic here. Paris is a cruel city, or hypocritical, in any case. All these smiles frighten me, the exquisite kindness of these people makes me nauseous. No blood, though, you see, just a bit of fluid, never any pus. You don't seem disgusted. Have I always had this type of problem?

Carl Sturm, 107 Unter den Linden. They say Berlin is a whore and a drug addict. Sturm, Sturm, what a stupid name. As to why I chose it for a pseudonym. . . . There is reason among idiots and little Carl Sturm does the best he can with his time on earth.

This blue that you see is for "Night" and the red says "Club." I'm so lucky to have this little neon sign in front of my window, don't you agree?

All night long blue-red, and blue, and red, blueredbluered. I have the whole night long to imagine the thighs gripped by sticky hands beneath the bar, the bar-girls with the suckers they've picked up. Oh, they all know their roles by heart. A little urine, no doubt, in the corners. Sometimes the thick laughter of the men penetrates my dreams as they leave—rarely a girl at their side—

although it seems there's a hidden door that allows a profitable traffic in drunken meat.

The boss is a strange woman. She whistles German tunes and scratches her asshole with distinction. The girls arrive at the club about 6 p.m., usually in pairs. They hop out of the taxi, half-dressed in terribly suggestive clothes that you'd love to rip apart just as a sort of joke. My poor Sturm, who told you they would laugh at that? Maybe I could insert a little nostalgia in their lives and they could keep it nice and warm inside their erudite cunts.

Does Carl Sturm want a virgin woman now? Something exotic and under age? Completely hairless? Why do I have this recurring memory of sodomizing that pretty whore on the Wilhelmstrasse? The one who spit into her hands? But it wasn't all that easy, though, was it Carl? Was it? WAS IT?

During the entire meal in that restaurant on the Right Bank, we spoke of publishing and journalism. Not a word about politics. Such scrupulous behavior got on my nerves. I was thinking: I must have money. Even a lot of money. But how much was one of those lousy poems worth? Or ten of them? Not a thing, poor Carl, your words are like failed suicide attempts. Who'd want any part of your Germanic blues? Sturm is so afraid of the simplicity of things, isn't that it? And these four bare walls that have plunged Carl Sturm into waiting—they have something to do with it. Something, yes. But what? So you suggested that we go somewhere and have a drink.

—I have some schnapps at my place, I said. If that tempts you. . . . You look-ed at me and said nothing.

—The schnapps, I said, is excellent. The room, on the other hand, is squalid.

—That doesn't frighten me, you said. In the taxi you took my hand. Why are you trembling? you asked.

In the grimy rear view mirror, the driver snickered in silence.

(*You show her into the room, she enters, then takes off her coat.*)

SHE: Strange for a writer. You don't have any books.
YOU: (*Serving the schnapps.*) I don't really like to read. And I don't really like books, either, as objects.
SHE: That's hard to believe.
YOU: I want to matter to you. To believe someone is to forget that he exists. Everywhere truth shields us from the real. I think you should leave.
SHE: Am I in danger?
YOU: Isn't that what you're looking for here, with me? Danger?
SHE: Tell me more.
YOU: Carl Sturm went down by the river. He imagines he will find peace there, the winged rhythm of writing. Making his way, he comes upon a multitude of people. The daily tasks they must fulfill have enslaved them. And Carl

Sturm envies them for having some faith to profess. And then there he is, seated on the stone of the quai, his feet dangling. The water, he thinks, is so green and so black. So deep.

But finally he calls upon "BLUE," since water must be so.

Then his eyes stare tirelessly at the orange peel disfiguring the undulating surface of the river's skin.

Or rather: mottled with wisps of silver-gray, he thinks, like the wind in Chinese paintings.

But no, instead: worried night, the mouth shut, an old man masticating. And the odor too, that smells good only alongside the river where the rocks grow woolly emerald hair, their oily locks eternally stroked by some invisible comb.

Did Carl Sturm see that, really?

SHE: (*After emptying her glass and staring at the bottle, then at the door.*) Go on.

YOU: Around four o'clock I look up when I hear the sound of a big barge laden with fuel or grain. I read the name in faded white letters. *Mallarmé* was its magic name. WHY? I shout. HEY! WHY! A little girl waves to me from the deck. In one hand she hugs her rag doll. The *Mallarmé* pulls away. Every verse since reminds me of that barge. Although it drifted past, it seemed not to be moving at all, its journey seemed to weigh upon it so.

SHE: And then? What else? I'll have some more of your schnapps, Carl Sturm.

YOU: I'm walking now.

A man adjusts the patch over his left eye. A prostitute is scolding her pet poodle. A cop yells at me to wait before I cross. A PAINTER IS PAINTING, do you understand? I burst out laughing, I say to myself, Oh my God, a painter is painting, a car passes by, and the sun is shining, hahahaha!

And the farce continues: a drunk approaches me. Two teenagers are smoking a cigarette on a bench covered with pigeon shit. A priest slaps a small girl. Two old men, standing in the middle of a crosswalk, kiss each other passionately on the mouth. The heat pins us all to the street, drools its diluted urine on us, a billion oppressive drops.

My head turns a bit, I feel buildings and trees, trucks and pedestrians unfold before me like I'm walking inside a small child's cardboard city.

And the whole of Carl Sturm's city is a sort of fold-up toy sold to God knows who in a little gift bag/   /on the back of the little game are the operating instructions I/   /I scrape the walls and groan/   /my nails crack my fingers wrench and twist/   /grinding into the rock/   /a bit of blood on the corner of a cement/   /block I bash/   /my head against an old iron/   /then I then I/   /then I

SHE: Take it easy.

YOU: . . . . I beg the toy city to leave me in peace. I toss a coin away somewhere, a ticket, a cigarette. I crawl the length of a sidewalk that reminds me of the river with its gentle lapping of leather shoes, and its WHAT'S THE MAT-

TER WITH HIM/LEAVE HIM ALONE.

I hear the voices and their threats that are really offers of help camouflaged in shouts and I explain sobbing to all the hands reaching for my head that I'm too hot too hot too hot!

The crowd parts, people growl and push each other, a man says LET HIM BREATHE YOU'RE GOING TO KILL HIM!

A glimmer of light precedes a kind of night filled with sounds of day.

Several flashes, a few near heart-attacks, a horrid little film drills through my skull. And in it we see that Carl Sturm's city is the city of dirty granite abutments, of bare mounds or moorings along the quai, a city of closed-down factories with shattered windows, a city of walled houses, of propped-up facades, of gutted buildings, of diseased neighborhoods, of waste land, of hairless dogs, muddy scrap heaps, smoking dumps, a city of rust and fault and age, that, yes that is the city of Carl Sturm.

SHE: Your eyes are like weapons, your words are like triggers.

YOU: Some more schnapps?

SHE: Yes, I want to get drunk. Did you die?

YOU: There is no hand to hold in a hospital. Just eyes that stare at you. And Carl Sturm counts the seconds that separate him from those eyes. But now words must be his weapon.

I remember the image he presented of himself then: unshaven, bruised, his face haggard, his jaw scarred.

He asks for a mirror, the nurse finds one somewhere. He looks at the face they offer to him, and begins to have doubts about the pink skin and the short hair too well-combed. This chubby somewhat flaccid thing stares smiling back at him and Carl Sturm asks it: Who are you?

—The nurse, answers the nurse. And Carl Sturm goes back to sleep.

In the middle of the night I am awakened by the light from a burning torch. A voice whispers to me: "Was machst du denn da, Carl?"*

The speaker moves, torch and shadow. A creaking sound, a man coughs. Will it speak again?

—Glaubst du nicht, Carl, das es zeit würde wieder zu die verschwundenen kameraden zu kommen?

—Kameraden?

—Ya. Deinen kameraden, Carl. Bist du nich auch ein verräter, Carl?

—Verräter?

Do you understand German?

SHE: "Verräter" means traitor. What "comrades" was he talking about?

ME: That's what I couldn't understand. Then the floor creaked. This time I hear the metal sound of a gun breech. A hand grabs me by the hair and shoves the gun barrel into my mouth. I see it for an instant in the light of the torch. Was there one man, or two, or three? "Warum nicht leufen, Carl?" another voice says to me.

---

*German in the original.

SHE: Why didn't you run?

ME: And then another: "Warum nich zu hilfe rufen?" I will! Yes! HELP! HELP! A hand grabs my shoulder and shakes me. I must have been dreaming, Madame, forgive me. You screamed, she says, what happened? The nurse doesn't understand German. It's my Berlin accent, I say to get rid of her, you'll pardon me.

The next day I return to these four bare walls.

And while shaving, Carl Sturm looks with disapproval at his own expression. Why this collapse, this illness? And the dream? Nothing, I say to myself. Nothing happened. That's when I telephoned you.

SHE: (*Pouring herself a full glass of alcohol.*) I was waiting for your call.

YOU: Impossible. We only met once, at the publisher's.

SHE: There was this poem of yours, *Exile*, on my table. Do you remember the first line?

YOU: "Your hands will snap a woman's fragile neck." I don't understand.

SHE: (*She downs the whole drink.*) A simple question of self-composure, *mon petit Carl*. A little schnapps. Tell me about a woman you loved.

YOU: I had a friend in Berlin.

SHE: What was his name?

YOU: Hermann. What difference does it make?

SHE: Go on.

YOU: His wife was very beautiful. For a whole year she was secretly my mistress.

I still think of her little round breasts that she loved me to kiss while I foraged around in her cunt. I had this epileptic look, she said, that love had plastered on my face.

I remember a piece of pink skin between two fields of gray silk when I got up under her long skirts, this quirk that she had of taking several distracted puffs from my cigarettes, the glimmer in her eye when she opened the door for me the nights Hermann was away, her make-believe perversity, her way of saying *mensch*, her clumsy fingers, how could any of that be forgotten? And yet.

SHE: And yet?

YOU: Carl Sturm is a man running from something. Don't you see? Hermann is after me, his blurred face screaming, VERRÄTER! VERRÄTER!

Stop drinking, you won't understand anything! . . .

Some days I suddenly run to the window suffocating, and have to beg for air. I'm bent double from the pain in my left side. My cramped fingers grope for the pulse in my neck, cling desperately to the rhythmic pumping of my life. A piece of flesh battling through the great crusade of life, you must be joking!

Meat, meat, just chunks of meat. All the rest is decoration.

SHE: What was her name?

YOU: Annah. GOOD GOD, WHAT DIFFERENCE DOES IT MAKE?

SHE: Go on.

YOU: They were both known as troublemakers. They were deported. Now Carl Sturm can only imagine forever all he has left behind in his irascible Berlin, at the corner of a little alleyway, on the front steps of a building, in a late-night café. A gathering of artists, the cover of a literary revue, a little art gallery. . . . We wrote with a paradoxical feeling of calmness then, which the acceleration of history soon drained out of us. We said to ourselves: so many beautiful things, still unthought of! And then all the most horrible things befell us. But we had known all that would happen, our literature was crammed with it. And Carl Sturm, too, spoke of THE APPROACHING APOCALYPSE in his little poems! And so? Who are the words we love? Who are the verbs that think? Who are all these things that we didn't take literally? And was the morbid complacency that we tortured ourselves with endowed only with conscience? All of this, I must say, seemed to Carl Sturm just a tiny bit romantic.

SHE: As if you weren't you. As if you yourself were all your books. Or the only soul of all your books.

Touch me, Carl Sturm. Put your hands on me, here.

YOU: You're right. I am a book, a dead tree. I'm full of dead trees. An artifact, an *assemblage*. Just a few words! A contagious disease. Yes. Yes.

SHE: I've finished your schnapps. What are you looking at?

YOU: Mama is seated there, smiling at me. I return a smile to her tired body. I tell myself that a miracle will surely occur. And then she gets up, very slowly, and puts her hand to her mouth as if to stifle an embarrassing sound. A look of sharp pain contorts her face and she falls to the floor before I can say anything, or do anything.

The day after her death, I composed my first poem. I wrote one each day for an entire year, following thus the schedule I foolishly set for myself. When I finished the 365th, I was surprised to discover that I had written a book. Five years have slipped by since. And five books. And her face now seems blank. A simple virgin space left to color in according to the day's mood.

Why didn't I keep all those poems? Each book contained only twenty or thirty. Hardly more than a hundred in all. One thousand five hundred days have been wiped off some map—the only one Carl Sturm ever possessed. Five little worn and yellowed books, signed with a strange pseudonym.

And just as you suspect: there will be no reprieve.

SHE: Your eyes are like two drops of blood. Is that how you always look at women?

YOU: Every living woman I call my mother, or Annah.

SHE: What do you want from me?

YOU: Come here.

SHE: You frighten me.

YOU: It's about time.

SHE: I want to go. Leave me alone. I said leave me alone. Let go of me! LET GO
  OF ME!
YOU: DON'T SHOUT! STOP SHOUTING!
. . . .
I remember squeezing a woman's fragile neck.
I remember straining to hear the cartilage popping,
absorbing with my legs the final convulsions
of her young body struggling in its last great effort.
I remember suddenly releasing her, letting her slide to the floor.
I was gasping for breath and sweating, my whole body was trembling.
I remember remaining motionless a long time, staring at her, and then,
as if coming to a sudden decision, relaxing and stretching
the way I do after making love, enjoying the air that my mouth
drew in hungrily, and the light touch of my right hand
through my hair.
I remember that some time passed
before I spoke to her again:

ME: Don't shout. Shouting distorts your face. You're so beautiful, so cruel, so
  distant. I have your photo. I collect them in my head. I take them with the
  eyes of a man-woman who, consuming himself at night, spends the days giving birth. Listen to my song of dead images.
    The first: A tree and flower bed. A child's swing. A sudden surge of the ef-
  fects of heroin four hours after the last fix. Memory of an almost cata-
  strophic dust. Testing a finger up the ass. Eternal regrets. The swing is
  perfectly still. To adjust the focus would condemn Carl Sturm—at least experience leads him to believe so—to vomit his guts all over the flowers. The
  tree doesn't budge despite a gale force wind. A general darkness, then long
  streaks of white. Case closed. And forgotten.
    The second: Cigarette out, the ashtray full. A fat woman's tit upon the
  newspaper, perhaps a photo of Adolph himself. Bitter laughter. The flank of
  a belly, rolls of quivering gelatinous matter. Lack of flame. Teeth eaten away
  by impossible cavities against a somewhat soft brownish prick. Turn to
  chapter entitled "Romantic fantasies." The laughter dies, a cigarette slowly
  burns down. Desire for a piece of raw meat. The ashtray ends up in the
  trash. Cut.
    The third: Sky, clouds, sun. No more sun. Clouds again, and rain. Rain-
  bow, sunset, dusk, the whole deal. Music in cube-form. A wounded bird on
  the beach. Helpless leaps. A long, red stain and tiny cries. A minor flaw on
  the horizon. Hold the pause. The lightning sweep of an army in dress
  uniform. Grosz dedicates a drawing of a general in a whorehouse to me, his
  pants to his knees, cigar between his teeth. I say: "He looks like he's drool-
  ing." And Grosz says: "How did you guess?" Carl Sturm telephones a friend

who suggests he call another. In the last scene we notice a pair of worn nylon stockings on a carpet. Little nocturnal moans heard through walls too thin.

. . .

   At dawn, a white hand upon the floor. This thing, that I'm always strangling but which never dies. Wake up, you'll catch cold lying there on the floor like that. Wake up, the silence frightens me. These four bare walls are watching me. Let her die, then. Or let me die. To strangle her every time, then forget her. Wake up, you rotten piece of schnapps-soaked meat! This thing that returns at dawn to tug at my legs. Always you who wakes me, and always you that I murder. At dawn, a white hand upon the floor. Mama. Mama. Annah. Mama. Mama. Mama. Mama. Mama. Mama. Mama. Mama. Mama. Mama. Mama. . . . . . .
. . . .
. . . .

END

The Workroom

Jean-Claude Grumberg

THE WORKROOM
South Street Theatre (U.S.A.)
Directed by Aaron Levin

CHARACTERS:

Helene
Simone
Gisele
Marie
Madame Laurence
Mimi
Leon
First Presser
Machine Operator
Jean
Max
Boy

(A tailoring workroom in Paris. There are two small tables. The women perch on stools next to the table which is by the window. There is also a cutting table and a third table for the Presser. There are two entrances: one leads off to the stairs; the other leads to Leon's apartment. A small spool table is optional.)

SCENE 1

THE TRY-OUT

(*Very early morning, 1945. Simone sits at the table, working. Standing near another table — Helene, the owner's wife, also works. From time to time she glances at Simone.*)

HELENE: In 1943 they took my sister, as well . . . .

SIMONE: Has she come back?

HELENE: No . . . she was twenty-two. (*Silence.*) You worked for yourself?

SIMONE: Yes, just my husband and me; during the busy season we took on a worker . . . . I had to sell the machine last month; he won't even be able to go back to work . . . . I shouldn't have sold it, but . . . .

HELENE: You can always find a machine . . . .

SIMONE: (*Nods in agreement.*) I shouldn't have sold it . . . . Someone offered me some coal and . . . . (*Silence.*)

HELENE: You have children?

SIMONE: Yes, two boys . . . .

HELENE: How old?

SIMONE: Ten and six . . . .

HELENE: Spaced just about right . . . at least that's what they say . . . I don't have children. (*Gisele enters.*)

SIMONE: They get along very well. The older one takes care of the younger. During the occupation we sent them to the free zone; when they came back the big boy had to explain to the little one who I was. The little one hid behind his big brother, he didn't want to see me; he called me "Madame" . . . .

HELENE: Without children you often wonder what you're here for . . . .

SIMONE: It's not too late . . . . (*Gisele, at the coatrack, takes off her jacket, hangs it up, puts on her smock and takes her place. With a nod, she greets Simone and Madame Helene.*)

HELENE: (*Introduces Simone.*) Madame Gisele . . . Madame Simone; here for finishing work. (*Simone and Gisele nod and smile to each other. Gisele is already at work as Madame Laurence enters, closely followed by Marie. They both greet Madame Helene.*)

MADAME LAURENCE & MARIE: Bounjour Madame Helene. (*They change into smocks. Marie finishes buttoning hers while already beginning her first piece. Madame Laurence takes her time—even takes off her shoes, which she swaps for slippers. Shuffling her feet, she goes to her place at the end of the table facing Simone, with her back to the window on a high stool. Thus, she dominates the situation. Helene, standing in front of her table, bastes the cloth onto the front of the jacket while glancing at the others from time to time. Mimi, coughing, enters hurriedly and is acknowledged by Helene.*)

GISELE: Did you fall out of bed again this morning? (*Mimi, putting on her blouse, gestures as if to say: "Don't talk to me about it."*)

HELENE: (*Introduces her.*) Madame Simone . . . Madame Laurence, Mademoiselle Marie, Mademoiselle Mimi. (*Simone smiles at them.*)

MADAME LAURENCE: (*As soon as Mimi begins to crowd Madame Laurence with her work, Madame Laurence backs her stool away slightly and speaks to her.*) Someday you're going to put my eye out . . . . (*Mimi disregards this and works in silence. Gisele hums mechanically.*)

HELENE: Things are going well today, Madame Gisele!

GISELE: (*Surprised.*) For me? No, why?

HELENE: Since I hear you humming . . . .

GISELE: I'm not humming, Madame Helene; I don't have the heart for it. Especially not these days . . . . (*Marie and Mimi join in on "not these days" and burst out laughing together.*)

MADAME LAURENCE: (*After glancing at Simone's work.*) You did finishing work? (*Simone agrees.*) It shows; you make pretty little stitches . . . . (*The owner, Monsieur Leon, suddenly pops his head inside the door and shouts loudly.*)

LEON: Helene, Helene! (*All the workers are startled; they let out a squeal and then burst into laughter. Helene sighs. Leon can be heard getting annoyed in the other room—perhaps on the telephone. Simone, who had been as startled as everyone else, laughs heartily. Madame Helene goes out and shuts the door behind her. She and her husband can be heard talking as they move away from the closed door.*)

GISELE: We're off to a fine start . . . If he's yelling this early in the morning . . . .

MADAME LAURENCE: There's trouble brewing . . . .

SIMONE: Is he always like that?

MADAME LAURENCE: Monsieur Leon? You haven't seen him yet? We'll let it be a surprise.

MIMI: (*In a very hoarse voice, nearly voiceless.*) He'll hear about this.

MADAME LAURENCE: What?

MIMI: He's going to hear about this.

MADAME LAURENCE: What?!

MIMI: (*Still hoarse; she'll speak this way until the end of the scene.*) I'm going to repeat that to him.

MADAME LAURENCE: (*Taking the others as witnesses.*) That's not fair. She's crazy,
the little slut. What did I say? What did I say? (*Mimi clears her throat without
answering. Marie chokes back laughter. Madame Laurence crushes her with a
glance.*) You find that funny?

MARIE: It's her voice . . . . (*She bursts out laughing. To Mimi.*) It's your voice.

MIMI: (*After coughing furiously.*) This is funny? You don't give a damn about my
sore throat? (*Marie nods her head.*) People's misery has always amused im-
beciles . . . .

MARIE: (*Laughing.*) Thank you.

GISELE: Nowadays you've got to laugh; it's a substitute for meat. (*Mimi coughs.*)

SIMONE: (*Looks in her purse and finds a box of cough drops which she offers.*) They're
good for the throat . . .

MIMI: (*Taking one.*) Thanks . . . . (*Simone offers some to the others, who accept
them.*)

MARIE: (*Reads.*) "Pectoides: candy cough drops, soothe the throat, sweeten and
refresh the breath."

GISELE: (*To Simone.*) You can tell who has children . . . . (*Simone nods in agreement.*) How many?

SIMONE: Two.

GISELE: It's a tough job, isn't it?

MIMI: Why don't you ever offer us candy? You're a mother, aren't you?

GISELE: I don't even give them to my kids; would you like me to buy some ex-
pressly for you?

MIMI: As a matter of fact, I would. You could never offer us anything . . . .
(*Gisele stays quiet.*)

MADAME LAURENCE: (*To Mimi.*) You'd be smart to avoid talking today. Give
your voice a rest for a change . . . . (*Mimi snickers and her voice quavers.*) It's
for your own good, isn't it? Of course if you think that what you have to say
is important . . . . (*Brief silence, she continues.*) Even so, a day of silence would
be a blessing. (*Mimi has a coughing fit; she ends up aiming it at Madame
Laurence, who pulls back slightly and then, dignified.*) Would it trouble you too
much to allow me a little breathing space?

GISELE & MARIE: (*Together.*) My dear . . . .

MIMI: What? What's she talking about? (*Madame Laurence puts down the piece
she's just finished, rises and goes out. Mimi is trying to speak in an undertone.*) The
bathroom brigade is starting earlier than usual; she needs a plumber to cork
that up . . . . (*Her voice gives out, she clears her throat and coughs. Simone takes
out her cough drops but Mimi refuses with a gesture.*)

GISELE: (*To Simone.*) You'd do better to save them for your kids.

MARIE: How did you catch that?

MIMI: (*Shrugging.*) I don't know . . . I went dancing last night; coming out I got soaked.

GISELE: Did it rain last night?

MIMI: (*Shaking her head "no."*) I fell in the gutter. (*Marie bursts out laughing.*) Go ahead and laugh. I was with Huguette, my friend Huguette. . . .

GISELE: The fat one?

MIMI: She's not so fat.

GISELE: Isn't she the one you called the "big cow?"

MIMI: (*Agrees.*) Yes, but that doesn't mean she's fat. She's a slob . . . . Yesterday we went to the dance hall together. I took off my shoes to dance and at the end I couldn't find them again . . . . (*Marie is doubled up with laughter. Simone begins to chuckle also.*)

GISELE: You lost your shoes?

MIMI: Yeah, somebody lifted them . . . .

GISELE: Since when do you have to take off your shoes to dance?

MIMI: To swing—to dance swing. So these two Americans sweetly offered to see us home; one carried me so I wouldn't get my tootsies wet and then I don't know what they were jabbering about, but the next thing I knew one of them asked me something—I didn't understand exactly what, but I nodded my head "yes" and my girlfriend did, too, and without warning the guy drops me smack bang into the gutter. I was soaked to the skin and then Huguette and the two Americans start laughing to beat the band, so we get into this big brawl. (*She clears her throat; it hurts more and more.*) This morning I woke up like this; I couldn't talk at all . . . . (*Gisele, Marie and Simone double up laughing.*)

MADAME LAURENCE: (*Returns to her stool and asks.*) Laughing at me again? (*Gisele, Marie and Simone shake their heads "no," laughing even harder. Madame Laurence addresses Simone, who forces herself to stop laughing out of politeness.*) So you've joined them already. It doesn't matter; I'm used to it. She turns everybody against me. (*Simone can't control herself; she laughs more and more nervously, constantly excusing herself.*)

GISELE: (*To Madame Laurence.*) Nobody said anything about you; not a word . . . .

MIMI: (*To Gisele.*) Quit it . . . it's not nice to lie; especially after what you said . . . (*Simone now has her handkerchief in her hand; she's no longer working, she mops her eyes while continuing to excuse herself at each burst of laughter.*)

MIMI: That's what you get when you don't understand American lingo. Huguette said to me that I shouldn't have nodded "yes."

MARIE: Were they drunk, or what?

GISELE: So you came back all wet and barefooted?

MIMI: (*Who laughs now in turn.*) My skirt stuck to me everywhere . . . It had shrunk; real trash this whore of a fiber . . . . (*They laugh all over again, Simone the most. Little by little, calm returns.*)

GISELE: How can you go dancing like that every night?

MIMI: I don't go every night; I went yesterday . . . .

MARIE: Simone, do you go dancing too? (*Simone shakes her head "no," laughing.*)

GISELE: She said she has children.

MARIE: It's against the law to go dancing when you have children? (*Gisele, irritated, shakes her head.*) You could even go dancing with your husband, right?

SIMONE: (*Simply to cut it short.*) These days I don't go dancing.

GISELE: There!

MARIE: But you used to go?

SIMONE: Yes . . . from time to time . . . .

MARIE: Your husband's the one who doesn't like it?

SIMONE: He's not here; he was deported. (*Brief silence.*)

MIMI: When I think what a skunk that GI was . . . I'll bet *he* was the one who pinched my shoes!

GISELE: Brilliant! All you had to do was not take them off . . . . Honestly I've never —

MIMI: (*Cutting her off.*) *You* go dancing?

GISELE: Sure.

MIMI: No kidding?

GISELE: When I was a girl . . . .

MIMI: *You* were a girl? No kidding!

GISELE: In any case, I never danced with Army trash . . . .

MARIE: Why not, if they're not German?

GISELE: Just because they're not German doesn't mean they're safe . . . . (*She turns toward Simone.*) I'm sorry to have to say it but sometimes the Americans . . . . (*She stops.*)

MIMI: (*After a while.*) C'mon, spit it out, let's have it all.

MADAME LAURENCE: Exactly what is it that you want to say, Madame Gisele?

GISELE: Nothing, nothing.

MADAME LAURENCE: (*Conciliatory.*) You'd rather have the Germans than the Americans?

GISELE: I didn't say that; don't put words in my mouth.

MADAME LAURENCE: (*More and more conciliatory.*) We're only talking about manners of course.

GISELE: When you put it that way I'd say yes, although like everything else there are two sides . . . .

MIMI: You want someone to ask them back; you miss the Krauts? (*She whistles under her breath. Gisele shrugs her shoulders. Silence.*)

MADAME LAURENCE: It's true that as long as the Americans weren't here we prayed for their arrival; now that they're here, we're praying that they go away.

MIMI: Speak for yourself. They don't bother me, except when they snitch my shoes and dump me in the water.

MADAME LAURENCE: I find that they lack a bit of . . . .

MARIE: Was there one who lacked respect for *you*, Madame Laurence? (*Mimi shouts with laughter. Madame Laurence raises her shoulders. The door opens. Helene calls.*)

HELENE: Madame Simone, come here please. (*Simone rises, puts down her work. Helene calls from the door.*) No, no, bring it with you. (*Helene disappears.*)

GISELE: Have you already discussed money? (*Simone shakes her head "no."*) You don't have to let yourself get taken, you know . . . .

MARIE: (*Whispers.*) Watch yourself, his hands are a little bit like a crab's . . . . (*Simone goes out.*)

MADAME LAURENCE: (*To Marie.*) What did you say?

MARIE: When?

MADAME LAURENCE: You said something about crabs?

MARIE: I said he had hands like a crab.

MADAME LAURENCE: (*After a moment.*) I don't understand. (*Marie shrugs. Mimi demonstrates Leon's "pinching."*)

GISELE: He's a good man anyway.

MARIE: (*Irritated.*) That doesn't prevent . . . . (*Silence.*)

MIMI: (*To Marie.*) She's one.

MARIE: What?

MIMI: (*Pointing to Simone's stool.*) She's another one.

MARIE: Another what? (*Mimi makes a gesture outlining a hooked nose.*) You're crazy.

MIMI: Really!

MARIE: I don't believe it . . . .

MIMI: I recognize them. I have the knack; I recognize them. (*Marie shrugs.*)

GISELE: In any case, she's a good person.

MIMI: Oh, la la, as far as she's concerned *everybody's* a good person today . . . .

GISELE: I happen to like her, that's all.

MIMI: I happen to like her, too . . . but that doesn't prevent her from being one . . . .

MADAME LAURENCE: She has an odd laugh! (*Silence.*)

GISELE: The poor thing can't have had much chance to laugh recently. Not with all her troubles.

MIMI: So what? Everybody has troubles; I lost my shoes but I don't make it a—

GISELE: (*To Marie with reproach.*) And you go and ask her if her husband likes to dance?

MARIE: How was I to know?

MADAME LAURENCE: Some things you can sense . . . .

MARIE: (*She finished her piece; she looks around for another. She's angry.*) I don't have any more work!

GISELE: Go look for some.

MARIE: (*Without getting up.*) That's not my job . . . .

GISELE: You prefer to lose a piece rather than move your ass?

MARIE: If I do it this time, I'll always be expected to go get it . . . . But why don't

I have any more work? (*Simone has come back and taken her place again.*)

GISELE: (*Asks her.*) Well?

SIMONE: Everything's fine . . . just fine.

MADAME LAURENCE: Did you get everything straight? (*Simone doesn't understand.*) You got what you wanted?

SIMONE: Yes, the usual, I guess . . . .

GISELE: You'll see, everything will go well; there's work here year 'round.

MARIE: (*More and more irritated.*) There's work *everywhere* these days!

GISELE: Right, there's another reason; here, too.

MIMI: What did you think of our boss—the monkey?

SIMONE: The usual, I guess . . . the usual . . . .

MIMI: Start making bigger stitches if you want to get through quickly, you've got to cut corners a little, otherwise . . . . (*Helene enters.*)

HELENE: (*To Mimi.*) You're always full of good advice, Mademoiselle Mimi.

MIMI: I didn't hear you come in, Madame Helene. You should wear your wooden-soled shoes for work, and save your rubber ones for Sunday.

MARIE: Madame Helene, I've finished my piece and . . . . (*Leon enters; he's very nervous.*)

LEON: (*To Helene.*) So, have you told them?

HELENE: No, I'm getting there . . . .

LEON: So what are you waiting for?

HELENE: (*Sighs.*) I've come to tell them, I'm getting there, all right . . . .

GISELE: What's up, Monsieur Leon?

LEON: She's going to tell you, she's going to tell you . . . . (*He goes out.*)

HELENE: (*Calling him.*) Since you're here already, tell them yourself.

LEON: (*From the other room.*) If I tell you to tell them, I don't want you to tell me "You tell them" . . . .

HELENE: (*Addressing the workers, while busily moving about the workshop.*) We didn't receive the fabric they were supposed to deliver so Monsieur Leon hasn't been able to cut . . . the machine operators are going home. So, in short, finish what you're working on and go home.

MARIE: What? (*Helene is already outside.*) What did she say?

GISELE: Wonderful! Now what do I do to kill the afternoon?

MIMI: You can hurry back home to your dear little man . . . .

GISELE: If you think that's funny . . . .

MARIE: Do you see: he doesn't receive his fabric and we're the ones left in the lurch; he doesn't give a damn if we come for nothing. I travelled all the way across Paris. "Go home!" They're so organized, it's scary . . . .

MADAME LAURENCE: It's all the same to me, mesdames. (*She gets up, puts her scissors in her box and begins to exit. Marie and Mimi go out. Gisele and Simone remain seated; they finish their work in silence.*)

SCENE 2

SONGS

(*A little before noon in 1946. All the workers are present. The Presser is at his ironing table. Gisele has a headache and is choking on a pill.*)

MIMI: What's the matter with you?

GISELE: I've a headache.

SIMONE: It's a long way from the feet. (*Gisele tries to get down her pill. She tries many times.*)

MIMI: Can't you get it down? (*Gisele shakes her head "no" and takes another swallow of water.*) Her hole's too small. (*Marie laughs.*)

GISELE: (*To Marie.*) C'mon . . . do me a favor . . . .

MARIE: A person can't laugh anymore?

GISELE: Not all the time.

MARIE: With you around, it averages out.

GISELE: I'd like to see you take it. (*She goes back to work.*)

MIMI: Just don't think about it anymore . . . .

GISELE: Don't think about the headache that's killing me? . . .

MIMI: Sing us something; that will make you feel better. (*They all insist. Gisele shakes her head "no" without answering.*) Shit, you're a pain.

GISELE: I don't feel like singing.

MIMI: C'mon, love, for my sake.

MADAME LAURENCE: She likes to make us ask.

GISELE: Fine, *you* sing . . . .

MADAME LAURENCE: If I had your gift—

GISELE: Here it comes, the soft soap . . . .

MARIE: (*Singing.*)
I have two great oxen in my stable
(*Speaks.*) Go on . . . . (*She picks it up again.*)
Two great white oxen.

GISELE: If I had two great oxen I wouldn't be here . . . . (*Pause.*) The butchers are going to be closed three days a week . . . .

MADAME LAURENCE: Not for everyone; when it's closed out front, it's open around the back.

MIMI: (*Sings.*)
From the front, from the back
Sadly as always
She's known love.

GISELE: (*While Mimi is singing, Gisele continues.*) It's true that for some people there's always plenty.

MADAME LAURENCE: (*Articulating clearly.*) There's plenty . . . but not for everyone!

GISELE: You wonder how they do it . . . .

MARIE: Ecch! Can't you talk about other things?

GISELE: I'd like to see you manage . . . .

MARIE: Isn't it just as tough for me?

GISELE: You – you haven't any children!

MARIE: So what? Madame Laurence doesn't . . . neither does Mimi.

GISELE: C'mon, it's easy when you're young . . . . (*Brief silence.*) Less bread than in '43!

SIMONE: And their bread isn't good . . . .

GISELE: To say nothing about how hard it is to get . . . .

SIMONE: It wasn't good during the war, either.

GISELE: Yes, but at least there was a war on.

MADAME LAURENCE: What could I cook on Saturday that would be good and filling?

MIMI: Horse balls.

MADAME LAURENCE: For heaven's sake . . . .

MIMI: What's the matter, they're good and they're filling.

MADAME LAURENCE: There will be eight of us; my husband is inviting –

MIMI: (*Cutting her off.*) Then get two pairs. (*Silence.*)

GISELE: It's true you have your husband . . . .

MADAME LAURENCE: What about my husband?

MIMI: Tough to be a policeman, isn't it?

MADAME LAURENCE: He has the same rights as everybody . . . the same rights. (*Gisele is about to say something, holds back, sighs and goes back to her work. Silence. Gisele continues to work, her nose stuck close to the jacket, begins to sing mechanically to herself in a soft voice. Mimi alerts the others and then accompanies her in a grotesque manner. Gisele stops abruptly.*)

MIMI: Well, hon? Gisou? What's up?

GISELE: You think I don't notice when you make fun of me?

MIMI: I was just doing the harmony to make it prettier.

GISELE: Thanks. (*They all insist, but Gisele quietly resists.*)

MIMI: Gisele, everyone's going to turn away so as not to disturb you; even the presser is going to turn away. O.k., presser of my heart, turn your head, right? Don't look at the artist; go on turn around, girls, that's it . . . . (*They all turn around. Mimi continues to look at the presser.*) There, you see, no one is looking at you and I won't add the harmony anymore since you don't like it. (*Silence. They are all turned away. Only Gisele is in her habitual place; she seems absolutely opposed to the idea of singing. The workers continue to work, search gropingly for their scissors or their spools of thread on the table without turning their heads back toward Gisele. Suddenly Gisele starts a very sentimental song, which she sings in a strong voice. Marie, on her chair, resists as long as she can; soon, little-by-little, laughter overcomes Mimi, Madame Laurence, then Simone. But already Gisele has stopped in the middle of a note. She now works in silence with ferocious energy.)*

MIMI: Well, why are you stopping?

GISELE: They're making fun of me . . . .

MIMI: Not at all; they were even moved . . . .

GISELE: She, she, she, she's making fun of me. (*Marie bursts out laughing.*) Because it's not swing, it's not zoot-suit music. (*She sings in a mocking voice.*) There are zoot-suiters in my quarter,

Boum, tra la la tsoin tsoin.

(*Speaks.*) —that's good, that's swell.

MARIE: I didn't say anything to you.

GISELE: As soon as I sing she makes fun of me . . . . You—all you can do is sing your jitterbug crap instead of letting other people sing; it's easy to make fun. (*She imitates another "zoot" song in a nasal voice.*)

MARIE: What's the matter with her?

MIMI: Good question. Gisou, what's wrong, did you eat some horsemeat?

GISELE: Everything is going to pot here because of your kind. You no longer give a damn for anything, you screech like something in the zoo, you jerk up and down, you respect nothing, you don't even know how to work·. . . .

MARIE: (*To Gisele.*) What are you saying?

GISELE: Young girls don't even know how to stitch anymore, that's what I'm saying, and I'm not the only one to say it, believe me . . . .

MARIE: (*Half-risen.*) Shut up, shut up . . . .

GISELE: All right, then, turd, tell me you're not the one who . . . .

MARIE: (*Gets up, throws her piece and shouts.*) Shut up, I tell you, shut up! (*Gisele gets up next. Mimi, Simone and Madame Laurence continue to stitch, all the while trying to hold onto the spools which are rolling about on the table.*)

PRESSER: (*Puts down his iron and tries to joke.*) Fight, murder each other, but whatever you do, don't hurt yourselves . . . .

MARIE: Mind your own business; nobody asked you to butt in . . . . (*The Presser beats a retreat. The sewing machine Operators stick their heads into the door to see what's going on. Gisele gives up first; she drops her work and goes out running past the machine Operators. Marie lets go of the table and sits back down on her stool.*)

OPERATORS: (*They persist.*) Hey—what's going on?

MIMI: (*Rises. Shouts at them.*) Will you leave us alone, you goons? Nobody needs men here. Nobody's broken into your tents to steal your women. It's incredible, just incredible . . . . (*The Operators beat a retreat. Marie suddenly collapses onto the table in tears; she very quickly gets control of herself and soon picks up her work again.*)

MIMI: Beautiful! There's one sniveling in the john and one sniveling here, shit! (*Madame Laurence shakes her head disapprovingly and whistles between her teeth.*) Stop it, that annoys me! (*Madame Laurence continues without noticing. Silence.*)

SIMONE: There are days when nothing goes right. Even the thread keeps breaking . . . .

MIMI: (*Has finished her piece. She doesn't take another one. She rummages in her basket and finds her lunchbox.*) This isn't going to stop my appetite . . . . Very warm, very Parisian, hmm? (*She hands her lunchbox to the Presser.*)

PRESSER: Lifts his iron from the gas plate and puts the lunchpail in its place.) Any more? (*Madame Laurence brings hers.*)

MARIE: (*Throws down her work, gets up and leaves, grumbling.*) I'm going out.

MIMI: (*Mocking.*) Oh well . . . .

MADAME LAURENCE: (*To Simone.*) You're still not bringing anything warm?

SIMONE: I didn't have the time to fix it.

MADAME LAURENCE: You didn't have the heart, I understand.

MIMI: You've got to eat shit . . . otherwise . . . .

MADAME LAURENCE: You've got to eat some meat! (*Mimi and Madame Laurence put their semblance of a table setting on the corner of a table. Having finished her work, Simone takes out a little package from her purse and begins nibbling on it. Madame Laurence speaks to Simone.*) Here, I'm going to give you a taste . . . .

MIMI: Is this a day with or a day without, Madame Laurence?

MADAME LAURENCE: Even when it's without I make it seem like it's with.

MIMI: How?

MADAME LAURENCE: When I make ragout, even if I don't have meat I put in a lot of sage so that later, when it comes back up, it comes back tasting like mutton.

MIMI: And when you fart?

MADAME LAURENCE: (*Primly.*) Please, we're eating . . . . (*Gisele returns.*)

GISELE: (*Sees Marie's empty stool.*) Where's she gone?

MADAME LAURENCE: She's eating out.

GISELLE: You see, some people never deny themselves anything . . . .

MIMI: Gisele! (*She signals to Gisele to button her lip. Gisele shrugs, takes out her lunchbox and brings it to the Presser.*)

PRESSER: So now I've got to do *two* servings?

GISELE: (*She says nothing; she fills an empty glass at the faucet behind the pressing table and carries it to the table, declaring:*) We ought to pool our money and buy some lithine so we could have bubbly water whenever we wanted.

MIMI: Buy, buy if you've got dough to throw away . . . .

GISELE: I'm not one for scrimping when it's a question of health . . . . (*They sit and eat. From the courtyard a man is heard singing "The White Roses." They listen while eating. Gisele opens up the window. Simone remains seated. Mimi and Gisele look up. The song continues through the end of the scene.*)

MAN: (*Sings "The White Roses."*)
He was just a child
A simple Paris kid.

His mother was all that he had.
She was very poor, sad and haunted eyes,
Knocked about by life's cruel troubles.
She loved every flower, roses best of all,
So every Sunday morning
He bought a bouquet of white roses
Instead of a candy or a toy.
First he smiled then he hugged her tight
And he said with his eyes burning bright:

Today is Sunday morning
These are for you, maman
Here are some white roses
For you love them so
And when I am a man
I'll buy all that I can
Hundreds of white roses
All for my dear maman.

But when Spring had come
Cruel destiny Struck down the blonde working girl
She was taken ill and a doctor came
Said she couldn't stay at home.
Breathlessly he ran to his mother's room
With the flowers clutched in his hands
But a nurse in white stopped him and whispered:
"My child, your mother is no more."
Then the boy fell down by the bed
And he shed not a tear as he said:

Today is Sunday morning
These are for you, maman
I brought you white roses
For you love them so
Now that you've gone away
To that garden above
All of these white roses
You'll have them with my love.

MIMI: Shall we give him some buttons?

MADAME LAURENCE: No, no, the poor man . . . .

MIMI: We'll put in twenty sous and some buttons; that'll make more noise . . . .

(Some of the women put on their jackets or drop their work over their shoulders to
protect themselves from the cold. Simone has stopped working. The others are

relaxing; Mimi is smoking. They all suddenly discover—even the Presser—that Simone is gently weeping.)

SCENE 3

NATURAL SELECTION

(The end of an afternoon in 1946. All the women workers are present, but the Presser's table is vacant.)

SIMONE: Yesterday a guy followed me.

MIMI: No? With the face you make when you're out alone . . . .

GISELE: Let her talk.

MIMI: I ran into you the other day and, my God, you scared me; an industrious mouse: one, two, one, two . . . .

SIMONE: You're right. Yesterday I was coming from the Red Cross; I had to leave a photo with them . . . .

MIMI: Of yourself?

SIMONE: No, of my husband. It annoyed me; I don't have many more because of leaving them . . . Anyway . . . as usual I run, I don't look in front of me, I stand in line, it's my turn—hop—I'm outside already and there I bump into this guy.

MARIE: What was he like?

SIMONE: Just a guy . . . . I excused myself, he excused himself, we stammered a bit and I guess I must have smiled at him automatically.

GISELE: Ah la la, never smile . . . never . . . you've got to insult them. . . .

SIMONE: I smiled, that was it, I was stuck, I couldn't get out of it: bla bla bla and bla bla bla . . . .

MARIE: What did he say to you?

SIMONE: How do I know, I wasn't listening . . . .

MADAME LAURENCE: Was he vulgar?

SIMONE: Not really. He talked to me about my eyes . . . more nonsense like that . . . . In the end I didn't dare step out of the metro.

MARIE: Did it happen on the street or in he metro?

SIMONE: I had to take the metro to get home . . . .

GISELE: He followed you into the metro?

MADAME LAURENCE: Some people have nothing to do.

SIMONE: That's just what I said to him: don't you have anything better to do?

GISELE: You talked to him? Ah la la never talk . . . .

SIMONE: Finally I got frightened . . . . I didn't dare get off at my station . . . .

MARIE: Was there a crowd in the metro?

SIMONE: Not many, luckily . . . .

MIMI: And what could he have done to you? A baby in the back through your coat?

SIMONE: You're a good one . . . . I'd like to have seen what *you* would have done—

GISELE: Not a chance—she's the one who collars them on the train and they have to scramble to avoid becoming a father.

MARIE: You can meet nice guys, too. I told everybody that it was at a dance, but it wasn't really true . . . . I met my fiancé on the bus . . . we took the same bus every day . . . . (*To Simone.*) So what happened?

SIMONE: I told a policeman that there's this guy who . . . .

MIMI: And after that it was the cop who scared the shit out of you, right?

MADAME LAURENCE: They're not like that.

MIMI: Oh yeah, pardon me; with a cop I'd have the shakes, but not with some ordinary guy who talked to me about my eyes . . . .

MADAME LAURENCE: They're not like that; they serve the public . . .

MIMI: Sure, tell her that . . . .

GISELE: It's like everything else . . . some cops are good and some are bad . . . .

MIMI: (*Overlapping.*) Yap, yap, yap.

MADAME LAURENCE: (*Agreeing with Gisele.*) Exactly!

SIMONE: In '42 the local police were helpful for the most part. There was one who insisted on carrying my bundle as far as the commissariat.

GISELE: They arrested you?

SIMONE: It wasn't me they wanted, it was my husband. But since he wasn't there they took me instead, along with the kids, to the commissariat, in the basement of City Hall . . . . There, the commissioner—very kind also—looked at my papers and told me to go back home because they were't arresting French citizens; they hadn't received orders for that . . . .

MADAME LAURENCE: Your husband wasn't French? (*Simone shakes her head "no."*)

MIMI: Whew, little chicken, you nearly got your tail-feathers singed.

SIMONE: So I grabbed up my little bundle, my two kids and—only my oldest didn't want to leave like that; he was upset: "Isn't there anyone to carry Mama's package?" He shouted: "They made us come for nothing." I yanked him by the arm, I thought surely I'd pull it off. We ran all the way home . . . . (*She laughs. Everyone laughs.*)

GISELE: (*Wiping her eyes.*) Poor darling . . . .

SIMONE: When we got home, there was something which I couldn't find: a large pocket watch that my husband got from his father and which always sat on the buffet in the kitchen . . . .

MIMI: The one with the hobnailed boots snitched it from you . . . .

SIMONE: That astonished me because they seemed to be the good kind, helpful and all . . . . Not like those who came afterwards and took away my husband; they kicked down the door.

MARIE: Why did they do that?

SIMONE: They knocked, we didn't open, so . . . . The manager said it was up to me to repair the door. I've already repaired it, but you can still see the traces. Apparently that upsets the other tenants . . . . it would be better if he'd re-paint the walls; they're peeling everywhere . . . . (*Silence.*)

MARIE: And the guy?

SIMONE: What guy?

MARIE: The guy, what was he like?

SIMONE: (*Evasive.*) Just a guy . . . .

MARIE: Young?

SIMONE: Average.

MADAME LAURENCE: You should have told him you have children, that you were in a hurry; there's always a way to show them . . . .

SIMONE: That's exactly what I did. I told him that I had two big kids. He says: "I love kids."

GISELE: Shit!

MADAME LAURENCE: Everything depends on the tone of the voice.

SIMONE: What's that supposed to mean?

MADAME LAURENCE: (*Repeats.*) Everything depends on the tone of voice. (*Brief silence.*)

SIMONE: I didn't do anything bad, you understand.

MIMI: Oh, let her talk, it's all piss.

MADAME LAURENCE: It's odd; that never happened to me. (*Mimi starts to laugh.*) Laugh, go ahead and laugh. They sense right away who they're dealing with.

SIMONE: All I did was tell him he was wasting his time. What else could I do?

MADAME LAURENCE: No one is accusing you.

SIMONE: She's finally beginning to get on my nerves . . . .

GISELE: You must never answer them, you must insult them, I mean it . . . insult . . . (*Silence. They work with a great energy now, hurrying to finish the pieces in order to leave. Night has fallen. Aften having finished, they put away their pieces, put away their things, then they change and leave. Helene has come in, and has gone to work during the workers' departure. On the pressing table there is a pile of clothing, unironed. Helene, once the last worker has gone, stops and begins to pace, visibly unhappy. Leon enters and glances at the pressing table.*)

LEON: He didn't come in all day?

HELENE: Who? (*Leon indicates the pressing table. Helene shrugs.*)

LEON: You should tell him to come at regular hours, whether it's in the morn-ing, or in the afternoon. . . . So we can know when we can count on him . . . .

HELENE: Tell him yourself. (*She sits down at her work table.*)

LEON: Why? Why me? (*Silence.*) What does that mean, "Tell him yourself?" (*Silence.*)

HELENE: (*Continuing to work.*) If you have things to tell him, *you* tell him, period, that's all.

LEON: He doesn't iron well, he works badly, I shouldn't have hired him? (*Si-*

lence.)

HELENE: (*With difficulty.*) I can't look at him.

LEON: Don't look at him . . . tell him without looking at him . . . (*Pause.*) All right . . . all right, I'll tell him, I'll tell him. (*He starts out but turns back and continues.*) "I can't look at him." What does that mean? He's a man like any other, yes or no? (*Helene doesn't answer.*) What's the matter with him? What's the matter with him? He's as strong as a Turk; all day long he has a five-kilo iron in his hands, when he's not ironing here, he works the small press at Weill's and I'm sure that he has a third place for the early evening and a fourth for the night . . . . The only thing is: I want him to tell me when he'll be at Weill's and when he'll be here, that's all . . . that's all. I wish I had nothing but workers like him, that's what I wish; of iron, he's of iron, never a word, never a complaint. He knows what it is to work, don't kid yourself, they know—those who've survived the camps. They know—that's called natural selection, madame. (*Helene says nothing, she has stopped working; she goes out abruptly, wiping her eyes. Leon begins to follow her, then stops.*) That's what you get for trying to hold a serious discussion with her. (*He goes out, extinguishing the lights.*)

SCENE 4

THE PARTY

(*In 1947. Late afternoon; everybody is at work. Marie and Gisele, after having looked at the time, get up and prepare for the party.*)

GISELE: (*To those who are still working.*) All right, all right, we're going to stop. (*Then pushing the table against the wall.*) Clear the way, we've got to set up.

MIMI: Is it all right if I finish my piece?

SIMONE: (*Getting up.*) You'll finish it tomorrow.

MIMI: (*Continuing to work furiously.*) Get her! She talks to men on the bus, but it's o.k. for me to lose a piece!

MARIE: (*Laughing and snatching the work from Mimi's hands.*) Come on, stop!

MIMI: You really piss me off; am I the one who's getting married? (*During this time, Madame Laurence has gotten up, taken off her smock and slipped on her coat. The women continue preparing for the party. The Presser sets up a record player.*)

MARIE: (*Fixing her make-up.*) What are you doing, Madame Laurence?

MADAME LAURENCE: I'm going home, dear.

MARIE: You're not staying for—

MADAME LAURENCE: Unfortunately I can't choose the people I work with, but when it's a question of pleasure . . . I value—

MIMI: When it comes to pleasure, she doesn't get to choose very often.

GISELE: (*Combing her hair.*) Come on, Madame Laurence, everybody here likes you a lot.

MADAME LAURENCE: La, la, la, I know what I know.

MARIE: For my sake; it would please me very much.

MADAME LAURENCE: I wish you happiness, my dear, and all that goes with it, but I've finished my day and I've a train to catch.

MIMI: (*Tidying up.*) Let her go then, if madame is too proud to have a drink with us.

SIMONE: (*After having fixed her make-up.*) Madame Laurence, why not take advantage of occasions like this to make peace? . . .

GISELE: It's certainly not a day to make trouble!

MADAME LAURENCE: As long as there are those who talk behind my back! (*She hesitates near the door.*)

GISELE, SIMONE & MARIE: Can you believe it! Go on then! She's imagining things, it's awful.

MIMI: (*To Madame Laurence.*) Was that aimed at me?

SIMONE: Forget it, she wasn't talking about you!

MIMI: Was that aimed at me?

MADAME LAURENCE: If the shoe fits . . . .

MIMI: Believe me, sweetie, it's out of politeness that I talk behind your back.

MADAME LAURENCE: Well, you'd better believe that I don't like it, and since we didn't raise pigs together, I'll ask you not to be so familiar.

MIMI: (*Cutting her off.*) What you've raised or not—

GISELE: C'mon, c'mon, shake hands and let's not talk about it anymore.

MIMI: Me, shake her hand! I should say not. I don't pretend to be something I'm not.

MADAME LAURENCE: Everybody knows what you are.

MIMI: Good, there it is, that's it! You want to know face-to-face what I think of you behind your back?

MADAME LAURENCE: I don't give a damn, believe me. Good night.

MIMI: (*Preventing her from leaving.*) Oh no, oh no! That would be too easy. She sows her shit, she fucks up our party and she expects to leave with her nose in the air? (*She pushes her back to the center of the workroom.*)

MADAME LAURENCE: (*Recoiling, hysterical.*) Don't touch me!

SIMONE: Mimi! Madame Laurence!

MIMI: You want to know what we think? We're fed up with your airs, we're fed up, understand? And something else you'd better get through your thick skull is that you weren't born with that stool up your ass!

MADAME LAURENCE: But what's she saying, what's she saying? Let me go . . . .

MIMI: (*Pursuing.*) While we wreck our eyes all year under a light bulb, madame is next to the window by divine right! No more . . . .

MADAME LAURENCE: It's my place. I've no reason to change it. I won't change it.

MIMI: Tomorrow, it's my little cheeks that will be plopping there. Me, too, I've the right to make eyes at the concierge from time to time, don't I?

MADAME LAURENCE: What? (*Leon enters, distracted. Helene follows him; she is dressed up and made up.*)

LEON: Now what's going on?

MADAME LAURENCE: Monsieur Leon, Monsieur Leon, there it is, it's beginning again.

LEON: What's beginning again?

MADAME LAURENCE: (*Pointing at Mimi.*) She wants to take my place.

MIMI: Why is she stuck to the window; why don't we take turns?

GISELE: One week one, one week another; that's the usual way, isn't it?

MADAME LAURENCE: You see, you see, they're all starting.

LEON: What does it matter — near the window or not near the window, there's a good breeze, right?

MIMI: Exactly, we're afraid she'll get sick.

GISELE: We'd like to be able to breathe too.

MIMI: Monsieur Leon, it's impossible to see anything in your dump of a workroom. We're ruining our eyes, do you know what that's like? And Madame wants to monopolize the window and the sunlight.

LEON: But who's talking about the sunlight; there's never any sun. In five minutes it will probably rain . . . .

MIMI: To get the window open you have to beg her; Madame is cold. And when you want to close it, Madame is having her period, she feels faint . . . shit!

GISELE: And then she takes advantage of it to look outside but she never wants to tell us what she sees. There, I've said it and I'm sorry but . . . .

LEON: (*Opening the window and looking out.*) But there's nothing to see, it's the courtyard, just the courtyard; there's absolutely nothing out there!

MIMI: Exactly; we want to see it ouselves.

LEON: Good, good . . . that's fine, that's fine, I get it; they tell me it's a party, they want me to stop early because Marie is getting married. I say yes, why not! I'm not an animal, I'm civilized. In short, it's the revolution. All right then, if that's the way it is, no more party, everybody sit down, back to work!

MIMI: (*Cuts him off, shouting.*) We want another light fixture; we don't want to ruin our eyes anymore or have any more favoritism here . . . Got that? Good! . . . And we don't want your rotten stools anymore; we want some chairs, do you hear?

MADAME LAURENCE: (*In a low voice.*) Monsieur Leon, they have it in for me because my husband is a civil servant. That's the truth, go ahead and admit it; you're jealous!

SIMONE: But Madame Laurence, no one said anything about your husband.

MADAME LAURENCE: Yes, my husband is a civil servant and I'm proud of it!

MIMI: (*Sings.*)
   From Vichy comes the call: collaborators, one and all.

MADAME LAURENCE: (*Advances toward her, fists clenched.*) Alright then, all right then! (*Brief silence. Mimi turns her back.*)

LEON: Good, are you finished now, are you finished?

MIMI: (*To Gisele.*) Now it's out in the open.

MADAME LAURENCE: You've said plenty of other things which you wouldn't dare repeat.

MIMI: Oh yeah?

LEON: That's enough, now; that's enough!

MARIE: (*On the verge of tears.*) You're wicked. The one time when I'm getting married.

LEON: Well done. That'll teach you to give yourself airs and make a fuss . . . . The result is that we've lost an hour and someone's crying . . . . (*Madame Laurence is taken aside by Helene and Simone.*)

HELENE: Stay; make the little ones happy.

MADAME LAURENCE: No, no, no! They can insult me . . . . (*She makes a gesture of indifference.*) But when they insult my husband, never!

SIMONE: No one said anything about your husband, Madame Laurence; we've never seen the man.

MADAME LAURENCE: That's the last straw. (*In a low voice to both of them.*) He saved some Jews, you know.

HELENE: Of course, of course.

MADAME LAURENCE: And he didn't do it for money like some. Oh no.

SIMONE: Go on, take off your coat; you'll be cold when you go out.

MADAME LAURENCE: (*Lets them take off her coat and continues in a lowered voice.*) He even went to warn them in advance.

HELENE: But who thinks about that anymore, Madame Laurence? Who still thinks about all that?

MADAME LAURENCE: He took risks, he—

LEON: Helene, what about the machine operators, what are they doing?

MIMI: Ah, not the guys; guys aren't allowed in here.

LEON: What about *me* then?

MIMI: You're not a man; you're a monkey. Does Chee-Chee want a banana?

LEON: (*Like a monkey.*) Ah! Ah! Ah! And the presser—I suppose he's not a man either! (*The Presser excuses his presence with a gesture.*)

MIMI: In a harem, there always has to be a eunuch. (*The sewing machine Operators enter.*)

OPERATORS: So *here's* where we get drunk! Who's pouring?

LEON: Marie's the one getting married. So . . . .

HELENE: The pressing machine girl has gone; we forgot to tell her . . . .

OPERATORS: (*Gathering around Marie.*) We're about to lose the only kissable one . . . . Where's your lover-boy, Marie, huh? (*While Gisele and Marie get the bottles, Simone goes to find the gift.*)

SIMONE: (*Waits for a silence, then:*) On behalf of all my friends . . . .

MARIE: (*Bursts into tears and hugs Simone.*) You shouldn't have, you shouldn't have.

SIMONE: (*Crying and hugging Marie very tightly, all the while repeating.*) Be happy, be happy . . . .

MIMI: There it goes, they're off like waterfalls. Music, shit, music. (*She sings. They all embrace Marie who cries looking at her unwrapped package.*)

MADAME LAURENCE: (*In her coat and dry-eyed.*) I also contributed toward the gift for the little one. My best wishes.

MARIE: (*Hugging her hard.*) Thank you, thank you. (*Leon puts on a record; it's a tango in yiddish.*)

MIMI: What's that?

LEON: A tango. Don't you know the tango?

SIMONE: (*Explaining to Marie and Giselle.*) No, it's not German; it's yiddish.

GISELE: What's this yiddish?

SIMONE: It's what the Jews speak.

GISELE: And you speak it?

SIMONE: Yes.

GISELE: Then you're a Jew?

SIMONE: Sure.

GISELE: Wow, am I stupid. It's funny.

SIMONE: What's funny about it?

GISELE: Nothing. I knew that Monsieur Leon was; his wife too. But you . . . . I just can't grasp it . . . . It's . . . . It's strange, isn't it? But it's true? You are? . . . Then you could probably tell me what *really* went on between you and the Germans during the war? (*Simone remains silent.*) I mean . . . how do you explain that you, the Jews, and they, the Germans . . . At any rate, I don't know how to say it, but you had many . . . many things in common, right? I was talking about it with my brother-in-law the other day, and he said to me: "Before the war, Jews and Germans were cut out of the same cloth." (*Simone doesn't answer; she looks at Gisele.*)

LEON: (*While dancing with Marie, pushes the Presser toward Simone.*) You know how to dance?

PRESSER: Me?

LEON: (*Pushing him into Simone's arms.*) Then ask her, ask her; she has only two children and she has a three-room apartment. (*The two couples begin to dance, but the music ends in their first step. Leon hurries to turn the record over.*)

HELENE: (*Near the machine.*) Don't you have anything else?

LEON: What?

HELENE: I don't know. Something more normal.

LEON: I don't know what you're trying to say.

HELENE: It's too yiddish.

LEON: What? (*Helene shrugs her shoulders. He tries to control himself.*) What's too yiddish? (*Helene shrugs her shoulders and then moves away. Leon follows her while the other song begins. It's a yiddish waltz.*) What's too yiddish?

HELENE: I didn't say anything, I didn't say anything. That sounds fine, that one!

LEON: Yes you did! Yes you did!

GISELE: (*Hugs Marie.*) I've got to go home. It'll soon be your turn; ten minutes late and there's a crisis.

MADAME LAURENCE: (*Gets up; she's a little tipsy.*) I'm going down with you. (*To Maria.*) You've got to train him, little one; you've got to train him, otherwise . . . .

SIMONE: (*To the Presser.*) Want to?

PRESSER: Can you dance to that?

SIMONE: It's a waltz.

PRESSER: I don't know if . . . .

SIMONE: You have to turn, that's all.

PRESSER: You like that?

SIMONE: To dance?

PRESSER: No, yiddish? (*Clasps Simone.*) Shall we take the plunge?

SIMONE: Let's plunge. (*The Presser and Simone dance. Leon and Helene, in a corner, are arguing.*)

SCENE 5

NIGHT

(*In 1947. The workroom is plunged into half-darkness. Simone works in silence. Before her, some candles or a gasoline lamp. The Presser sits by his pressing table and waits without doing anything.*)

SIMONE: I'll be finished in a moment.

PRESSER: (*Grumbles.*) No one is waiting for me . . . . (*Silence.*)

SIMONE: They still won't give me the death certificate; a woman told me she was told that a missing-person certificate was enough . . . . But that depends . . . to get a pension it's not enough . . . . They always make us fill out new papers; you never know what your rights are . . . . No one knows anything . . . . They toss us from one office to another. (*Pause.*) Because you've stood in line everywhere, you end up knowing each other . . . ah the tall stories go on and on . . . . There are some who always know everything . . . . The mothers are the worst . . . . Did you have to go through the Hotel Lutetia? (*He nods "yes."*) They sent me there at the very beginning to get information; someone who might have seen him, who—you know what I mean. The photos, the—good. I was only there once, I didn't dare go back. There was a woman who grabbed me by the arm and shoved a photo in my face; the kind they take on Awards Day. I can still see the little boy—he was the same age as my eldest—in short pants, wearing a tie, clutching a book he was given as the prize for excellence." She was screaming: "He always got the prize for excellence." She didn't want to let go of me; she kept repeating: "Why are you crying? Why are you crying? Look, look, they're coming back—they'll *all* come back. It's God's will. It's God's will." Then another woman shouted at her and began to push her . . . . Someone ought to tell them there's no hope for the children. Yet there they are, they keep coming, they keep talking . . . . I've seen her time and again in the offices, more and more crazy . . . . I spotted another one of them—this one never likes to stand in line; she always wants to be waited on first. Once I said to her: "You know, Madame, we're all in the same boat here; no need to elbow your way to the front. There's enough unhappiness for everyone . . . ." At the Prefecture, I met a Madame Levit, Levit with a "t" on the end. She was very nice, a good woman, but she was truly unlucky. Her husband was taken in '43, also, but he wasn't even Jewish, you see, his name was Levit, that's all . . . . She hasn't stopped running since. At first during the war it was to prove that he was— (*She searches for the exact word.*)

PRESSER: (*Whispers.*) Innocent?

SIMONE: (*Nods "yes."*) And now, like us, she runs around just trying to find out what's become of him . . . trying to get a little something . . . . She's a woman alone, with three children; she has no trade, she doesn't know how to do anything . . . . (*Silence. The Presser looks at her without saying anything. Silence.*) The hardest thing is not knowing . . . thinking that perhaps he's lost somewhere, no longer able to remember even his name . . . having forgotten me and the children. It happens . . . it happens, but I tell myself that kind of illness cures itself with time . . . . The other day I was coming out of the market and I saw a man, with his back to me, holding a basket. I don't know why but I said to myself, just for a second, I thought: It's him! With a basket! It's funny because he wouldn't even go out to buy bread; he never ran errands. He didn't like to . . . . Anyway . . . I mean you think of the times . . . Here, I'm finished . . . . (*She hands him the piece. The Presser lights his lamp on the table and begins to iron it.*) Anyway, if the Prefecture doesn't want to give out the death certificate it means they still have some hope; it means even they aren't sure of anything. Otherwise they'd be only too happy to make out all the papers and file all the records, so that everyone would be in order and no one would have to mention it anymore. (*The Presser pounds on the back of the jacket to put it into shape and to force the steam out of it. He seems to strike some blows furiously, but in fact he's only doing what's necessary. Leon enters; he is joyous and excited.*)

LEON: So you're fighting it out in the dark, huh? Our President fires some cabinet members, there's a strike and—hop!—all France finds itself in blackness; happily they've left us the gas . . . .

PRESSER: (*Hands the jacket to Leon.*) There it is . . .

LEON: (*Forming a coathanger with his open hands, delicately receives the jacket under the shoulders, then bringing it closer to the light, he turns it around.*) A new model again: pockets on the back of the sleeves . . . oh, well, if that pleases them and if it brings in orders, who am I . . . . (*As he exits.*) I'll be a minute; just the time it takes to dispose of the self-styled new model with the self-styled representative. I don't like him at all; he's a . . . (*He makes the gesture of tightening a necktie. Simone hasn't budged; she remains seated, eyes fixed.*)

PRESSER: (*Sits down next to her. Silence. He speaks with difficulty.*) He left when?

SIMONE: '43.

PRESSER: End of '43?

SIMONE: (*Shakes her head "no."*) On the missing person certificate it says: "Left Drancy in March, 1943 . . . ." (*A pause.*)

PRESSER: They say for where?

SIMONE: In the direction of Lublin Maidanek . . . (*Silence.*)

PRESSER: How old was he?

SIMONE: Thirty-eight. We married late; we were ten years apart.

PRESSER: Did he look older or younger? (*She doesn't understand.*) Than his age?

SIMONE: (*Without looking at him.*) Perhaps a little more when they took him; he was a convalescent. He stayed at Compiegne for a little while as a prisoner of war. He got sick over there. Then they released him. When he got back to Paris, he got some papers for himself at the Jewish Association so he'd be legal. It's funny: he who'd lived in France for years without identity papers, decides he wants to be absolutely legal. At the Association they gave him a sort of residence permit. He wasn't French; he was still Rumanian, so in the end they wrote: "Country of Origin: Rumania."

PRESSER: (*Without looking at her.*) He wear glasses?

SIMONE: Yes, but not all the time.

PRESSER: His hair? (*She doesn't understand.*) Did he have all his hair?

SIMONE: A little bald perhaps, but he looked good that way. (*Silence.*)

PRESSER: Face the fact that he never go beyond the camp gate. (*Brief pause.*) When we arrived, those who survived the trip were separated into two groups . . . those who were going to enter the camp and the others. We, we left on foot. The others, the majority, climbed into trucks. At the time we envied them . . . . (*He stops.*) The trucks took them directly to the showers . . . . They didn't have time to realize . . . . (*A pause.*) They've told you about the showers? (*Silence.*)

SIMONE: How can you be sure? (*The Presser is silent.*) Everyone says some of them are still going to come back. There are some everywhere: in Austria, in Poland, in Russia, and they're being taken care of, they're being rehabilitated and sent home! (*The Presser shakes his head in silence.*) Thirty-eight is not old, not old at all. Granted, they did what you said to the old, to those who couldn't work anymore, to the women, to the children . . . everyone knows that, but— (*She is interrupted by Leon, who enters carrying a tray on which there's tea, a liter of eau-de-vie and some dry cakes. Simone rises, slips her coat over her smock, and goes out after having placed her hand, in passing, on the Presser's shoulder. The Presser hasn't moved.)*

LEON: *(Flabbergasted.)* She's stubborn that one! *(He goes out after shouting.)* How about a drink? Wait, don't go home all alone. At least let someone go with you. *(He returns.)* She's gone. She's nuts, right? What's the matter with her? If she didn't want to stay she should have said so . . . . There it is: ask for extra work today . . . if you've agreed to do it, do it willingly, right? I would have done it myself, this miserable piece. You saw that . . . . *(Toward the door.)* Go on, smart-ass. *(To Presser.)* Did she say something to you?

PRESSER: It was me who talked to her.

LEON: Ah! Good! Ah, good . . . . You want some tea or a glass of . . . . *(He shows him the liquor bottle.)*

PRESSER: *(Without getting up.)* I'm going home, too . . . .

LEON *(Serving him.)* No, no I absolutely insist. How about a glass of . . . huh? *(The Presser doesn't move. Leon serves himself.)* You did well, you did well . . . . Me, too, I've wanted to speak to her for a long time, but . . . .

PRESSER: *(As if to himself.)* If only you could cut out your tongue.

LEON: Yes, you're right: "If only you could cut out your tongue." *(He shouts suddenly as if he's suffocating.)* Helene! Helene! *(To the Presser.)* What do you want? In this world, a person needs a certain amount of give . . . . *(Points to Simone's stool.)* That's what she's missing . . . so inevitably she . . . . *(He searches for words.)* She . . . .

PRESSER: *(Rising.)* I'm going home . . . .

LEON: Out of the question; we're going to drink together. Otherwise . . . . *(He makes a vague gesture. He turns over two glasses. Helene enters wearing no makeup; she has a bathrobe over her nightgown.)*

HELENE: Has Simone left?

LEON: Yes. *(Pointing to the Presser, in a low voice.)* He spoke to her. *(Helene looks at the Presser without saying anything. Leon raises his glass and offers the other to the Presser, who accepts it mechanically.)* Go on, drink, drink. *(They drink.)* I wanted to speak to her myself, yes . . . yes, only . . . . I was afraid of what I might say—really afraid! I plan to say something kind, full of good sense and human understanding, but what comes out is a disgusting mess. It's as if I had verbal diarrhea. It's horrible; it always happens like that. *(He spits, then to Helene.)* Isn't that true? Oh, I know myself, believe me, I know myself . . . .

HELENE: Please stop drinking. Do you want—

LEON: *(Indignant.)* Me? I haven't drunk anything . . . . *(He turns toward Simone's stool and howls suddenly.)* On the stock shelves where the German housewives keep their stock of brown soap, there's where he is, that's where you have to look for him; not in offices, not in files, not on lists . . . .

HELENE: *(Rises and pushes him with all her strength to get him to sit down again.)* That's enough; have you gone crazy or what? *(The Presser hasn't reacted.)*

LEON: (*Tries to laugh, wagging his finger at her.*) Tss tss tss . . . she's never had the slightest sense of humor. Never . . . what can you do: a German Jew? Each country gets the yids it deserves. (*He laughs.*) The dregs of the dregs of the earth, madame, that's what you are. (*He pretends to spit on her.*)

HELENE: (*Shrugs and murmurs.*) Polack humor! Very subtle . . . . (*She yawns.*)

PRESSER: I can't stay in bed in the morning . . . .

LEON: Why? It'll be a strike for Weill, too, you know!

PRESSER: I got into the habit; I can no longer manage to stay in bed in the morning . . . . (*Silence. The Presser pours himself a glass.*)

LEON: (*Getting a drink.*) That's it, that's it, let's drink, let's drink. (*He sings quietly.*) Let's drink a glass, let's drink it, two jolly companions of Burgundy. (*He sighs and then picks up his drinking song.*)

HELENE: (*Without stirring.*) Good, as for me, I'm going to bed. (*She remains seated. She yawns.*)

LEON: That's right, that's right, run to the free zone, go, go. That one went to rejoin her mother with the peasants. Me, I didn't want to go; no, I stayed . . . the whole war in Paris, me, monsieur! I even had false papers and everything; Richard, I was called, Leon Richard . . . yes . . . I went everywhere; some days I was myself wearing my Jewish star; some days I was Richard without the star. I even worked a little under that name at a fashionable dress shop . . . An Italian . . . People said to me: "Be careful, Monsieur Leon," but I said to myself, even if I'm caught what could they do to me; another kick in the ass? . . . No one realized at that time . . . we were blind . . . totally blind . . . I even went to play cards in a cafe with some Armenians . . . And then at the end of '43, beginning of '44, people everywhere began to say that they were taking us away to burn us. That's when I began to get the shakes for real! They sealed off the free zone; our last escape was gone . . . One day I come home and the concierge he signals for me not to go. They were up there; three youngsters with berets. I saw them come back down, disappointed. They said several words to the concierge. He's the one who hid me in a room on the top floor; he brought me things to eat and the news. I stayed there, blinds down, and waited like a mole, and waited . . . And then one day, knock, knock, knock. Who's there? "Monsieur Leon, this is it—it's all over; the Krauts are busy making themselves scarce." It hit me like a bombshell. (*A pause.*) I raced into the street like a real madman—you realize I had nowhere to go—I looked at all the people, at the faces above all; they seemed happy, certainly but, how can I say it? (*A pause.*) There was still gunfire here and there, especially from the roofs. I went from one barricade to another . . . one time they even stuck a rifle in my hands, they soon took it away from me because—according to them—I was holding it upside down . . . And then somehow I fell in with a group near a truck. A very young man was climbing into it, arms high on the air, hands on his head. It was a blond German youngster. We exchanged glances and I don't know why but I had the impression that this asshole was asking me for help. The French soldiers who were making him get into the truck shoved him a little to give themselves a more military air. The women were making jokes and he seemd to shout at me: "And you, yes, you who know, you who have some experience, help me, teach me." Suddenly I threw myself toward him, screaming, "Ich bin yude, ich bin yude, bin leibedick!" Then he closed his eyes and turned his head away and disappeared in the back of the truck . . . Suddenly panic broke out; the women dragged their brats into the shelter of the doorways: "Another German, a civilian and a surly one at that!" The soldiers surrounded me; the leader, pointing his machine-gun at my chest, repeated: papers, papers . . . I tried to laugh; a miserable rumble came from my belly, and after I caught my breath, I said as calmly as possible: "I am a Jew, monsieur officer of the resistance. I wanted him to know that I was Jewish and alive. That's all, that's why I shouted . . . excuse me . . ." The leader looked at me for a minute without moving. I saw clearly in his eyes that he didn't understand why I'd shouted, that undoubtedly he would *never* understand. I was afraid that he'd ask me to explain; I stepped backward. Finally he gave the signal and the soldiers jumped into the truck, maginificent! . . . I could still feel the others staring; I spread my arms, lowered my head and then, despite myself, my body – my whole body – apologized. A lot of good it did to me to repeat to myself that it was over, that I was again a free man with nothing to do . . . Then a voice, very much "old soldier" from Verdun, said very loudly, detaching each syllable: "Here in France, we respect prisoners of war!" My belly rumble became more resounding. Then I became transparent – you know, like the invisible man in the movie, and I left them all together: all those people who respect prisoners of war, the Geneva Convention, the Hague meetings, the Munich agreements, the German-Soviet pacts, and the cross, *all* the crosses, and I went home. A few days later the German (*he indicates Helene with his chin*) returned and we laid out our first interfacing in a kind of felt, half-cardboard, half-blotting paper; at the moment they weren't difficult to do because everything pulled apart like little loaves of bread. It was a good time except that you found neither fabric nor supplies . . . (*Silence.*) And you, how did they take you?

PRESSER: (*After a time.*) They took me!

LEON: (*Nods agreement. Silence.*) In the beginning I did it all, with Helene. I was the cutter, the presser, the machine operator, and Helene worked by hand. After that we took on the cop's wife . . . (*He points to Madame Laurence's place.*) After that we stumbled onto the crazy one . . . (*He points out Mimi's place.*) Later, there was an operator who brought me his cousin, and then, and then, voila, from thread to needle as they say, I found myself in shit up to here. (*Silence.*)

PRESSER: (*Getting up.*) I'm going home. (*He takes a step.*) I won't be coming in Monday.

LEON: Good, what do you want me to say to you? You want your Monday, *take your Monday; take advantage of me like the others . . .* What do you want me to do about it?

PRESSER: (*Takes another step.*) You'll have to look for another presser! (*He gathers up his things and prepares to leave.*)

LEON: What, what does that mean? What does that mean? Are you looking for a raise? Speak frankly with me, okay; none of that between us, not between us! (*He is on the verge of tears and holds the Presser by the arm.*)

PRESSER: I'll come by during the week to settle up; get my tally-sheet ready.

LEON: But you're crazy, what's gone wrong? Are you mad at someone? Is it me? Have I said something? Somebody's gotten on your nerves?

PRESSER: No, no, it's . . . (*He doesn't finish his phrase and makes no gesture.*)

LEON: At least finish out your week, we'll see after that. We're not savages, right? We'll talk about it again . . . Things are going to work out . . . Just give me a chance to catch my breath, all right?

PRESSER: No . . . no . . . it's better like this . . . Salut, Leon.

LEON: (*Without shaking his hand.*) You're not comfortable here, you're not comfortable?

PRESSER: Yes, yes, very comfortable . . . doesn't matter, Salut. (*He leaves.*)

LEON: (*Following him.*) They warned me, they told me never to get involved with your kind. Never! You're all crazy, all crazy. But you're not the only one who has suffered; shit, not the only one! There's *me* too; I've done dirty things in order to survive . . . (*He comes back and knocks over the bottle and teapot; he howls, kicking them.*) Ah shit!!

SCENE 6

THE COMPETITION

(*The workroom. A day in 1948, before noon. The pressing table is unoccupied. Gisele stands working at the pattern table. Marie is very obviously pregnant.*)

GISELE: (*While working.*) I said to her: "You can do what you want later on, when you're married; right now *I'm* still giving the orders . . . ."

MARIE: What did she answer?

GISELE: (*Shrugging her shoulders.*) Nothing. She was already on the landing; I don't even know if she heard me.

MIMI: That's what you get when you bawl them out all the time.

GISELE: Sure, it's easy for *you* to talk!

MARIE: You know, it's normal at her age to want to go out . . . when you're married you can't go out as much . . . .

MADAME LAURENCE: You'd like to "go out" in your condition?

MARIE: I didn't say that . . . .

GISELE: "At her age"; you'd better believe that at her age I couldn't stay out late.

MIMI: And look where it got you! (*Gisele looks at her without understanding.*) Would you like your daughter to turn out like you?

GISELE: I'm not so bad; there are worse. I've got no complaints . . .

MADAME LAURENCE: You don't look your age, that's certain . . . .

GISELE: (*Annoyed.*) Thanks a lot. (*Silence. Then to herself.*) Go out, go out, that's all they can say. Me, I'd rather go home . . . .

MIMI: To fight with your Jules?

GISELE: We don't fight all the time!

MIMI: Oh, I can see that from here: a hot love affair! (*She hums a java.*)

SIMONE: (*To Gisele.*) And your youngest?

GISELE: Oh, she's got no problems.

MIMI: She hasn't got the itch yet.

GISELE: (*To Mimi.*) Oh, how disgusting you can be! It's easy to see you don't have any kids . . . . (*To Simone.*) She's doing well in school and all in all, she's fine—knock on wood . . . let's hope it lasts . . . .

MARIE: What do you want your daughters to do later?

MIMI: (*In an undertone to Simone and Marie.*) There's always the sidewalk!

GISELE: You see, I'm not complaining but I wouldn't want them to end up like me, pulling a needle the whole blessed day. Pardon me for being blunt but it's not a very interesting life . . . . Frankly, I'd prefer that they learn to stitch by machine; you wear yourself out less, it pays better and the work is more interesting, right?

MADAME LAURENCE: Machine operator? It's a man's job!

MIMI: Why, do you have to pump the pedal with your balls?

MADAME LAURENCE: (*Lets out an "oh" of suffering while the others burst out laughing.*) It's a pleasure to have a serious discussion with you; you can see immediately what fascinates you . . . .

MIMI: Balls? They don't fascinate me more than something else; actually somewhat less . . . . I thought I understood, that's all . . . .

MADAME LAURENCE: (*Between her teeth.*) Always dirty things . . . .

MIMI: They're not dirty things, Madame Laurence; of course you have to run them under the water from time to time, otherwise—like everything else—they end up smelling . . . . You ought to tell your husband: when he washes his ass he ought to rinse his organ as well . . . . (*The others are now under the table, crying with laughter.*)

MADAME LAURENCE: (*Covering her ears.*) Please don't talk to me anymore, leave me alone; I'm sorry I said whatever it was. Oh my God, my God! (*Madame Laurence drops her work and runs toward the door.*)

MIMI: What do you know: maybe she's going to get her pedal fixed . . . (*Madame

Laurence goes out, bumping into Leon, who enters, a jacket under his arm.)

GISELE: (*Who didn't hear Mimi's last reply.*) What did she say? . . . What did she say? (*Simone and Marie are still crying with laughter, wiping their eyes, and gasping. Mimi works seriously. Gisele begs her to repeat her last line.*)

LEON: (*Looks at Simone, Marie and Gisele, who blow their noses, each one louder than the other. Then he asks.*) Are you laughing or crying?

MARIE: We don't know anymore, monsieur Leon; we don't know anymore. (*She groans.*)

GISELE: Something to drink, help!

MIMI: (*Serious.*) It's hard to keep them quiet; I do what I can, but there are some days . . . . (*Gesture of futility.*)

LEON: (*With unaccustomed calm, he waits for Madame Laurence to come back to her seat and then he lets go.*) Good . . . in your opinion, Madame, who are we sewing for, the dead or the living? (*No response. Leon studies the jacket fom every angle – it's a poor specimen.*) If we're sewing for the dead, I'd say this garment is a very fine garment for a dead man . . . but just between us, a dead man can do very well without garments, right? You toss him into a bit of rag, roll him up, and – plop! – into the hole. You can even save money on the rag and on the hole. We know about that, right? If we're sewing for the living, it's necessary to make provisions for certain gestures which a living man will inevitably have to make: like moving an arm, sitting down, breathing, rising, buttoning, unbuttoning. I won't even mention wartime when frequently the living, in order to remain living, are obliged to raise both arms in the air at the same time. No, I'm talking about ordinary moves, made during ordinary life, in ordinary clothes. Look at this piece; Monsieur Max has just returned it to me with a little paper pinned on the back. Gisele, will you please read what's on this paper. It's written in big letters. (*He shoes her the paper.*)

GISELE: (*Reads.*) "This is sewing for the dead."

LEON: A customer had just left . . . (*Brief silence, then.*) That the lining of the sleeve, yes, Madame Simone, has split . . . All right, I know it's not serious, not yet worth crying over; these things happen. That's what the salesman immediately said; a poor quality thread, a stitch too loose, let's go on . . . Next the buttons fell off one-by-one when the customer wanted to . . . (*He makes the gesture of buttoning.*) Automatically, the customer cast a glance down at the buttonholes. Yes, madame Mimi, look at them, as well; buttonholes done by hand?

MIMI: Sure; what the matter with them?

LEON: You could say that they shit and vomit at the same time . . . That's what's the matter. Next he raised his eyes and saw himself in the mirror. Then he tore this thing off his body, raced out of the store, and threw himself head-first into a store run by our competitor. Perhaps you've already heard of the competition; you know, all those people who are a lot less expensive because they have less overhead . . . Seeing the customer leave on the run, the owner of the store dumped all the merchandise which he had just received right into Max's lap, with this little paper pinned to the back, and then he, too, went running to the competition with his order. Monsieur Max received the package, he examined it, he called me. I examined it next and I must admit that the client was right. It's sewing for the dead! (*Silence. He begins again, in a professional manner.*) Now I must warn you, those who wish to continue sewing for the dead are going to have to do it somewhere other than here. From now on, my workroom will dedicate itself solely to the living; and those people, believe me, want something for their money today. The time is over when we stuck them with the worst rubbish: raincoats with two left sleeves, jackets which button in the back, etc., etc. Fini! The war has been over a long time; with a little luck we'll get another one soon. Who knows; things are going beautifully everywhere . . . We are no longer in the post-war era; we are once again in the pre-war period. Everything is normal again, everything is available today – at all prices. They're even talking about ending rationing. Now I demand a minimum of professional integrity, you understand . . . a minimum. (*He puts on the jacket. It is too big for him and hangs badly on all sides.*) Look at this, look at this "half-size!" One shoulder's already on the second floor while the other's still in the basement . . . Madame Laurence, it's necessary to pay a little attention to what you're doing instead of constantly watching the others . . .

GISELE: The color looks good on you . . .

LEON: "Color?!" On top of everything else, you're making fun of me?

GISELE: No, no, I'm sincere, monsieur Leon. (*Marie lets out a crazy nervous laugh.*)

LEON: (*Howls.*) It's over now, enough joking. Each piece will be checked, and re-checked and re-checked, and if the stitches are too large or if it's bungled you'll work on it again until it's right! Doing and undoing are both work but they're not paid the same; you're going to learn that right now. Oh you've had a cushy life so far but all that's finished, you understand, fini! I want it to be hard labor here from now on, like it is elsewhere – like everywhere – like at our competitor's. I've been a sucker, right? (*Simone has risen as discreetly as possible, placed the piece she's just finished on the pressing table, taken off her smock, and slipped on her coat. Leon sees her near the door.*) What! Sit down! Sit down immediately. What's that? What's that mean? You come in, you go out; it's a revolving door here?

SIMONE: I've an errand to run and since it's almost lunch time, I thought I'd take advantage of . . .

LEON: I'm the one who decides when it's lunch time or not.

SIMONE: I warned Madame Helene that I'd have to be gone; it's important.

LEON: I don't want to know about it. Around here I give the orders; I'm the one you've got to ask!

SIMONE: You weren't there so I asked your wife.

LEON: (*Shouts.*) You ask *me*, and me – I say no, there! When someone spends half the time on errands or on sick leave—

SIMONE: (*Protesting.*) I had to stay away from work for eight days once in three years and even then I brought things home to finish.

LEON: Blah, blah, blah. If you can't stick to your job, we can't let you occupy a stool here. Positions like this are hard to come by; every day I get requests, there's work here all year—no off seasons. Either do the job or get out for good! If you want to groan, or cry, or run errands, this isn't the place. This isn't the Bureau for Widows and Dependent Children. I want you to work, to turn out impeccable merchandise which we can deliver and which won't be thrown back in our teeth . . . Who's going to have to swallow this whole series Max got back? It's me, me! I don't want to hear laughter anymore, or shouts, or tears, or songs; from now on no one will be allowed to take off an hour, you hear me, an hour, even if your children perish, even if your old folks rot, even if your husbands blow up, I don't want to know about it, understand; for errands you have Saturday afternoon and Sunday.

SIMONE: (*Bursts out, on the verge of tears.*) The offices are closed!

MIMI: (*To Simone.*) What are you arguing with him for, honey? Go on, don't be afraid; I'll tell you how it comes out. (*Simone glances at Leon and turns away. Simone goes out. Silence. Leon sits down in Simone's place and remains there for a moment without saying anything, as though empty. The workers return to their work again in silence.*)

LEON: (*To Mimi.*) You've got a big mouth, eh?

MIMI: It's fine, thanks; I do what I can . . . (*Silence.*)

LEON: Then explain to me with your big mouth what she's going to gain by ruining her health running like that from one office to another . . . .

MIMI: She has a right to a pension, doesn't she? A woman alone with two children!

LEON: It's here, her pension is here! (*He taps on the table.*) She stays an extra hour every evening, she runs her errands every day and she gets her pension, right?

GISELE: She can't stay any later.

LEON: Why, who does that upset; we're open, I stay myself . . . .

MIMI: Yes, but when you want to eat, all you have to do is slide your two flat feet under the table; your stew is hot, whereas she has to run errands and get supper for her kids.

LEON: Where there's a will, there's a way; you have to know where your interest lies. Why should they give her a pension, in whose honor?

GISELE: Her husband was deported, wasn't he?

LEON: But he wasn't even French, madame, not even French. She has a right to nothing! They provide pensions for the French, not for stateless persons of Rumanian origin; who's going to provide it, huh, who—the French? Why? The Rumanians? Don't know him, the Rumanians; he left Rumania when he was twelve. They don't give a damn, the Rumanians. The stateless? Ah, the stateless can't help, they all left with him, the stateless, and those who came back, they're all cracked like the former presser, you remember? Anyway, who still cares about all that? New camps are springing up, no one's got time to spend on the old ones when already there are new ones.

MIMI: She has been to a legal committee; they're going to tell her.

LEON: That's right, a legal comittee . . . they're going to tell her . . . (*He makes a gesture which seems to say: "Who am I talking with?" He gets up, gathers up the jacket which was on the floor, hesitates, then wads it into a ball and throws it under the pressing table. The workers work without looking at him.*)

MIMI: (*Keeps her eyes on her work.*) It's not the sewing which is off; it's his cutting. He cuts any which way . . . Are my buttonholes to blame if it hangs badly, if the sleeves are screwed up? Where are you going to find buttonholes like that? . . . If there was a competition I'm sure that I'd hold the world championship for buttonholes . . . Look, look, I'm not shitting you: wouldn't you say it lives, that it sees you, that it lacks only speech, and at that, I don't even have cord—just rotten thread which breaks and knots . . . Honestly . . . there are days . . . I ask myself *why* am I doing this? (*Ironically.*) Obviously because it's fashionable . . . I upset myself and . . . I've nothing . . . I've nothing . . . I don't have nylons . . . I don't have a suit . . . I don't have soap, nothing . . . First of all, I want some chocolate. I want some chocolate!

GISELE: Hey, what's the matter with you, Mimi?

MARIE: Have *you* got a craving?

MIMI: What, what, aren't I right? The end of rationing? For *them* it is, but what do we have, what do we have; there isn't even toilet paper in the johns, not even toilet paper . . . (*Helene enters with more jackets. Madame Laurence and Gisele try to warn Mimi by coughing.*)

MIMI: (*After noticing Helene's presence, immediately curbs herself.*) What, what . . . I'm not ashamed. I can say it before Madame Helene: it's the cutting which is off, it's the cutting, not my buttonholes . . . (*Helene continues to hang jackets on the high bar, perhaps those which Max just returned.*)

SCENE 7

THE DEATH CERTIFICATE

(*1949. Afternoon. Working are: Mimi, Madame Laurence, Jean—the "new presser," and Helene at her pattern table. Simone is in the midst of taking off her coat and slipping on her smock.*)

HELENE: You have it? (*Simone nods "yes."*) Let me see it. (*Simone takes a sheet of paper out of a large envelope which she hands carefully to Helene. Simone sits down and begins to work. Helene reads in a low voice.*) Death certificate . . . by a judgment of the civil tribunal of the Seine . . . on these grounds the tribunal states and affirms monsieur . . . deceased at Drancy, Seine. Deceased at Drancy? Why have they put deceased at Drancy?

SIMONE: (*Without looking up from her work.*) That's how they do it!

HELENE: (*Raising her voice in spite of herself.*) What do you mean, that's how they do it? (*Simone doesn't answer; she stitches with great energy. Helene reads on to the end.*) Deceased at Drancy, Seine, March 3, 1943. What does that mean? He slipped on a sidewalk in Drancy, Seine, and died? (*Jean approaches, takes the death certificate and reads it. Helene tries to control herself. Simone works indifferently.*)

JEAN: (*After having read it.*) They put down the last place where the deceased left a trace . . . legal . . . That's the date and the place of his departure for . . . That's so it will be more . . . (*searching for the words*) more . . . legal.

HELENE: (*Cutting him off.*) The date of the departure for where? For where? They don't say that it's a date of departure . . . They say deceased at Drancy, Seine, period, that's all. (*Jean goes back to the pressing table without saying anything. Silence. Helene now walks up and down the workroom and then returns to Simone.*) In your missing persons certificate, it's clear he left Drancy the third of March '43 in the direction of Lublin-Maidanek, right? I didn't invent it. Why didn't they put that again? Simply that?

SIMONE: (*After a time.*) On a death certificate you can't put in the direction of . . .

HELENE: Why?

SIMONE: It's necessary to be more precise.

HELENE: Why? (*Simone doesn't answer; she works more and more energetically. Silence. Helene suddenly shouts.*) You've got to refuse! You must refuse, you don't have to accept that on top of everything, you don't have to accept that. (*Leon arrives, the cutting scissors in his hand.*)

LEON: What's going on, what is it now? What's she done?

HELENE: (*Holding out the certificate.*) Here, read!

LEON: What's that?

HELENE: Read.

LEON: (*Skims the paper and returns it to Helene.*) Very good . . . very good . . . With that she won't have to run from one office to another any more; maybe she'll be able to stay put from time to time, right there. (*He points to the stool.*)

HELENE: (*Giving him back the paper.*) Read to the end!

LEON: I've read, I've read to the end. It's good, very good, all the stamps are there, it's perfect!

HELENE: Nothing there shocks you?

LEON: Shocks me? You think it's the first time I've seen a death certificate? (*He laughs derisively and shakes his head.*) If I only had as many orders this winter as I've already seen dea—

HELENE: (*Crying out.*) Deceased at Drancy! Deceased at Drancy!

LEON: So? Drancy or somewhere else . . . . It's a paper, isn't it?

HELENE: Poor idiot; "Drancy or somewhere else." But if the truth doesn't exist on their papers with all their stamps and all their official signatures, look . . . Tribunal of the Seine . . . . Clerk of the Court . . . registered . . . certified . . . then no one got sent over there, no one ever got into their railroad cars, no one was burned; if they're simply deceased at Drancy, or Compiegne, or at Pithiviers; who will remember them?! Who will remember them?!

LEON: (*In a low voice.*) They will be remembered, they will be remembered. There's no need for papers, and above all there's no need to shout.

HELENE: Why do they lie, why? Why not simply put the truth; why not put "thrown alive into the flames?" Why? . . .

LEON: A paper, it's a paper; she needs this paper in order to try to get a pension, that's all. Maybe she's got no right to this pension, certainly no right, but she wants to try, she still wants to run and run again to the offices; it's stronger than she is, she loves it—to fill up files, card-indexes, papers, it's her personal vice and that paper is good for nothing else . . . it's a paper for obtaining other papers, that's all!

HELENE: And her children, how will they know? They'll see "deceased at Drancy," and that's all?

LEON: They'll know, they'll know; they always know too much.

HELENE: Certainly with you, the less one knows the better one gets along.

LEON: Those who ought to know, will never know; and we, we already know too much—much too much . . . .

HELENE: Who ought to know according to you?

LEON: (*After a pause, in an undertone.*) The others.

HELENE: Which others?

LEON: Don't scream like that, this is a workroom here; we're here to work, to work, not to philosophize . . . . (*To Simone.*) And you, settle down . . . why do you have to go spreading out your papers here; we don't give out pensions here; we work here, period, that's all . . . no need for certificates or documents.

HELENE: Stop shouting at her; I'm the one who asked her for it.

LEON: And who are you: judge, witness, laywer, Minister for the Veterans and War Victims? You want to set everything to rights. You, with your big mouth, huh? Straighten out *my* problems first, then if you've got a little time left, you can worry about *their* problems.

HELENE: What problems do you have?

LEON: Me? None! I'm happy, so happy I'm dying from so much happiness. What problems do I have, what problems do I have? . . . And who's going to remember me, madame, huh, who's going to remember me, in your opnion, who? (*Helene goes out. Leon sighs and then moves restlessly around the workroom; everyone works in silence. Leon questions Simone.*) Everything all right?

SIMONE: (*Shrugs her shoulders as if all that didn't concern her at all.*) Fine . . . .

LEON: Good . . . good. (*He exits.*)

SCENE 8

THE MEETING

(*In 1950. The workroom working at top speed.*)

LEON: (*To Jean while unhooking some jackets hung at the back of the room above the pressing table.*) Can you stay later tonight?

JEAN: I'm leaving at 6:30 . . . .

LEON: Six-thirty; you're a civil servant now?

JEAN: Is today Friday?

LEON: That's right, it's Friday, the day before Saturday.

JEAN: I leave at 6:30 every Friday. I have a meeting.

LEON: You have a meeting Friday night and I've got to deliver Saturday morning! (*Jean doesn't rise to this; he works calmly. Leon shrugs his shoulders and then reaches the door. On the verge of going out, he changes his mind and then the idea connects.*) Your revolution, you're going to start it tonight, at this meeting?

JEAN: I don't think so.

LEON: (*A sigh.*) Too bad! It would be a good excuse for delivering late tomorrow morning . . . a pity . . . It's just a meeting to discuss then, to prepare? For once couldn't they discuss a little bit without you?

JEAN: No!

LEON: You're such a big leader, that even to discuss they can't do it without you?

JEAN: (*Slamming down the iron.*) If you want a presser who works day and night to please you . . . .

LEON: No one works here to please me . . . .

JEAN: We're not married, eh! It's not as if jobs were scarce . . . .

LEON: (*Using the workers as witness.*) It's a real disease: all the pressers want to leave here! This table is no good, it leans; the iron is too heavy, you want tea at five o'clock; this monkey isn't pleasant enough! (*He makes a horrible grimace; the workers protest and offer him bananas.*)

JEAN: Friday, every Friday I have a meeting and I go at 6:30.

LEON: Go, go ahead leave, leave; may God protect you! You know what, we're going to reassign the tasks: You, you go to your meeting and concern yourself with the happiness of all humanity and me, I'll come back here tonight and concern myself with tomorrow's delivery. There, how about that? At least don't forget to tell them that regularly, every year, I buy an ad in the Peasant Workers' Almanac and I support the Labor Festival which I never attend, however, because it never fails to rain.

JEAN: Don't worry—I'll fix it so they shoot you among the last!

LEON: My wife, too?

JEAN: Your wife, too.

LEON: Thanks, it's good to feel you're protected. Simone, you stay with me to sew on buttons; at least you don't have a meeting. (*He goes out without waiting for an answer.*)

MIMI: You're stupid—why do you take that? Why don't you tell him to go to hell?

GISELE: Can't he ask his wife?

MIMI: Think—she might chip her nail polish. (*Simone stitches, indifferent.*)

GISELE: And your kids?

SIMONE: When they don't see me Friday evenings, they come looking for me.

MIMI: Fine; everything's perfect, if you like that . . . .

JEAN: You could shit on her head, and she'd still say thanks . . . . You have rights you haven't even found out about; how are you going to make them respect you? (*Silence. Everyone works. Suddenly Simone throws herself onto the table, head in her hands, and bursts into sobs. Everything stops.*)

MIMI: There it is, it's starting again . . . .

MARIE: All right, what's the matter, Simone?

GISELE: He didn't say that spitefully.

MADAME LAURENCE: You see, you see what I've gotten mixed up in? "Rights!"

JEAN: I didn't say anything . . . .

MADAME LAURENCE: Oh, sure, we're not deaf.

MIMI: What's wrong, why are you still crying? You want me to go tell the monkey you aren't staying tonight; it wouldn't be any skin off my nose. (*Simone shakes her head "no."*)

MADAME LAURENCE: (*Rising.*) Come sit in my place, you'll have a little more air. It's so hot today and with these winter fabrics on top of that . . . (*Simone thanks Madame Laurence with her hand but doesn't move.*)

MIMI: (*In a low voice.*) Have you got the curse? (*Simone shakes her head "no." Mimi continues, still more quietly.*) Were you thinking about your . . . ?

SIMONE: (*Still shaking her head.*) I was thinking of nothing, of nothing . . . I've nothing . . . nothing . . . .

MIMI: And what do you need with their pension; you can do plenty well without it. Go on . . . . It's not worth getting sick over . . . . Let 'em keep their pension, let 'em choke on it! (*Simone shrugs, as if to say that's not it either.*)

GISELE: It's your kids, they're still fighting, right . . . . Listen my good friend, when my youngsters get on my nerves I'd rather have *them* cry, not me; and believe me, last night when I got home, the oldest stained her blouse—she'd just put it on—and now it needed to be washed again. "Slut," I said to her, "*you're* the one who's going to wash it again . . . ." So of course her father took *her* side and everyone started shouting and crying. I cried all night . . . . I didn't close an eye . . . . Ah, I swear there are days . . . . (*Gisele begins to sniffle also.*)

MIMI: (*Between her teeth, threatening Gisele with her fingers.*) You shut up, huh?

GISELE: (*Picking up again.*) What's wrong? I don't have the right to say anything? (*She is now sobbing, pretending to blow her nose.*)

SIMONE: (*Beating on the table.*) But why am I crying, why am I crying? I don't even know why . . . .

MIMI: Good; stop and laugh.

SIMONE: I can't, I can't.

MIMI: Tickle yourself under the arms! (*Simone still sobs. Silence.*) Good then, cry, my friend; you'll piss less! (*Simone laughs under her tears.*) There, you see . . . it's coming. Do you want me to tell you about the hunchback's tool . . . . It was all twisted, all crumpled; you had to touch it to make it straighten itself out . . . . (*Simone shakes her head and her sobbing redoubles.*)

JEAN: (*While getting dressed.*) Leave her alone; you're making her dizzy with all your nonsense.

MIMI: You, buzz off . . . .

JEAN: If you all got together and insisted on being paid by the hour, he'd think twice before making you stay late. You've got to know how to make yourselves respected. Otherwise . . . .

GISELE: Personally, I prefer to do piece-work . . . .

JEAN: By the hour, you put in your hours and the rest is paid in overtime.

GISELE: You must feel less free . . . .

MIMI: Especially you, who piss every five minutes . . . .

GISELE: Me, I piss every five minutes?

MADAME LAURENCE: That's nothing to be ashamed of . . . go on . . . .

GISELE: I'm not ashamed; I never go there, that's all . . . .

MADAME LAURENCE: It's not really a criticism . . . .

GISELE: I don't go there, I never go there . . . .

MIMI: Then why do you go out?

GISELE: I don't go out; it's the others who go out . . . .

MADAME LAURENCE: It's terrible; you'd think someone was accusing you of . . . .

JEAN: (*After a brief silence.*) You really have water on the brain.

MIMI: (*Showing him the time.*) You'd better run, darling, or you're going to be late for clocking in. (*Jean leaves, slamming the door. To Simone, who continues to weep, working all the while.*) Now we're alone; you can let down your hair . . . go on . . . . (*Simone sobs.*)

MARIE: She's going to end up choking herself.

GISELE: Do you want to stretch out for a bit? (*Simone is lifted onto a table.*)

SIMONE: (*Shakes her head, sighs a great gasp, then, between two sobs.*) Everything's going to be fine, everything's going to be fine, everything's going to be fine. (*Brief silence.*)

MIMI: (*To Simone.*) Do you want me to tell you?

GISELE: Leave her in peace.

MIMI: A good healthy screw from time to time brushes away the cobwebs and chases away the blues.

GISELE: Pouah . . . that's great . . . she hasn't enough troubles without that as well? A man would give her more laundry, that's all; she already spends half the night washing her kids' underwear.

MIMI: And laundresses, they're for the dogs?

GISELE: She doesn't need that, I tell you.

MIMI: (*To Simone.*) Don't listen to her . . . . Hey, Sunday I'll take you dancing; you'll pick up some handsome guy . . . .

GISELE: You can be so disgusting . . . really . . . some days . . . .

MARIE: What she needs is someone who helps her, who supports her . . . .

MIMI: (*Sings.*) Prosper yop la boum . . . He's the king of asphalt.

MARIE: (*Cutting her off, irritated.*) No, I mean someone who's good and hard-working.

MIMI: That's right, when it's hard it's good. When it's soft, it's not working. (*Everyone bursts out laughing.*)

MADAME LAURENCE: (*To Simone, without laughing.*) Are you feeling better?

SIMONE: (*Wiping her eyes and laughing now.*) I don't know what came over me. I was fine and then I felt as if I was choking . . . .

MIMI: (*Weeping with laughter.*) Yes, in the long run you can choke on it . . . .

GISELE: Oh shut up; let her talk . . . . Me, too, sometimes I feel like . . . I feel like . . . and then it won't come out. It's like . . . like . . . . (*She searches for words.*)

MIMI: Like what, sweetie?

GISELE: Like cotton wool, here. (*She taps on her chest. To Simone.*) Isn't that right, isn't that right; like a wad of cotton wool? (*Simone shrugs her shoulders as a sign of ignorance.*)

MIMI: (*To Gisele.*) Yeah, but you've no reason; you're happy, you've had a nice husband, a nice little house, some nice little daughters . . . .

GISELE: Sure, sure . . . .

SIMONE: But it's the same with me; my kids are fine, they're doing well in school, there's work here all year, no off-seasons . . . .

MIMI: What you miss . . . .

GISELE: Give her some peace.

MIMI: Come dancing with me on Sunday; I'll tell my Joe that I have to see my mother, since he can't stand her.

SIMONE: You're crazy; what would I do with the kids?

MIMI: They stick to you like leeches even on Sunday? Listen, my friend, you're not smart; send them to play soccer . . . or go camping . . . .

GISELE: Thanks a lot . . . so they'll catch cold . . . thanks a lot . . . .

SIMONE: Sunday is their day; we go to the movies . . . .

MIMI: Every Sunday?

SIMONE: Except when the weather's good; then we go for a walk . . . at the end of the afternoon we stop by to visit my father . . . .

MARIE: Grandpapa's, every week? (*Simone nods "yes."*) With the children?

SIMONE: What choice do I have?

MIMI: Oh boy, what a charming day . . . looking back on it you're dazzled.

Then when do you get a change? (*Brief silence.*)

SIMONE: Here, with you . . . . (*Mimi looks at her a minute and then plunges back into her work. Everyone works in silence now. The alert has passed.*)

SCENE 9

TO REBUILD HER LIFE

(*A summer evening in 1951. The windows are wide open. Simone, seated in Madame Laurence's place, sews on buttons. Helene, at a table, tries to put some garments in cartons, crumpling them as little as possible. She gets irritated.*)

HELENE: These are going to be real rags . . . .

SIMONE: Where are they going?

HELENE: Belgium . . . . (*Leon enters, sits down at the table next to Simone and laughs for no reason.*)

HELENE: Have you finished?

LEON: Guess what just happened to me?

HELENE: What?

LEON: I've got three aces, a black king, a red queen; I ask for two cards, I discard the king and queen and guess what I got?

HELENE: Two aces?

LEON: "Two aces?" One ace! There are only four aces in all; I already had three . . . .

HELENE: What do I know? Why isn't Max doing this shipment?

LEON: (*To Simone.*) Do you play cards?

SIMONE: I play war, with the kids . . . .

LEON: A full hand of aces the first time in my life, and it has to be with my own machine operators . . . . It's finished now, if they want to play we'll play seriously; we're no longer the age where you play for buttons. Furthermore they're *my* buttons; they won't risk anything!

HELENE: Oh, I give up, I can't do it; the cartons are too small!

LEON: Leave it, leave it, I'm going to do it; I've got to do everything here, it's simple . . . .

HELENE: Sure, sure . . . . Why isn't it Max?

LEON: I have the right to have my own customers without going through monsieur Max; I'm not tied to monsieur Max for life . . . .

HELENE: You're sure that they'll pay at least?

LEON: Why wouldn't they pay?

HELENE: I'm asking, that's all . . . .

LEON: Because I've had some unpaid bills, you're going . . . . (*He rises and helps Helene do the package. Simone has finished her piece. She hangs it up and takes another. Leon to Simone.*) Any news from the children?

SIMONE: Yes, I received a card.

LEON: Everything all right?

SIMONE: Yes, thanks . . . .

LEON: Where are they by now?

SIMONE: In the Federal Republic.

HELENE: So are you helping me or chatting?

LEON: I'm helping you and I'm chatting; I can do two things at once, I don't have two left hands like you . . . .

HELENE: (*Watching him do it for a minute.*) Sure, it's not difficult like that, but you don't realize; they're going to be real rags when they arrive . . . . Go ahead and roll them into balls while you're at it . . . .

LEON: They don't know how to iron in Belgium?

HELENE: Good, good, leave it, leave it; you're irritating me even more. I prefer to do it alone . . . .

LEON: (*To Simone.*) Federal Republic? That's Germany, isn't it?

HELENE: The air is very good there.

LEON: Yes, yes, that's what they say . . . .

SIMONE: They're very happy.

LEON: You've warned them, at least?

HELENE: Leon, I beg you.

LEON: What, I haven't said anything?

HELENE: Exactly, don't say it.

LEON: It's awful, she knows in advance . . . .

SIMONE: (*To Helene.*) I didn't want to send them over there and then I said to myself, after all, if the Jewish Federation is organizing it . . . .

HELENE: You did well; the climate is very healthy . . . .

LEON: Sure, sure . . . .

SIMONE: The oldest wrote me that they took them by bus to visit Ravensbruck . . . .

LEON: (*To Helene abruptly.*) But why are you doing up this carton now? You want them to stay crumpled up all night, eh?

HELENE: You told me that they have to leave tomorrow morning at dawn . . . . I've purposely kept Simone . . . . (*Simone has hung up the piece which she's just finished and gets ready to leave.*)

LEON: I'll do it tomorrow; leave it . . . .

HELENE: You won't have time tomorrow . . . !

LEON: Leave it, I tell you!

HELENE: No, I've started, I'll finish!

LEON: (*To Simone.*) Stubborn, eh? . . . You're going to bed now?

SIMONE: Yes. I mean I'm going home . . . .

LEON: You're not taking advantage of the kids being on vacation to . . . .

HELENE: Leon!

LEON: What now?

HELENE: Will you stop?

LEON: What've I said? She's not at the age where . . . . Do we have to talk to her like a little girl—by hints?

SIMONE: (*She smiles.*) You know, in the evening I always have things to do in the house and then . . . and then . . . . (*She laughs.*)

HELENE: Certainly . . . certainly . . . they don't realize . . . .

LEON: Who realizes here? It's you who don't realize . . . . If you don't take advantage of the fact that the kids are going to go out, to see people, make acquaintances, how do you expect to rebuild your life, huh, how?

SIMONE: I'm not interested in that at all, monsieur Leon; I'm fine as I am . . . just fine . . . .

LEON: (*Peremptorily to Simone.*) Sit down . . . . (*He sits next to her.*) You know the Thermometre, place de la Republique—no, it's a cafe at the angle of the boulevard Voltaire or the avenue of the Republique, a big cafe—good. Every Sunday morning there's a woman, madame Fanny, very nice woman, who busies herself with rebuilding the lives of people who . . . . You go there, at my suggestion, you talk to her and if she has someone, eh . . . go find out, someone who sounds interesting, she introduces you . . . . That doesn't commit you to anything, right; if it works out, it works out; if it doesn't, good-bye and thanks. You're not obliged to buy; entrance is free . . . . Anyhow, you understand . . . . (*Silence. Helene looks at Simone. Simone abruptly bursts out laughing. To Helene.*) What's the matter with her, what did I say that's funny? Why stay alone when you can still make someone happy; there are so many men who have suffered and who are alone . . . . She's normal, isn't she; then she can live normally . . . . And even if she were ugly as sin; with a three room apartment you can always find someone who's interested . . . . (*Simone laughs again.*) Good, let's pretend I didn't say anything . . . .

SIMONE: (*Calming herself.*) Excuse me monsieur Leon, I've never been to the cafe Thermometre, but I *was* introduced to someone, not very long ago . . . .

LEON: Ah, ah, you see? You see?

SIMONE: (*Laughs again.*) He even came to the apartment.

HELENE: (*Stops working on her package and runs to sit beside Simone also.*) But that's wonderful! Wonderful!

SIMONE: The kids made his life so impossible that he left and I've never seen him again; they were hateful to him . . . . (*She laughs.*) Happily, because the person who introduced him to me has since learned he was a guy already remarried, thanks to madame Fanny, and since he wasn't pleased with his new wife's apartment, he was looking for a larger one. That's why he'd asked to visit mine . . . . (*Laughs.*) You know what he said to me as he left: "It's a three room, but a *small* three room." . . . I don't regret it, I'm not eager at all. To begin with, I think that even if I wanted to, I wouldn't be able to . . . .

LEON: People say that . . . . Not all of them are jackasses; there are good men who're looking for someone.

SIMONE: The children are too big, they'd be unhappy, they're used to being the men of the house and then, you know, when I was married to my husband it was an arranged marriage; they introduced us . . . . I must say I was fortunate; I never had any reason to complain, he was a good husband . . . but today . . . it would have to happen differently; if not, I don't think I'd be able to . . . . When this guy came over — I'd seen him once at the home of the person who introduced us — anyway, when he came over . . . .

HELENE: How was he?

SIMONE: Fine. He had a slightly crooked mouth, but he wasn't so bad; he was a man who'd had misfortunes, *many* misfortunes . . . it was hard not laughing out loud in front of him . . . As soon as he had his back turned, all three of us would have a fit; the littlest began to imitate him, he did the whole apartment visit for us with comments . . . . The guy had a bit of a yiddish accent; the little one imitated him so terribly well, we laughed and laughed . . . . No, it's too complicated and then, you know, I'm comfortable like this. I feel free; I'm able to . . . anyway . . . good night . . . . (*She leaves.*)

HELENE: See you tomorrow — good night. (*Silence.*)

LEON: Well at least I told her . . . .

HELENE: You and your ideas. (*Silence.*)

LEON: Good, let's go to bed.

HELENE: (*Pointing out the still-unwrapped package.*) You'll do it tomorrow?

LEON: I'll do it tommorow.

HELENE: You need a bigger carton . . . .

LEON: No, I don't!

HELENE: And the letter?

LEON: Which letter?

HELENE: You know very well . . . .

LEON: I'll do it tomorrow . . . .

HELENE: Tomorrow you'll tell me tomorrow and still tomorrow . . . .

LEON: I don't have paper . . . .

HELENE: Do a draft on that and I'll recopy it . . . .

LEON: Have you got a pencil? (*Helene gives him a pencil. He reflects a minute and then.*) What should I say?

HELENE: Please, we've talked and talked about it . . . .

LEON: What do I say to begin? What do they use?

HELENE: "Dear cousins."

LEON: "My dear cousins."

HELENE: If you want . . . .

LEON: "My dear cousins and children of my cousins."

HELENE: Go on; I'll take care of that part of it.

LEON: You want to write it?

HELENE: No, it's your cousin; you write . . . .

LEON: My cousin, it's not even a real cousin, it's a distant cousin and her, I don't know her; I've never seen her. Him already I must have seen two times in my life at the absolute maximum and I was a kid; I can't even remember what he looks like, so . . . . (*Helene sighs without responding.*) Good! "Dear distant cousins" or "Dear distant cousins and distant children of my distant cousins." (*He writes it down.*) There! Next?

HELENE: (*Dictating.*) If you are still planning to come—

LEON: Ts, ts, ts . . . not so quick . . . Don't you think that we ought to warn them that things are tough here as well—very tough—and that it's necessary to work? I don't know . . . what do they hope for; why are they leaving there?

HELENE: We're not going over all that again; they're leaving because they can't stand living there any more . . . .

LEON: (*Nodding agreement.*) They can no longer stand it . . . . and that, that's a serious enough reason for leaving everything and depositing yourself in a strange country with people you barely know?

HELENE: You don't want them to come? It's simple you write that you can't receive them, period, that's all. But don't drive me crazy; we've already talked and talked it over, if you please!

LEON: I'm asking if we shouldn't warn them, that's all, that things will be tough here, too; that it's necessary to work hard. Above all they mustn't have any illusions . . . .

HELENE: Who has any illusions?

LEON: I don't know, maybe they think that here all you have to do is lean over to scoop up the dough?

HELENE: (*Getting up.*) Write what you want; I'm going to bed.

LEON That's awful . . . you're the one who tells me to write and when I start to write you go to bed.

HELENE: Good, write: "Dear cousins, you will be welcome and we are waiting for you. See you soon." Signed Helene and Leon.

LEON: If that's what you want to write, you don't need me.

HELENE: I want *you* to do the writing!

LEON: Why?

HELENE: I know you, come on . . . .

LEON: (*A sigh.*) Good. "Dear distant cousins, come; we are waiting for you—" no . . . "If you are still determined to come, write to tell us when you intend to arrive so we'll be better prepared to house you during the beginning of your stay." . . . There, it's good like that? (*Helene doesn't answer.*) You don't like "the beginning of your stay?"

HELENE: It's simple: if you don't want them to come, write "don't come" . . . I've got a headache . . . .

LEON: I could write "don't come" to my own cousin who asks for help after all they're suffered? I simply wish that . . . we have a responsibility, right? Do I know what they have in their heads, why they want to leave Poland, why they want to come here, precisely here? I don't know why they don't go to Israel, for example . . . . Maybe they imagine that I've an immense factory, that I'm rolling in gold and diamonds . . . .

HELENE: (*Beside herself.*) They're communists; they don't give a damn for gold, they don't give a damn for diamonds. They have no one in Israel, their children speak French; they want to come to France, to live in France, to work in France!

LEON: If they're communists, why don't they stay over there where everyone is a communist these days?

HELENE: Good, I'm going to bed.

LEON: Can't we discuss anything anymore? I'm trying to—

HELENE: (*Cutting him off.*) Discuss with the walls; me, I'm tired, I've got a headache. It's your family, you do what you want, you write them what you want . . . . (*Leon nods agreement. Helene goes out crying.*)

LEON: It's awful; what did I say, what did I say? Is it my fault, is it my fault if the whole world is shit?

SCENE 10

MAX

(*An end of an afternoon in 1952. Everyone is at work; only Simone is missing. There is a pile of jackets at her stool. Mimi hums. Leon enters panic-stricken and running as if he were pursued. He hurries to hide under the pressing table, behind a pile of unironed jackets, while the voice of Helene is heard coming from the corridor.*)

HELENE: But since I tell you he's not here . . . .

MAX: Where is he then, where is he?

HELENE: How would I know; we're not hooked together . . . .

MAX: I want my merchandise, you understand, I want my merchandise; I'm not going away without my merchandise.

HELENE: As soon as it's ready . . . .

MAX: I know, I know; you'll put it all in a taxi . . . . (*Max has entered followed by Helene who tries to calm him. Max is at his wits' end; for an instant he contemplates the workroom with a haggard air, then, discovering the pile of pieces waiting to be finished by Simone, he groans.*) But nothing is ready—nothing. . . .

HELENE: (*Smiling.*) You see, monsieur Max, everything which is ready has already been delivered to you.

MAX: (*Shouting, piling the pieces on the floor or even tearing them from the girls' hands.*) Only 40s, only 40s, I need all sizes, you've delivered only 40s. (*Max continues to gather up the pieces and put them down further on. He moves the pile under the pressing table and discovers Leon.*) Leon!

LEON: (*As if waking up.*) Huh?

MAX: You're hiding under the table now!

LEON: Me, I'm hiding?

MAX: Why haven't I received—

LEON: (*Emerging.*) Who's hiding here? Why would I hide at home in my own house . . . ? I've hidden enough in my life . . . Thanks . . . that's terrific . . . so I no longer have the right to come and go under my own pressing table?

MAX: (*Controlling himself.*) Leon, Leon, Leon. Why'd you tell me on the phone this morning that you'd put the rest of my merchandise in a taxi and that it was going to arrive at any minute?

LEON: (*Shouts.*) Me, I said that? I said whatever it was on the telephone? I have the time to answer the phone?

MAX: Not you, your wife.

LEON: (*Pained.*) Helene, why do you say such things? (*Helene looks at Leon without saying anything.*) Good, let's not talk about it any longer.

MAX: I have customers who are waiting for their merchandise; I've got to know, I've kept them waiting since last month—last month! This morning there was one who came into my place, sat down on a folding chair and didn't want to budge without the rest of his order.

HELENE: Surely we're not going to start waiting in each other's places of business! Soon we won't be able to work . . . .

MAX: Madame, he's in his shop, he also has customers who wait, whether it's for a marriage or for a burial . . . . You can't make people wait indefinitely. When you promise delivery on a certain date, it's necessary to hold to it, otherwise . . . . Leon, do something; we've always worked hand-in-hand, right?

LEON: Yes, but it's always *my* hand doing the work!

MAX: I swear to you that if you don't deliver everything owed to me this evening, you understand, everything, it's finished between us, finished!

LEON: It's finished? Good, then, it's finished; what should I do now; weep, hang myself?

MAX: (*With a hand on his midsection.*) Leon, if one day I get an ulcer . . . .

LEON: (*Cutting him off.*) An ulcer—he talks about *an* ulcer. I already have two, two and gastritis.

MAX: Good, it's finished; I can stand everything, everything, except bad faith!

LEON: (*To Helene.*) Where is the bad faith? I'm not sicker than he is, maybe?

MAX: If you'd get organized a little, instead of working like a Jew.

LEON: Ah! I see what he's up to; he wants to stick us with an Aryan production manager. With pleasure, let him come; I'm leaving him the keys and this time *I'm* heading for the Free Zone on the Riviera . . . .

MARIE: Why did I have all 40s?

LEON: (*Cutting him off.*) At my place it's like that: all or nothing!

MAX: (*Continuing.*) It does me no good—all 40s—that's not usable. If I don't have a little of each size I can't deliver, I can't . . . .

LEON: Do you think I keep your merchandise at my place to be perverse, huh? To deliver, to deliver – what other goal do I have in life, what other do I have?

HELENE: Leon, I beg you . . . . (To Max.) We're going to do the maximum, don't worry . . . .

LEON: "The maximum!" Look, look! (He points to the workers.) All the deprived, all the neurotic, all the unstable and even the revolutionaries come to plant their buttocks on my chairs and pretend to work; all of them have a brother, a father, a mother, a sister, children, a husband, and by turns that one gives birth, this one dies, that one gets sick. What can I do, eh, what can I do?

MAX: And at my place no one dies; no one is born at my place? I'm missing two warehousemen and my bookkeeper wants to become a singer; he practices in my own office, he drives me crazy and, me, I've got to deliver piece-by-piece, chase after merchandise which you give me with a medicine dropper, keep the books, make out the bills, the out of town consignments.

LEON: Sure, sure, but at least you sleep at night . . . .

MAX: (Irritated.) Me, I sleep at night? Me, I sleep at night?

LEON: As soon as I close my eyes, that one (he indicates Helene) jabs me with her elbow; "Are you asleep?" Definitely not, and that does it, she's off: Do you remember this one and that one . . . it so happens they're all dead and you know how; she talks to me about them and then afterwards she weeps. She weeps and then she goes to sleep, but for me it's finished, finished, I can't sleep any longer; I get up, I go into the kitchen and I shout . . . I don't want to have anything to do with the dead; the dead are dead, right, and ours are a thousand times more dead than any others because there's nothing left of them . . . fine . . . . You've got to think of the living, and by chance the only surviving relative left to her is me, me. And she kills me at night while the others murder me during the day . . . . (Brief silence.)

MAX: What's that got to do with my merchandise?

LEON: Who's talking about merchandise here, who?

HELENE: Leon, I beg you . . . . (Max, a hand on his stomach, abruptly bends over in misery.)

LEON: Look at him, look at him, my word, he wants to hit me over the head with his ulcer but if I had only ulcers, I'd go dancing every night in the jazz clubs . . . .

MAX: Leon, seriously, let's speak man to man.

LEON: That's right, let's talk: what is your fabric in fact, huh? Special, pure chemical synthetic; that's what you wanted in order to make things more chic, right? You think I don't know where it comes from?

MAX: It comes from Switzerland!

LEON: That's right, that's right; it goes through Switzerland, it crosses Switzerland . . . .

MAX: (*To Helene.*) What's he trying to say?

LEON: I said to myself, at least with Germans, we'll get deliveries on time; never a train, never a convoy late—the best shippers in the world! Only for us, you and me, monsieur Max, the fabric is late. So what? I don't say anything, I don't get upset; above all don't get upset with those guys . . . . And when their magical pure chemical fabric arrives, once cut, once mounted, it has a life of its own: it does what it wants, ask them . . . . (*The workers make some timid gestures as to the problems with the material.*) Put the iron on it, put it on. Dry: it hardens like a plank and shrinks in width. Moist: it shrinks in length and becomes as supple and agreeable as a sponge. You hang it up: it stretches, it pouches, it gets shiny, but tell him, tell him . . . .

JEAN: It's drek!

LEON: And me, I have to watch all that and organize!

MAX: (*Shouting like a madman.*) Fifty percent natural fiber, fifty percent nylon, the last word in modern technique, the last word!

LEON: (*In a mutter.*) Yes, yes, the last word; what is that they have in stock over there, tons and tons? Ashes and hair, yes monsieur, don't bother shrugging your shoulders; hair, mountains of hair . . . .

MAX: But what's he saying, what's he saying? (*Leon suddenly tears the clothes from the workers' hands and throws them at Max's feet, then he attacks the hanging clothing. Helene and Jean try to hold him back. Max, maddened, gathers up the clothes and refolds them, muttering some incomprehensible words. A Child appears in the doorway. He's between ten and twelve years old, wears glasses, is only slightly astonished to discover the workroom, now in absolute disorder.*)

MIMI: (*Seeing the child, calls to him.*) Come in, it's okay . . . come in . . . .

CHILD: (*Plants himself in front of Leon and then in one breath.*) My mother says to tell you she's sorry but she won't be able to come to work today . . . .

LEON: (*Shouting like a madman.*) You wait until five o'clock in the evening to come and tell me that?

CHILD: (*Not at all impressed.*) I couldn't come before. I was at the hospital.

LEON: And your brother?

CHILD: He was at the hospital, too.

LEON: Oh wonderful; you're both sick together now, bravo!

CHILD: No, it's mother.

MIMI: She's in the hospital?

CHILD: Yes.

HELENE: What's wrong with her?

CHILD: She can't stand up; she got up to go to work this morning but she couldn't manage it, then my brother went to look for a doctor and he said that they would have to send her to the hospital. At the hospital, they said they were going to keep her under observation.

LEON: (*To Max.*) "Under observation"; you see, you see, what can I do, what can I do?

MAX: That's right, I'm going to tell my customers to tell their customers that they won't have their clothes for getting married or going to the ball because one of you workers is in the hospital under observation.

LEON: (*Shouting at Helene.*) What are you waiting for? Telephone, place an ad: "Seeking qualified finish-worker without family, without child, neither widowed, nor married, nor divorced, not mixed up in politics and in good health . . . ." There, perhaps one time—who knows—I'll get a good hand . . . . And you, what're you doing clustered like flies around this kid? You're here to work, yes or shit, then work, work. But look at them, look at them, my Lord you'd think that I was already paying them by the hour . . . . (*Helene has gone out.*)

MAX: Leon, seriously . . . .

LEON: Shh, we shouldn't talk in front of . . . (*He indicates the workroom with his chin.*) No one is to leave this workroom until monsieur Max's order is ready for deliver. (*To Jean.*) Meeting or no meeting. . . . (*He has gone out. Max and Leon can be heard arguing, then laughing. The women crowd around the Child. They pose a lot of questions about Simone's health.*)

MARIE: What's wrong with your mother?

CHILD: (*Shrugs, then says.*) I don't know, she's tired . . . .

MIMI: How are you and your brother going to get along?

CHILD: Doing what?

MIMI: Eating and all that.

CHILD: Oh! We're going to find a way; I know how to cook and at noon nothing's changed; we eat at the school.

JEAN: The hospital, it's Lariboisiere?

CHILD: No, I put the name of the hospital and all that on a piece of paper; it's in the suburbs . . . . (*Mimi takes the paper.*)

GISELE: You kill yourself raising kids . . . .

MARIE: You've got to love her very much, your mother . . . .

MIMI: Always.

MADAME LAURENCE: You're nice to her at least?

JEAN: Leave him be . . . .

GISELE: That's a beautiful coat; is it the one the Americans sent you?

CHILD: I don't like it . . . it's a girl's coat.

GISELE: They're still very nice, the Americans, to send coats to young French children . . . .

CHILD: I don't like the Americans.

GISELE: Why not, my rabbit?

CHILD: I'm not a rabbit, I like the Russians, the Americans want war . . . .

JEAN: Bravo . . . for your trouble I'm going to give you a piece of candy . . . .

CHILD: I don't like candy, thanks, I've got to go . . . .

MIMI: Tell your mother to come back quickly; that we'll go to see her and . . . you can give us a good-bye kiss or are you already too grown-up a monsieur to kiss the ladies? (*The Child comes back, he hugs Mimi; Mimi slips a bill into his hand; the Child refuses it.*) Yes, yes, you're to buy something for yourself and for your brother, too. (*The others also embrace him.*)

GISELE: What does she complain of, your mother?

CHILD: She doesn't complain; she just can't stay on her feet.

GISELE: Does she still cry as much?

CHILD: Maman? She never cries . . . .

MADAME LAURENCE: She'll soon be well enough to come back to work . . . .

CHILD: (*Kissing Madame Laurence.*) Later, my brother and I, we'll work and she'll never have to work again. (*They all approve. The Child starts to leave.*)

JEAN: What about me; you don't kiss me!

CHILD: Men don't kiss. (*Everyone works.*)

GISELE: (*Sings "The White Roses" mechanically.*)

Today is Sunday morning
These are for you, maman
I brought you white roses
For you love them so
Now that you've gone away
To that garden above—

MIMI: (*Cutting her off.*) Shut up . . . . (*Gisele stops singing. The work continues a moment in silence.*)

END

ON THE EDITOR

Philippa Wehle is the author of *Le Théâtre Populaire selon Jean Vilar* and (with Hubert Nyssen) translator of *Jimmy's Blues*, a selection of James Baldwin's poetry, both published in France. She also writes frequently about contemporary European theatre, dance and performance for *Theatre Journal*, *The Drama Review*, *Theatre Crafts*, *American Theater*, and *Performing Arts Journal*. Philippa Wehle is also Associate Professor of French Language and Culture and Contemporary French Theatre at the State University of New York at Purchase, New York.